JUDAISM ON TRIAL

Dedicated to the memory of
LOUIS THOMAS SIDNEY LITTMAN
who founded the Littman Library
for the love of God
and in memory of his father
JOSEPH AARON LITTMAN
יהא זכרם ברוך

'Get wisdom, get understanding:
Forsake her not and she shall preserve thee'
PROV. 4:5

Judaism on Trial

Jewish–Christian Disputations in the Middle Ages

◆

Edited and Translated by
HYAM MACCOBY

London
The Littman Library of Jewish Civilization

The Littman Library of Jewish Civilization

Published in the United Kingdom by
Vallentine Mitchell & Co. Ltd.
Newbury House, 900 Eastern Avenue
London IG2 7HH

Published in the United States and Canada by
Vallentine Mitchell & Co. Ltd.
c/o ISBS, 5804 N.E. Hassalo Street
Portland, Oregon 97213-3644

First published 1982
First issued in paperback 1993
Paperback reprinted 1996

A catalogue record for this book is available from the British Library

The Library of Congress cataloged the hardback edition as follows:
Judaism on trial
(The Littman Library of Jewish Civilization)
Bibliography: p.
Includes translations of the disputations at
Barcelona, Paris, and Tortosa.
1. Christianity—Controversial Literature.
2. Judaism—Apologetic works. 3. Judaism—Controversial literature.
4. Christianity—Apologetic works. 5. Disputations, Religious.
I. Maccoby, Hyam, 1924– II. Naḥmanides, ca. 1195–ca. 1270.
Vikuaḥ ha Ramban. English. 1981. III. Jehiel ben Joseph, of Paris, d. 1286.
Vikuaḥ de-Rabi Yeḥi'el 'im Nikola'ush. English. 1981.
IV. Tortosa Disputation. English. 1981.
V. Series: Littman Library of Jewish Civilization.
BM590.A1J83 230'.2 80-70239
ISBN 1–874774–16–1 AACR2

Cover design by Pete Russell, Faringdon, Oxon
Printed in Great Britain on acid-free paper by
Bookcraft Ltd, Bath

Introduction to the Paperback Edition

SINCE *Judaism on Trial* was first published in 1982, many works have appeared that have furthered understanding of the Jewish–Christian Disputations. The book has been much cited and discussed in this literature, though not always with full comprehension of my standpoints.

Jeremy Cohen's *The Friars and the Jews* also appeared in 1982. It is an excellent treatment of the whole friar campaign from the foundation of the Mendicant orders to the work of Raymund Lull, showing that the Disputations formed part of a broad pattern of conversionary activity that transcended and transformed the old Augustinian policy of limited toleration of the Jews. Cohen's treatment of the Barcelona Disputation, however, erred in exaggerating the originality of the Dominican argument in this Disputation. Here I agree with Robert Chazan's criticisms of Cohen in his *Daggers of Faith* (1988), pp. 170–3.

Chazan's *Daggers of Faith* gives a valuable account of the literary exchanges between Christians and Jews that followed in the wake of the Barcelona Disputation. Raymund Martini's *Pugio fidei* achieved a higher level of argument derived from rabbinic sources than Pablo Christiani had been capable of. This required a more serious response, which was given by Solomon ibn Adret (Rashba), Meir ben Simon of Narbonne, and Mordechai ben Joseph of Avignon. Chazan argued, against Cohen, that there was no fundamental change of Christian attitude in the friar campaign, only a greater investment of time and money. Here I am inclined to agree with Chazan, but he gives no sufficient explanation of the new intensity of conversionary activity. I would stress (in line with Cohen) the influence of thirteenth-century apocalypticism. There was no repudiation of the Augustinian policy of toleration of the Jews (as Cohen thinks); but that policy had always been regarded as an interim solution, which would become obsolete if ever it was thought that the End of Days was approaching. Also, the Augustinian policy was always predicated on the understanding that Judaism was a fossilized form of Old Testament religion. The discovery of the existence of the Talmud shifted the status of Jews from followers of a 'licit' religion to that of heretics. If, however, apocalyptic hopes were to die down, and if the Jews could be induced to repudiate the Talmud, the old Augustinian compromise would be as valid as ever.

An unfortunate misunderstanding arises in Chazan's comments on an interpretation of mine in *Judaism on Trial*. I offered a solution (p. 120) to the problem of why Naḥmanides apparently said at the Barcelona Disputation that he knew of no other Messianic claimant in history apart from Jesus. The term 'apart from' is ambiguous in Hebrew as well as in English; it can mean 'except' or 'in addition to', and it was the latter meaning that I suggested was more appropriate here. In my slightly emended version, Naḥmanides said that he disbelieved in all messiah-figures in addition to Jesus, i.e. that his disbelief extended not only to Jesus but to all other Messianic figures who had so far appeared. Chazan strangely misunderstood me to say that Naḥmanides believed in Jesus, a manifest impossibility, and therefore dismissed my suggestion.

David Berger, in his review of *Judaism on Trial*, criticized my statement on p. 54 that Naḥmanides regarded the coming of the Messiah as not inevitable and as depending on Israel's repentance. This, according to Berger, showed a lamentable ignorance of Naḥmanides' views as expressed in his *Sefer ha-ge'ulah*. In my reply (*JQR*, 1986) I pointed out that, on the contrary, it was Berger who had misread that work. The passages that Berger cites where Naḥmanides speaks of the Messiah's coming as 'unconditional' are all found to mean, on closer inspection, that the Messiah's coming is not conditional on *perfect* fulfilment of the commandments. Naḥmanides, however, does insist that a basic standard of fulfilment is required, and that if it is not forthcoming, the Messiah may never come. Though he believed that there is a pre-ordained date for the Messiah's coming, Naḥmanides' view, based on the Talmudic sources, was that this could be hastened by extraordinary repentance or delayed indefinitely by extraordinary sinfulness.

In *Barcelona and Beyond* (1992), Robert Chazan queried some of the emphases of *Judaism on Trial*. In particular, he criticized my approach as too 'partisan'. He chided me for using the expressions 'Jewish scholar' and 'Christian scholar', asserting severely that there are only two categories of scholar: those who are objective, and those who are partisan. It is now generally accepted, however, that a researcher can never be totally dispassionate. As Stefan Reif has recently remarked, 'Scholarship does not exist in a human vacuum.' Even the attempt to achieve objectivity has its sociological and psychological traps. In the case of the Disputations there is a special danger of over-compensation. I would add to Robert Chazan's two categories a third category: those scholars who by leaning over backwards to demonstrate their objectivity fall into the pit of negative partisanship.

Chazan certainly avoids some of the traps into which previous pursuers of unsullied objectivity have fallen. Thus he upholds the sincerity of Naḥmanides' standpoint in relation to *aggadah*. In other respects, however, Chazan fails to free himself from the fallacies of some previous commentators. For example, he again asserts that Naḥmanides cannot have been consulted in the matter of the agenda (contrary to Naḥmanides' own assertion), since, if he had been consulted, he would not have suggested as a central theme a topic which was not central to Judaism (according to his own statement), i.e. the topic of the Messiah. I argue at some length in *Judaism on Trial* that this is mere confused thinking. The main topic of discussion had to be a topic that was central to Christianity even if it was not central to Judaism: in fact, the main bone of contention between Judaism and Christianity was about how central the topic of the Messiah ought to be.

Chazan also subscribes to the view that Naḥmanides cannot have really said the more daring things that he claims to have said in the Disputation. Chazan fails to take into account that when Naḥmanides was brought to trial for publishing his account, it was not alleged that he had *added* to his contribution in the actual debate. Moreover, Chazan misunderstands some of Naḥmanides' remarks. For example, Naḥmanides never criticized King James for having an army: he simply pointed out that the biblical prophecies of world peace had not yet been fulfilled. He did not criticize King James for maintaining an army against his enemies in this non-Messianic age.

Some of the more daring things included in the texts of the *Vikuaḥ* that have come down to us may indeed not have been said in the debate; but this, I argued, was because they were added by a later editor in the course of transmission of the manuscript. Chazan accused me of being unscientific here: why distinguish between the work of Naḥmanides and that of a later editor in the absence of definite manuscript corroboration? All the passages in question, he argued, are equally authentic (in being the work of Naḥmanides) and equally inauthentic (in being apocryphal additions to the actual debate). However, he failed to appreciate my argument that a distinction must be made between passages pertinent to the debate (however daring) and those that are irrelevant and gratuitous attacks on Christianity, out of keeping with Naḥmanides' general style of argument.

Having thereby dealt with the critics of *Judaism on Trial*, I should like to thank Dr Jonathan Sacks (now Chief Rabbi) for his very full and appreciative review in the *Jewish Journal of Sociology*. I also welcome the support given both by Marvin Fox and by Bernard Septimus to my view that Naḥmanides' stance on the authority of the *aggadah* was in full accordance with traditional Judaism.

I dedicate this work to the memory of my mother, Zipporah Maccoby, and of my father, Ephraim Meyer Maccoby, with deep gratitude for everything I learnt from them.

H.M.

London
April 1993

ADDITIONAL BIBLIOGRAPHY

Berger, David. 'Maccoby's *Judaism on Trial*'. *Jewish Quarterly Review*, 76 (1986), 253–7.

Chazan, Robert. *Daggers of Faith: Thirteenth-century Christian Missionizing and the Jewish Response.* University of California Press, Berkeley, 1988.

——. *Barcelona and Beyond: The Disputation of 1263 and Its Aftermath.* University of California Press, Berkeley, 1992.

Cohen, Jeremy. *The Friars and the Jews: The Evolution of Medieval Anti-Judaism.* Cornell University Press, Ithaca–London, 1982.

Fox, Marvin. 'Nahmanides on the Status of Aggadot: Perspectives on the Disputation at Barcelona, 1263'. *Journal of Jewish Studies,* 40 (1989), 95–103.

Maccoby, Hyam. 'Het dispuut van Barcelona en zijn achtergrond'. *Ter Herkenning,* 19/4 (1991), 234–42.

——. 'Nahmanides and Messianism: A Reply'. *Jewish Quarterly Review,* 77 (1986), 55–7

——. 'Review of Robert Chazan, *Barcelona and Beyond*'. *Jewish Quarterly* (forthcoming).

——. 'Review of Robert Chazan, *Daggers of Faith*'. *Religion,* 22/3 (1992).

——. 'The Tortosa Disputation and its Consequences'. In *Proceedings of the International Colloquium on the Expulsion of the Jews from Spain, at the Catholic University, Louvain, 1992* (forthcoming).

Merhavia, Ch. *Ha-Talmud be-Re'i ha-Natzrut.* Jerusalem, 1970.

Sacks, Jonathan. 'Review of *Judaism on Trial*'. *Jewish Journal of Sociology,* 25/2 (1983).

Septimus, Bernard. '"Open Rebuke and Concealed Love": Nahmanides and the Andalusian Tradition'. In *Rabbi Moses Nahmanides (Ramban): Explorations in His Religious and Literary Virtuosity,* ed. Isadore Twersky, 11–34. Cambridge, Mass., 1983.

Contents

List of Abbreviations 10
Introduction 11

PART I
THE THREE DISPUTATIONS: GENERAL CONSIDERATIONS

1 The Paris Disputation, 1240 19
2 The Barcelona Disputation, 1263 39
3 The *Vikuaḥ*: Textual Considerations 76
4 Biographical Notes on the Chief Persons Present at Barcelona 79
5 The Tortosa Disputation, 1413–14 82

PART II
THE BARCELONA DISPUTATION: TEXTS

6 Introductory Note on the *Vikuaḥ* 97
7 The *Vikuaḥ* of Naḥmanides: Translation and Commentary 102
8 The Christian Account of the Barcelona Disputation 147

PART III
THE PARIS AND TORTOSA DISPUTATIONS: TEXTS

9 The *Vikuaḥ* of R. Yeḥiel of Paris: A Paraphrase 153
10 The Christian Account of the Paris Disputation 163
11 A Hebrew Account of the Tortosa Disputation 168
12 The Christian Account of the Tortosa Disputation 187

Notes 216
Bibliography 225
General Index 233
Index of Quotations 240

Abbreviations

AM	*anno mundi*
Av. Zar.	Avodah Zarah
b	Babylonian Talmud
BB	Bava Batra
BCE	BC
Ber.	Berakhot
BQ	Bava Qamma
BM	Bava Metzi‘a
C.	Chavel (1963)
CE	AD
Cohen	Cohen (1964)
E.	Eisenstein (1928)
Gen. R.	Genesis Rabbah
Gitt.	Gittin
Ḥag.	Ḥagigah
j	Palestinian Talmud
Kidd.	Kiddushin
m	Mishnah
Ma‘as.	Ma‘aserot
N.	Naḥmanides
P.	Pablo Christiani
PL	*Patrologia Latina* (Migne, 1844)
R.	Rabbah
RH	Rosh Hashanah
Rankin	Rankin (1956)
Roth	Roth (1950)
S.	Steinschneider (1860)
Sanh.	Sanhedrin
Shabb.	Shabbat
Sof.	Soferim
Sukk.	Sukkot
t	Tosefta
Yalq. Sh.	Yalqut Shimoni
Yev.	Yevamot

Introduction

Of the disputations which took place in the Middle Ages, there are only three of which any detailed record survives: the Paris Disputation of 1240, the Barcelona Disputation of 1263, and the Tortosa Disputation of 1413–14.[1] Of these, the most celebrated is the Barcelona Disputation of 1263. There are many good reasons for its pre-eminence. The Jewish spokesman at Barcelona was Moses ben Naḥman (known variously as Naḥmanides, Naḥmani, and Ramban, the last being an acronym formed from the name *R*abbi *M*oses *b*en *N*aḥman), who was one of the greatest figures in the history of Jewish learning and religion—no comparably great figure took part in the other disputations. Even more important, the Jewish account of the Barcelona Disputation was written by the chief participant, Naḥmanides himself, while the Jewish accounts of the other disputations were written by people of minor status. Further, Naḥmanides' account in Hebrew of the Barcelona Disputation is a classic in its own right, written in a clear, logical style which yet rises to the drama of the occasion, in contrast to the inferior workmanship of the Hebrew accounts of the other disputations.

Finally, it becomes clear after some investigation, that the Barcelona Disputation was the only one in which the conditions of debate were relatively fair, and the Jewish side was allowed to develop its argument in relative freedom.

The general conclusion one reaches is as follows. The Paris Disputation was not really a disputation at all, but an interrogation in which the Jewish spokesman, Rabbi Yeḥiel, was given very little scope for the exposition of fundamental Jewish ideas; he was severely hampered both by the restricted role he was given, and by the limits of the interrogation itself, which was confined to allegedly anti-Christian passages of the Talmud. This was not really a disputation between Christianity and Judaism, but a trial of the Talmud, in which Rabbi Yeḥiel was merely witness for the defence. The Tortosa Disputation, on the other hand, was a true disputation, in which the same areas were covered as in the Barcelona Disputation, but under much inferior conditions. As the voluminous Christian records show, as well as the Hebrew accounts, the Jewish participants were intimidated, kept in fear for their families, bullied and harangued at enormous length, and listened to with very little patience. In the circumstances, they behaved with great courage and showed considerable powers of argument, though they could not speak with the same authority as a Naḥmanides. There was no classic confrontation, as in the Barcelona Disputation, but a sprawling, untidy, long-drawn-out debate, presenting many points of interest among its *longueurs*, including many points of comparison with the Barcelona Disputation itself.

At Barcelona, however, many factors came together to form the greatest confrontation between Christianity and Judaism in the Middle Ages. There was a freedom of debate which was due partly to the personality of the presiding King James of Aragon, partly to the status and personality of Moses Naḥmanides, but most of all to the historical circumstances in which the disputation was held. The fact that the disputation was held at all was a sign that the position of the Jews in Spain was beginning to deteriorate; yet enough remained of the confidence and *élan* of the Jewish 'golden age' to make it into a real occasion, when Jewish attitudes towards fundamental matters such as the meaning of the Messiah, the scope of Original Sin, and the semantics of Biblical and Midrashic exegesis, were expounded in the manner of one giving instruction and enlightenment, not, as at Tortosa, in desperate self-defence. Even Naḥmanides was forced to some extent to take a defensive role, as he himself complained; for he was not allowed to put questions against Christianity, but only to answer questions put to him by his Christian opponent. In Naḥmanides' hands, however, and with the latitude allowed him, this structure of debate did not work to his disadvantage.

The Barcelona Disputation took place at a turning-point in Jewish history. The Dominican movement had not long been founded, and the Inquisition had begun. Catholic Europe was entering upon its period of flowering, and this meant the oncoming of a black night for the Jews, who had contributed so much to the recovery of European learning. As the Christians, their erstwhile pupils, gathered intellectual independence and turned on them, the position of the Jews became worse and worse. Naḥmanides stands at the end of the old dispensation; not yet overwhelmed, beaten down and diminished by the new. There is about him still the glory of the Babylonian academies of which he is the heir, together with the philosophical grasp of the school of Maimonides and the subtlety of the French school of Rashi—not to mention the esoteric mysticism of the Kabbalah, which had recently achieved a new development in Spain, and of which he was a master—though he revealed almost nothing of this last aspect at the disputation. He is a highly complex figure, in some respects profounder than the great Maimonides himself. In the disputation, he is the last great representative of Jewish dignity and nobility before the ages of humiliation.

The present work is in three parts. In Part I, the three disputations are given general historical and thematic consideration. I have tried to treat the doctrinal and theological points at issue between Jews and Christians in all three disputations with seriousness and sense of present-day relevance. Scholars (principally, I think, because of contemporary ecumenical considerations) have tended to regard the issues as entirely outdated. This, in my view, is a mistake. Only the medieval vocabulary of the disputations is outdated; the issues remain vital.

In my discussion of the Barcelona Disputation in Part I, I have given special attention to the views of modern scholars (Yitzhak Baer, Cecil Roth, and Martin A. Cohen). Though I have been compelled to disagree with them to varying degrees, I am grateful to them for the stimulation provided by their attempts to reach a new level of objectivity.

In Part II, I give a full translation of the *Vikuaḥ* of Naḥmanides. I have given pride of place to this translation, contrary to the historical order of the documents, because of its outstanding literary and human interest; and I have supplied the translation with a detailed historical, theological, philological and textual commentary. I consulted two previous translations. M. Braude's was made from an unsatisfactory text. O. S. Rankin's is based on a good text, but is unfortunately very imperfect, as that excellent Biblical scholar was not well acquainted with medieval Hebrew or with its Talmudic background. Since Rankin's translation is much used, especially by Christian students, I have thought it worthwhile to draw attention to its errors in some detail in my commentary.

While the present work was going through the press, a new translation of the *Vikuaḥ* of Naḥmanides appeared in Vol. II of C. B. Chavel's *Ramban (Nachmanides): Writings and Discourses* (1978, New York). This is an excellent translation, yet it differs from my own sufficiently to make comparison interesting. Chavel translates accurately from the best text. My translation, however, is sometimes based on emendations (argued fully in the commentary), where even the best text seems to me to require correction because of theological or historical difficulties. An example is Naḥmanides' apparent assertion (see p. 120) that he knows of no person other than Jesus who claimed to be the Messiah. In view of Naḥmanides' own references to other messianic claimants in his other writings, this assertion, as it stands, is amazing. A small and plausible emendation, however, gives a much more understandable meaning to Naḥmanides' statement. Another such emendation comes in Naḥmanides' argument about the Trinity, where a small correction produces much better philosophical sense (see p. 145). My most drastic emendation is my excision of almost all the introductory paragraph of the *Vikuaḥ* as inauthentic. This, of course, requires very detailed argument (see pp. 97–101).

A translation (from the Latin) of the Christian account of the Barcelona Disputation completes Part II.

Part III gives the Jewish and Christian documents of the Paris and Tortosa disputations. The Jewish account of the Paris Disputation is given only in paraphrase, but the Christian account is translated in full. In the case of the Tortosa Disputation, however, the Jewish account is translated in full, while only selected extracts are translated from the very long Christian account. (See pp. 21 and 187 for further explanation of this varied treatment.)

I wish to acknowledge gratefully the helpful suggestions and criticisms I have received from Dr David Goldstein. My heartfelt thanks go to my wife Cynthia for her incalculable support and assistance. I should like to thank Mr Louis Littman for his encouragement of my work.

JUDAISM ON TRIAL

PART I

THE THREE DISPUTATIONS: GENERAL CONSIDERATIONS

1

The Paris Disputation, 1240

The Paris Disputation, the earliest of the three disputations, shows a less developed concept, on the Christian side, of how Judaism could be attacked than is seen in the Barcelona Disputation and the Tortosa Disputation. At Paris there was a single-pronged attack against the Talmud. In the later disputations, the attack was double-pronged: an attack on the Talmud combined with a building-up of the Talmud as the source of evidence for the truth of Christianity. This apparent inconsistency was reconciled by a two-tier theory of the Talmud somewhat similar in structure to modern critical theories of ancient texts. The Talmud, in its final redaction, was regarded as evil, the later strata and editorial revisions being the product of anti-Christian tendencies; but the earliest strata, dating from the time of Jesus and before, were thought to contain material as yet undefiled by rabbinism, and this material could be adduced to show that Christianity was the true fulfilment and continuation of inter-Testamental Judaism. This approach is very similar to that of modern Christian scholars (e.g., W. D. Davies in his *Paul and Rabbinic Judaism*) who seek to show that characteristically Christian doctrines, such as the doctrines of Original Sin, of predestination, and of grace have Jewish origins from which post-Christian Judaism has diverged.

The less sophisticated approach of the Paris Disputation is also shown in the line actually taken against the Talmud. The main line taken was that the Talmud had no right to exist, since its claim to sanctity set up a rival to the unique authority of the Scriptures. It is ironic that many of the arguments used in the Paris Disputation against the authority of the Talmud were used two hundred years later by the Protestant reformers to attack the authority of the Church. The Jews had already had their Protestant schism, namely the rise of the Karaite heresy in the eighth century, and there was a direct link between Jewish Karaism and the Paris Disputation. The Christian protagonist in the disputation was Nicholas Donin, a converted Jew who had first come into conflict with the Jewish religious establishment because of his Karaite leanings. It is doubtful whether he had any real interest in specifically Christian doctrines; his conversion to Christianity was motivated more by his opposition to the rabbinic tradition in Judaism.[1]

In attacking the Talmud as having no right to exist, the Christians were indeed laying the ground for a critique of the authority of the Church. For the Talmud was the direct analogue of the main institutions by which the Church claimed to be the guardian and interpreter of the Scriptural revelation. The legal parts of the Talmud correspond to the Christian canon law. The stories of the rabbis correspond to the Christian hagiographies, and the Talmudic Biblical homilies and exegesis correspond to the similar works of exegesis, exhortation and reflection in the Early Fathers and the scholastics. Christians thought of the Talmud as a book, which had somehow usurped the role in Jewish life that ought to be occupied by the Bible alone. They did not realise that the Talmud is not a book, but a whole library of books, covering many centuries of continuous Jewish religious experience, all centring on the Scripture, but interpreting that Scripture in the light of changing historical conditions. In attacking the Talmud, the Christians were not attacking a book, as they thought, but the Jewish Church, and Jewish historical experience. Nicholas Donin, on the other hand, had the typical Protestant's desire to commune with Scripture without the intervention of the centuries of history which had elapsed between the Revelation and his own day. He wished to stand on Mount Sinai and receive the Law in its pristine purity. It is not surprising that not many years after the disputation we find Donin in serious conflict with the authorities of the Franciscan order which he joined to escape from rabbinism.

There is unfortunately no very reliable source for the detailed facts of the Paris Disputation. The Jewish record was written by Rabbi Joseph ben Nathan Official (known as *ha-meqan'e,* the Zealous), about twenty years after the event. The style is turgid, and would be unreadable in a literal English translation, because of the frequent recourse to stock literary devices, such as rhymed phrases and Biblical allusions, which do not travel well from their medieval Hebrew setting. The account is frankly partisan; Nicholas Donin is never mentioned without some opprobrious epithet, while Rabbi Yeḥiel is introduced for each speech with expressions of fulsome praise. Instead of a full translation, therefore, I have provided a paraphrase, giving the gist of the points made on both sides in the argument, according to the Hebrew account.

Rabbi Yeḥiel ben Joseph of Paris, the main speaker on the Jewish side, is known from other sources as a prominent Talmudist and teacher. He is mentioned by name several times in the Tosafot commentary on the Babylonian Talmud, and is also mentioned with great respect in the travel diary of Benjamin of Tudela. Rabbi Yeḥiel was the pupil and successor of Rabbi Judah ben Isaac (known as Sir Leon), the head of the academy *(yeshivah)* of Paris. His main fame, however, comes from his part in the disputation of 1210. Here he differs both from Naḥmanides (whose fame is mainly independent of his part in the Barcelona Disputation of 1263) and from the rabbis of the Tortosa Disputation, most of whom would be almost unknown were it not for their part in the disputation of 1413.

Three other rabbis, apart from Yeḥiel, took some part in the disputation: Judah ben David of Melun (who was interrogated at some point and gave answers similar to Rabbi Yeḥiel's; see p. 166), Samuel ben Solomon of Château Thierry, and (most famous of all) Moses of Coucy, who later wrote the *Sefer Mitzvot Gadol* (Semag) and was a well-known preacher. On this occasion, however, his role was minor.

On the Christian side, apart from those who actually took part in the disputation itself, the great figures of the Pope, Gregory IX, and the King of France, Louis IX, were involved. It was a letter from the Pope, condemning the Talmud (at the instigation of Nicholas Donin) which set the disputation in motion. This letter was sent to all the kings of Christendom, though the King of France, the pious Louis IX, was the only one who acted on it (even the Pope did not act on it, within his own domains). The letter reads:

> If what is said about the Jews of France and of the other lands is true, no punishment would be sufficiently worthy of their crime. For they, so we have heard, are not content with the Old Law which God gave to Moses in writing: they even ignore it completely, and affirm that God gave another Law which is called 'Talmud', that is 'Teaching', handed down to Moses orally. Falsely they allege that it was implanted within their minds and, unwritten, was there preserved until certain men came, whom they call 'Sages' and 'Scribes', who, fearing that this Law

> may be lost from the minds of men through forgetfulness, reduced it to writing, and the volume of this by far exceeds the text of the Bible. In this is contained matter so abusive and so unspeakable that it arouses shame in those who mention it and horror in those who hear it.
>
> Wherefore, since this is said to be the most important reason why the Jews remain obstinate in their perfidy, we earnestly urge and warn your Royal Serenity that on the first Saturday of the Lent to come, in the morning, while the Jews are gathered in the synagogues, you, by our authority, shall seize all the books belonging to the Jews of your Kingdom, those subject to your authority as well as those subject to the authority of your vassals, the nobles of the said Kingdom; and you shall have these books held in custody of our dear sons, the Dominican and Franciscan Friars.[2]

This letter clearly shows the influence of Nicholas Donin, since it follows the wording of Donin's charge-sheet against the Talmud.[3]

Louis IX (1214–70; Saint Louis, canonised in 1297) was an implacable enemy of the Jews, regarding it as an act of Christian piety to harass them. On one occasion he asserted that the best way to carry on a disputation with a Jew was to plunge a sword into him. This advice, however, was meant for laymen rather than the clergy, whom he encouraged to dispute with Jews. King Louis provides a link between the Paris Disputation of 1240 and the Barcelona Disputation of 1263, for Pablo Christiani, the Christian opponent of Naḥmanides at Barcelona, was a protégé of King Louis, who gave orders that the Jews of Provence should be compelled to listen to Pablo's missionary sermons. It was under Pablo's influence too that Louis issued an edict that the Jews of his realm should be compelled to wear the distinctive badge instituted for them by the Fourth Lateran Council of 1215.

Louis, however, did not personally preside at the Paris Disputation. This task was performed by the Queen Mother, Queen Blanche of Castile. She was a woman of great character and ability, who acted as sole ruler of France later when her son went on his first Crusade (1248–52). The Jewish sources, which avoid mention of Louis, refer to her with some warmth, as one who was fair and humane in her dealings with the Jews.

The Christian clerics who acted as judges or assessors at the disputation were Walter, Archbishop of Sens, William, Bishop of Paris, Geoffrey of Belleville, Chaplain to the King, Adam de Chambly, Bishop of Senlis, and probably Odo of Châteauroux,

Chancellor of the University of Paris, later Papal Legate. Of these, the most famous was William of Auvergne, the Bishop of Paris. Though he drew extensively in his philosophical writings on the Jewish writers Ibn Gabirol (Avicebron) and Maimonides (the latter of whom he never mentioned by name), William of Auvergne was strongly anti-Jewish. The Archbishop of Sens, on the other hand, often showed a friendly disposition to the Jews.

The procedure of the disputation is not entirely clear. According to the Hebrew account, Rabbi Yeḥiel faced his antagonist, Nicholas Donin, and answered him directly. Yitzhak Baer (1930–31), however, takes the view that this is an idealised account, and that Rabbi Yeḥiel never spoke to Donin face to face. Baer thinks that the procedure was that of a session of the Inquisition, and that in fact the whole inquiry was under the aegis of the Inquisition; and under Inquisition rules, the defendant was not allowed to see his accuser. Judah Rosenthal (1956–57), however, disagrees, and is inclined to accept the picture given in the Hebrew account of a face-to-face confrontation. One thing that is clear is that the rabbis were interrogated separately and not allowed to consult each other about their replies. This seems to confirm Baer's view, since this was the procedure of the Inquisition, and was never followed in other disputations. Jewish religious opinions did not come under the Inquisition since Judaism was not classified as a heresy but as a licit though erroneous religion. But the limits of this classification of Judaism (as well as the rules of the Inquisition procedure) may still have been in process of definition at this time, since the Inquisition was still in its early years. The fact that the decision at Paris to burn the Talmud was later reversed suggests that it was felt later that the Paris proceedings had been irregular.

Even in its final formulation, however, the authority of the Inquisition did extend to *some* regulation of Judaism. The Inquisition was entitled to step in if Jews blasphemed Christianity or did anything to hinder its practice (e.g., by converting Christians to Judaism or encouraging Jewish converts to Christianity to lapse). The Inquisition even claimed the right to interfere in matters of heresy within Judaism, on matters which were held to be common doctrine between Judaism and Christianity; for example, the authority of the Old Testament as holy writ. The actual accusations made at the Paris inquiry, as Baer points out, do fall into the above categories. The reverence given by Jews to the Talmud was arraigned as a heretical attack on the authority of Scripture, which, it was alleged, the Jews had weakened by setting up a second Scripture. Secondly, it was alleged that the Talmud contained blasphemous attacks against Christianity. The first charge is an interesting one. It means that Christians were prepared to tolerate Judaism only as long as it remained fixated in pre-Christian Judaism; i.e., if it remained as a fossilised witness to the kind of Judaism which Jesus came to supersede. (Here, of course, Christians were not aware that Judaism had moved on considerably even by the time of Jesus from the kind of Judaism found in the Old Testament.) The basic Christian view was that the only legitimate continuation of Old Testament Judaism was Christianity itself.

Rabbi Yeḥiel's impassioned reply that the Talmud *was* Judaism must have come as something of a surprise to his Christian interlocutors. They had thought of the Talmud as something new-fangled and extraneous to Judaism. As Inquisitors, therefore (and Baer seems to be right that they were Inquisitors), they were in something of a quandary. For it was not their business to interfere with Judaism itself, which had to remain in a state of suspended animation, so to speak, until the time of the conversion of the Jews as a body to Christianity. The very existence of the Talmud (which had been the central feature of Judaism for the previous thousand years or more) was a surprise to them, since they were used to identifying the Jews with the people of that name in the Old Testament and the Gospels (though in fact, the Pharisees who feature so prominently in the Gospels were the originators of the Talmud). Their first impulse was to sweep the Talmud out of existence altogether as an annoying irrelevance and a 'heretical' innovation, in that it complicated needlessly their picture of what it meant to be a Jew. The Paris Disputation represents this reaction. Its object was to annihilate the Talmud, and turn the Jews back into Old Testament Jews, from which point their conversion to Christianity could eventually proceed as planned. The call of the Pope, instigated by Donin, to the secular and ecclesiastical leaders of Christendom was directed against the very existence of the Talmud. 'For they, so we have heard, are not content with the Old Law which God gave to Moses in writing: they even ignore it completely, and affirm that God gave another Law which is called "Talmud". . .' Only secondarily does the Pope complain also that the Talmud contains 'abusive' and 'unspeakable' matter. The main charge is that it is heresy on the part of the Jews to have a Talmud at all. The logical consequence of this would be the complete suppression of the Talmud. That this aim was, in the event, abandoned, and the policy of *censoring* the Talmud by erasing allegedly offending passages was substituted, shows that the Church learnt to change its definition of Judaism. One of the results of the Paris Disputation (a result which did not show itself immediately, since a full-scale burning of the Talmud took place in Paris in 1242) was that the Church did tacitly acknowledge the paramount place of the Talmud in the definition of Judaism and no longer regarded it as heresy, within the jurisdiction of the Inquisition, for a Jew to study the Talmud.[4] Instead, the second charge, that the Talmud contained blasphemies against the Christian faith, continued to be pressed, as a matter on which the Inquisition was entitled to regulate Jewish conduct.

Another category of charges against the Talmud, made both in the Paris Disputation and in the collection of thirty-five charges previously submitted to the Pope by Nicholas Donin, was that of allegedly anti-Christian remarks in the Talmud directed not against Christian belief itself but against Christians; for example, that it was permitted to kill a Christian, and that Christians were cursed in the Jewish prayer of the Eighteen Benedictions. Such charges were also probably the business of the Inquisition, since they could be construed as attacks on Christianity, in the sense that the Christian faith was thereby denigrated as inferior to Judaism.

On the other hand, some of the charges did not relate to Christianity or Christians at all. These were the charges of alleged imbecilities and obscenities *(stultitiae)* in the Talmud. Here again the standing of the Inquisition in the matter was open to doubt. It could be argued that such charges were relevant to the general charge that the Talmud was superfluous for Judaism and a harmful excrescence on the true basis of Judaism, the Old Testament. On the other hand, it could be argued that it was not the Inquisition's business to interfere in the Jews' private reading, provided that it did not affect their relation to Christendom. The latter view eventually prevailed, for when the censorship of the Talmud went into operation, it concerned itself only with Talmudic remarks which could be construed as anti-Christian.

We may now consider in more detail the above two categories of charges against the actual content of the Talmud, namely the charges of anti-Christian content (both against Christianity and against Christians), and the charges of stupidity, obscenity and blasphemy against God (i.e., blasphemy directed against doctrines held in common between Judaism and Christianity).

The Charge of Anti-Christian Content

(a) *Blasphemies against Christian Religion.* These consisted of alleged attacks on Jesus and Mary. Nicholas Donin, the accuser, had a good knowledge of the Talmud, and he cited nearly all the passages used in subsequent Christian attacks on the Talmud up to the present time. The Talmud contains a few explicit references to Jesus and also a few references to 'Ben Stada' otherwise known as 'Ben Pandira' (also the Tosefta twice refers to 'Jesus ben Pantiri', but Nicholas Donin did not cite these references; i.e., t Hullin II, 22 and 24). These references are certainly not complimentary. In one (b Sanh., 107b) Jesus is described as a pupil of Joshua ben Peraḥia, and as having lapsed into idolatry as a result of a rebuff from his teacher. In another (b Sanh., 43a) Jesus is described as having been executed on Passover eve by stoning on a charge of seducing Israel to idolatry. In another (b Gitt, 56b) Jesus is described as suffering in hell by being immersed in boiling excrement.

Rabbi Yeḥiel's defence to these charges was that the above Talmudic passages refer not to the Christian Jesus, but to some other Jesus. When the judges expressed incredulity at this, Yeḥiel made his famous remark, 'Not every Louis is King of France.' Yeḥiel, in this line of argument, relied on the fact that Jesus was a not uncommon name (he might have mentioned that a Jesus, other than Jesus of Nazareth, is mentioned in the New Testament itself, Colossians, 4: 11, and several figures called Jesus are mentioned in Josephus); and also, more convincingly, that the references to Jesus in the Talmud do not tally chronologically with the Jesus of Christianity. The Jesus who was the pupil of Joshua ben Perahia lived long before the Christian Jesus, in the reign of Alexander Jannaeus (126–76 BCE). As for (Jesus) ben Stada, or Ben Pandira, he lived long after the Christian Jesus, in the time of Pappos ben Judah (about 130 CE). Moreover, as Rabbi Yeḥiel pointed out, Ben Stada was executed at Lydda, not Jerusalem.

Yeḥiel's argument, therefore, was sound as regards several of the alleged references to Jesus in the Talmud, but not in relation to all of them. There seems little doubt that the account of the execution of Jesus on the eve of Passover does refer to the Christian Jesus, especially as the designation 'Jesus of Nazareth' is used. (Actually, the designation 'of Nazareth' does not appear in recent editions of the Talmud, but is found in early MSS.[5]) Yeḥiel's answer in relation to this passage is given in a confused form in the Hebrew narrative, but the gist of it seems to be that there may have been two Jesuses, both from Nazareth. This reply was received with even greater incredulity than his first formulation.

The passage in which Jesus' punishment in hell is described also seems to refer to the Christian Jesus. It is a piece of anti-Christian polemic dating from the post-70 CE period (since the person who is supposed to have conjured up the spirit of Jesus in order to inquire about his fate is Onqelos ben Qaloniqos, the proselyte, reputed to have been a nephew of the emperor Titus). The surprising thing is that such anti-Christian polemic is so infrequent in the Talmud, amounting at most to half a dozen short passages out of many millions of words. When one compares this with the mountains of vituperation against Judaism by Christian authors of the Patristic period and later, one can only wonder at Jewish restraint. The Talmud, in fact, almost completely ignores Christianity.

Rabbi Yeḥiel's contention that the Christian Jesus 'is nowhere mentioned in the Talmud' is thus almost true. The search for 'blasphemous' material about Jesus thus narrows down to two short passages out of a voluminous literature. One is the passage about Jesus' punishment in hell (stated not as a fact, but as a necromantic vision); the other is the account of Jesus' execution, which is clearly a late (second- or third-century) concoction, intended to counter Christian missionary propaganda. Its unhistorical nature is shown by the statement that Jesus was executed by stoning by the Jewish authorities, whereas the Gospels show that he was executed by crucifixion by the Roman authorities. The intention of the story is to say, 'If Jesus really did declare himself to be God, as the Christian missionaries say, then he deserved to be executed by the Jewish authorities as an idolater and one who sought to seduce others to idolatry.' The Jews of this period (second and third centuries CE) had no independent information about Jesus, the memory of whom had died (it should be noted that the Talmud contains no reference to other would-be messiahs such as Judas of Galilee and Athronges, who are mentioned either by Josephus or the New Testament). Only Christians had kept alive the memory of Jesus.

The two passages were thus indeed 'blasphemies' of Christianity, if it was blasphemy to take the Christian story of Jesus' self-idolatry as historically true and place a Jewish valuation on this. As a matter of historical fact, Jesus probably never did declare himself to be God. But it was not until the fourteenth century, in the work of Profiat Duran, that Jewish controversialists began to make the distinction between the historical Jesus and the Jesus of the Christian Church which later became the basis of what has been called the Jewish position on Jesus. In the thirteenth-century disputations, it was assumed that Jesus had, as the Church asserted, claimed to be God. Yeḥiel did not deny that he himself, and all other Jews, regarded this alleged claim as idolatrous, and that this Jewish view, if expressed in the Talmud, would come under the Christian definition of blasphemy. He denied, however, that this Jewish view of Jesus' claims ever finds expression in the Talmud, which therefore ought not to be suppressed by Christians as a blasphemous work.

The question may be asked, however, whether Yeḥiel really believed that Jesus was not mentioned in the Talmud, or whether he put this forward as an ingenious ploy in the desperate situation in which he found himself. All copies of the Talmud in Paris had been seized and were being held for burning, if the result of the inquiry were unfavourable. The question of the mere censorship of the Talmud had not yet offered itself; at present, it was a question of the complete suppression of the Talmud and of the academies devoted to its study. It would certainly have been pardonable of the rabbi to attempt some condonation in which he did not fully believe, to prevent such tyrannical proceedings by one religious culture against another.

It is certainly the case that Yeḥiel's contention on the passages mentioning Jesus was not the view generally held among the Jews. It appears from the commentaries of Rashi and the Tosafists on the Talmud that all the passages mentioning Jesus by name were regarded as referring to the Christian Jesus. Moreover, the popular anti-Christian account of the life of Jesus known as *Toledot Yeshu* built many of its incidents on these very Talmudic passages. In particular, the passage referring to Jesus as the rebuffed pupil of Joshua ben Peraḥia was accepted as referring to the Christian Jesus by no less a person than Moses Naḥmanides, the great Jewish disputant at the Barcelona Disputation thirty-three years later. (Naḥmanides considered that the Talmud's dating of Jesus at about one hundred years earlier than the date derived from the New

Testament account should be regarded as historically correct.) But of course, in that disputation, Naḥmanides was not defending the Talmud from extermination. On the contrary, the Talmud was held up by the Christian side as the source of Christian truths—a new mode of arguing against the Jews having been developed.

An interesting point is that the other rabbi whose evidence was taken, Rabbi Judah ben David of Melun, also argued that the Talmudic Jesus was a different person from the Christian Jesus, though he was not allowed to consult with Rabbi Yeḥiel during the course of the disputation. This was no doubt an argument currently in common use among the Jews even before this occasion. There is no actual literary instance of the argument being used, however, before this time. The famous book of Jewish history, *Sefer Ha-Qabbala* by Abraham ibn Daud, written about 1160 CE, assumes that the pupil of Joshua ben Peraḥia is the Christian Jesus.

The argument had probably been in use for about a hundred years in France, where Christian persecution and pressure had demanded some explanation of the Talmud's uncomplimentary references to Jesus.[6] The argument would probably never have developed except under such pressure, but that does not mean that it is a bad argument. In modern terms the argument may be stated as follows. The Talmudic references to Jesus which show great chronological discrepancies with the Gospel story (i.e., the Joshua ben Peraḥia story and the Ben Stada story) probably never referred originally to the Christian Jesus, or even to the same person. They are stories about rebellious disciples of various kinds, whether called 'Jesus' or not, which existed in the Talmudic corpus. When some counter to Christian missionary propaganda was required, these stories were found and were assumed to refer to the Christian Jesus, and were thus included in the Talmud as counter-propaganda. The wide discrepancies between these stories and the Gospels show that the original subjects of the stories were not in fact the Christian Jesus. (The exception is the story of the execution at Passover, which seems to have been adapted from the Christian Gospel story rather than from Jewish sources.) Thus Yeḥiel was right in saying that these stories did not *originally* refer to the Christian Jesus, but wrong in saying that in the context of the Talmud as finally redacted they were not intended to denote the Christian Jesus. The root of the matter is that the Talmudic rabbis had no authentic information about Jesus of their own, since his memory had been allowed to die out as a failed messiah.

Only the pressure of Christian missionary activity led to the resuscitation of the name of Jesus in the Talmud, when varied material, only sketchily relevant, was brought into use.

At any rate, Yeḥiel's desperate argument, wrung from him by concern for the survival of the Talmud, was not accepted, and when the censorship of the Talmud came into operation, the few passages referring to Jesus were the first to be excised.

As for the alleged references to Mary, the mother of Jesus (under the name of Miriam, 'the women's hairdresser', b Sanh., 67a), it is doubtful whether these were even secondarily intended to denote the Christian Mary. Rabbi Yeḥiel was able to point out convincingly that Miriam's deceived husband, Pappos ben Juda, lived long after the period of Jesus. Nevertheless, the identification of Miriam with Mary had been made by Jews living *after* the completion of the Talmud, and is found in the *Toledot* literature, so Donin was not entirely beside the mark in making this charge.

(b) Alleged Remarks against Christians. The Talmud undoubtedly contains some remarks hostile to gentiles *(goyim)*, idolaters (*'akum*, an acronym formed from *'ovedei kokhavim u-mazalot*, i.e., 'worshippers of stars and constellations') and heretics *(minim)*. The Mishnah declares (Av. Zar., 2: 1), 'Cattle may not be left in the inns of the *'akum** since they are suspected of bestiality; nor may a woman remain alone with one of them since they are suspected of lewdness; nor may a man remain alone with one of them since they are suspected of shedding blood.' The question is whether these strictures, dating from the ancient world, applied to thirteenth-century Christians. Nicholas Donin, in this part of his arraignment, was in bad faith, for he had enough Talmudic knowledge to be aware that his substitution of the word 'Christians' for the word *'akum* in this kind of saying was unjustified and unhistorical. Yeḥiel pointed out, quite correctly, that many of the Talmudic laws in relation to *'akum* were not applied to Christians; for example, the prohibition against trading with *'akum*, and that therefore Jewish law manifestly distinguished between *'akum* and Christians, not regarding Christians as idolaters, but as monotheists who respected the Hebrew Scriptures. Moreover, Donin's blanket charges against the Talmud took no account of the fact that the Talmud is not an apodictic code, but a developing legal system, in which laws have to be considered in relation to the time and circumstances in which they were promulgated. A law relating to gentiles promulgated at a time of persecution or war might have

*The earliest reading, here and elsewhere, is actually *'goyim'*.

no application in a time of toleration and peace. Any nation or religious community could easily be indicted on the basis of laws taken out of context from codes promulgated many centuries ago. Further, by no means all pronouncements in the Talmud had the force of law even at the time they were made. It is clearly unfair that Talmudic Judaism should be held responsible for every passing testy observation recorded in the name of some individual rabbi whose views were not adopted as binding law, especially as the Talmud is not just a law code, but a compound of biography, history, jests, tall stories, parables, sermons and everything else that goes to make up a picture of Jewish life over a period of several centuries.

The wonder is that, given the careless, unguarded nature of the Talmud and its freedom from pedantic restrictions on subject-matter, there are so few passages in this vast corpus which fall below a general standard of humanity, urbanity and intellectual acumen.

All the above considerations apply to the quotation from the Talmud out of which Donin sought to make the greatest capital; a quotation which has been used time and again by anti-Semites as proof of the depravity of the Jews and their animosity to mankind. This is the saying of Rabbi Simeon ben Yoḥai: 'Kill the best of the Gentiles' (b Sof., 15). This saying never had the force of law. It was the agonised cry of a rabbi who was a fugitive from Roman persecution—a persecution so bitter (after the Bar Kokhba revolt) that it invites comparison with the Nazi era. Moreover, the text of the saying, in some redactions, has the qualification 'in time of war.' This, in fact, was Rabbi Yeḥiel's immediate rejoinder, quoting from the text given in the Tractate Soferim. It is a universal principle, even among the most civilised nations, that in wartime an enemy may be killed without consideration for his personal character, however admirable. It is true that the qualification 'in time of war' was probably not part of Rabbi Simeon ben Yoḥai's original saying, but was added at a later date. It had certainly been part of the text for some hundreds of years before the Paris Disputation. Clearly, Rabbi Simeon's cry of agony had been softened into something more like a permanent principle by a later hand. There is no ground here for supposing that the Jewish ethic condoned the shedding of gentile blood. Even in its original setting, the saying is justified by a reference to the Egyptians pursuing the Israelites to kill them; and Rabbi Simeon's own circumstances were those of war and persecution; so the qualification was an unspoken one even before it was made explicit.

Apart from this, Rabbi Yeḥiel's main argument was that Talmudic sayings about 'gentiles' or 'idolaters' did not necessarily apply to Christians, since these sayings, in their original context, applied to the nations of the ancient world. Rabbi Yeḥiel pointed out, in evidence, that in actual practice various laws of the Talmud about 'gentiles' or 'idolaters' were not observed with regard to Christians. 'Jews have undergone martyrdom countless times for their religion,' observed the rabbi, 'and would not disobey the Talmud if they really thought the people called "gentiles" in the Talmud included Christians.' He goes on to say, 'We sell cattle to Christians, we have partnerships with Christians, we allow ourselves to be alone with them, we give our children to Christian wet-nurses, and we teach Torah to Christians—for there are now many Christian priests who can read Hebrew books.' All the above forms of social intercourse are forbidden by the Talmud in relation to *goyim* or *'akum,* on the grounds that they were presumed to be guilty of unnatural vice, murder and idolatry. It is interesting that the rabbi turns the very knowledge of Hebrew, through which the Church was beginning to attack the Talmud, into an argument for leaving the Talmud alone; for this knowledge, now turned against the Jews, was gained through the co-operation of the Jews, on the understanding that Christians, unlike *'akum,* would not misuse it.

It is undoubtedly true that many of the Talmudic laws against *'akum* were not applied to Christians. In fact, the main laws that prevented social intercourse between Jews and Christians in the Middle Ages were those passed by Christians against Jews. From the early councils of Elvira and Laodicea (300 and 360) which forbade sharing feasts and fasts with Jews or attendance at Jewish banquets, various laws were enacted to prevent Christians from becoming friendly with Jews: Jews were not to be employed as doctors, Christians were not to bathe with Jews, Christian clergy were not to eat or have business associations with Jews, the Jews were to wear a special badge to mark them out, etc. It is ironic, then, that in the midst of all this discrimination against Jews, the Jews should be taken to task for discriminating against Christians, on the basis of laws enacted eight hundred years previously against quite different people.

At the same time, it must be acknowledged that the distinction between the Talmudic *'akum* and Christians was not as clear-cut as Rabbi Yeḥiel represented it to be. As Jacob Katz has shown,[7] the state of Jewish law on this matter was somewhat confused. Though considerable steps had been taken towards nullifying the Talmudic *'akum* laws in relation to Christians, this had been done on a piecemeal basis. Ad hoc adjustments had been made in relation to particular laws, but no general distinction had been laid down by any authoritative rabbi of the kind which Rabbi Yeḥiel enunciates. In fact, in stating categorically that Christians were not *'akum*, Rabbi Yeḥiel was somewhat in advance of the state of the Jewish law in the thirteenth century.

It was not until the fourteenth century that a leading authority, Menaḥem ha-Meiri, stated in measured, legal form (and not under pressure of public harassment, like Yeḥiel) that, as a matter of general principle, Christians were not *'akum*, but belonged to the category of civilised peoples *('ummot ha-gedurot be-darkhei ha-datot)*.[8] Even so, some *'akum* laws continued to be applied to Christians, for example the prohibition against drinking their wine. Jewish law continued to be somewhat inconsistent in this area even up to the present day, the situation being that some *'akum* laws have been repealed in relation to Christians and some have not; where historical circumstances enforced a change, this took place and was justified by Meiri's principle or something like it; but where there was no pressure, the law remained, sanctioned by ancient custom.

In the time of Yeḥiel, though many statements existed in the codes and *Tosafot* modifying the status of Christians, there would have been no general assent to the blanket statement made at the disputation by Yeḥiel that Christians are not *'akum* in any respect. After all, massacres of Jews by Christians had only recently occurred[9] and were in daily danger of recurring. The ghastly massacres of Jews during the Crusades had had the blessing and connivance of the lower clergy and only half-hearted condemnation by the Church. The new horror of the blood-libel accusations was beginning to be heard. The life of a Jew was not worth much. There was thus little to contradict the idea that Christians, like the *'akum* of old, were congenital shedders of blood and uncivilised people, against whom a Jew should be on his guard. On the whole, Jews in the Middle Ages took Christians as they found them. When Christians were civilised in their behaviour, they were dissociated from *'akum* and the Talmudic laws, which were declared to be inapplicable. When, as often happened, Christians were bloodthirsty, vicious and idolatrous, Jews tended to identify them with the Talmudic *'akum*. Yehiel's statement, therefore, though in accordance with advancing concepts of Jewish law, was more sweeping than the condition of Christendom at that time warranted, and would not have been made in so general a form if Yeḥiel had not been under pressure. Indeed, Yeḥiel expressly made his distinction between Christians and *'akum* on the ground that Christians of the period applied standards of justice and humanity towards Jews. The implication is that where those standards were lacking, Christians did indeed revert to the condition of *'akum*.

It should be borne in mind that through a large part of the Middle Ages, Jews, with much justification, regarded themselves as a civilised people who were living among savages. When they saw, for example, Christian judicial procedures in which torture was used to produce confessions which were then used as valid evidence, they could hardly avoid contrasting this with their own law in which even a voluntary confession was not regarded as valid evidence. Signs of advancing civilisation among Christians were noted and welcomed, and the Jewish legal codes altered accordingly, but this was not a process that could be hurried in anticipation of actual improvements.

The Charge of Unedifying Material in the Talmud

(a) Blasphemies against God. In pursuance of the Christian claim to be entitled to regulate Jewish beliefs and doctrines, even when they did not bear on Christianity, if they were in contravention of the basic principles of monotheism common to Christianity and Judaism, charges were brought against certain passages in the Talmud which were alleged to be blasphemous by reason of their anthropomorphism or their lack of respect for the dignity of God. Such were passages which represented God as grieving over the Jewish exile, or as acknowledging a mistake on His own part, or as acknowledging defeat in an argument with a human.

At first sight, it may seem surprising that Christians should object to passages in which God is described as weeping and suffering. After all, the suffering of God is a central concept of Christianity. The answer is that, in Christian doctrine, God the Father is 'impassible'. Only God the Son is capable of suffering, and then only when in the flesh. This is the orthodox Nicene doctrine, as opposed to heresies such as Patripassianism. Aquinas insists on the impassibility of God the Father, but some modern Christian theologians have attempted to qualify this doctrine.[10] The criticisms made of the Talmud in this matter are thus an interesting example of the theological error of equating God the Father of Christianity with the God of Judaism, who is not impassible, and has attributes which in Christianity belong not to the Father but to the other Persons of the Trinity. The fact is that the concept of the God of the Old Testament as a figure held in common between Judaism and Christianity is a mistake. By adding God the Son, Christianity altered God the Father considerably, too. In seeking to regulate Jewish ideas of God, therefore, in the light of their own conception of God the Father, Christians (quite apart from the general inadmissibility of their claim to such jurisdiction) were acting on false premises.

Rabbi Yeḥiel was thus able to answer convincingly that the Talmudic conception of God is a valid continuation of the 'passible' God of the Old Testament. The Christian idea of an 'impassible' God was derived not from the Old Testament but from Greek philosophy. As Yeḥiel indicated, the God who answered Job out of the whirlwind was not to be contained within such bloodless categories.

An even more interesting example of the gap between Christian and Jewish theology arises from the accusation that the Talmud sometimes portrays God as being defeated by man. One passage cited here was the extraordinary story of Rabbi Eliezer, Rabbi Joshua, and the voice from Heaven *(bat qol)*. In this story (b BM, 59b), a debate goes on between Rabbi Eliezer and Rabbi Joshua on a point of law. Rabbi Eliezer, outvoted, causes miracles to happen, to prove that he is in the right. But the rabbis decide that miracles do not constitute arguments. Then Rabbi Eliezer calls for a voice from Heaven to support him—and the voice from Heaven duly comes to his support. But the rabbis, after a speech from Rabbi Joshua, decide that the voice from Heaven is out of order and should be disregarded; for the Torah has given to the council of rabbis the right to decide such matters by majority decision, right or wrong. Later, Rabbi Nathan, meeting the prophet Elijah, asked him what God thought of these proceedings, to which Elijah replied, 'He laughed, and said, "My children have defeated me." ' This story was cited by Nicholas Donin at the Paris Disputation as a compound example of absurdity, disrespect to God amounting to blasphemy, and illicit exaltation of the status of the Talmudic rabbis, who held their decisions to be irreversible even by God. The story thus sums up in itself the whole range of the Christian objections to the Talmud.[11]

Many opponents of the Talmud, since the Paris Disputation,

have cited the above story as an example of absurdity; yet it is in reality one of the great religious stories. It shows the humanism of Judaism, and its sense of a compact or covenant between man and God, in which God must keep his part of the bargain and not overstep the bounds of freedom which he has allotted to man. As for the possibility of successful argument of man against God, the Hebrew Bible affords many examples, of which perhaps the most striking is Abraham's cry, 'Shall not the Judge of all the earth do justice?' (Genesis, 18: 25.) That God is the kind of good father who is pleased when his children show their independence of him is a concept not to be found in Christianity at all, but it is characteristic of Judaism, which regards the object of human life as being the fulfilment of human possibilities, not as self-negation and self-annihilation before God. And the power of independent decision on the part of the rabbis is simply a sanction for the working-out of God's Word in human life—a concept which Christians understood in relation to their own synods and papal councils (though even here they had to introduce a notion of infallibility and direct divine inspiration that Judaism was able to do without).

(b) Allegedly Foolish or Obscene Passages. The Talmud contains a large element of folklore. Some of this consists of exaggerated 'tall stories', such as the tales of the huge Og, king of Bashan (b Ber., 54b). Some of the folklore consists of stories which offend against the canons of good taste, as these have been understood in later times; for example, the story that Adam copulated with all the animals before finding his true mate in Eve, or the story that Ham's offence was that he castrated his father, Noah. Nowadays, we are accustomed to see folklore of this kind as an uninhibited expression of infantile desires and fantasies, and as having psychological value and interest. When we read of Kronos castrating his father Uranos (a story to which the Talmudic story of Ham and Noah has obvious affinities), we relate the story to Freud rather than to sadistic pornography, bearing in mind especially the function of such stories in the sexual and social orientation of primitive peoples.

Have such stories any place in the canonical religious texts of advanced monotheistic religions? Here we have to bear in mind the status of these stories within the Talmudical canon. The distinction between Aggadah (narrative and homiletical material) and Halakhah (legal material), crucial to the understanding of the Talmudic literature, was here raised by Rabbi Yeḥiel; a distinction that proved important in later disputations, though in a rather different way. Yeḥiel indicated that the Aggadic parts of the Talmud were not regarded as having the same authority as the Halakhic parts. 'You may believe them or disbelieve them as you wish, for no practical decision depends on them.' Later, Yeḥiel declared that the stories of Og were mere hyperboles, and were not to be taken literally, any more than Biblical expressions such as, 'The cities are great and fortified up to Heaven.' However, he also advances arguments to show that they can, after all, be taken literally, for they are no more miraculous than stories in the Bible which were believed literally by Christians and Jews alike. There is no real contradiction here. Yeḥiel is saying that the Aggadic stories *need* not be believed literally, but in many cases, they *can* be believed literally. When not believed literally, they should be regarded, not as stupidities, but as figures of speech. Yeḥiel might have added, but did not, that they might have some allegorical or mystical meaning. He certainly thought this, for Jewish mysticism took much of its sustenance from these very passages, understood in a figurative or coded sense.

In the later disputations, the question of the status of the Aggadah became even more important, because Aggadic passages were now being used, not as *stultitiae* through which the Talmud could be attacked, but as proofs of the truth of Christianity. Again, the Jewish disputants made the assertion that they were not bound by the literal meaning of any Aggadic passage. The whole question of the status of the Aggadah will be discussed more fully in relation to the Barcelona Disputation.

Some of the alleged 'blasphemies against God', or anthropomorphisms, in the Talmud are, again, examples of the figurative or poetic style of the Aggadah (e.g., the passage which describes God as wearing phylacteries). Rabbi Yeḥiel was able to point out that such anthropomorphisms are common enough in the Bible, where, for example, God is called a 'man of war' or described as having a 'right hand'.

Judah Rosenthal, in his article 'The Talmud on Trial', says strangely, 'In general the Rabbis [at the Paris Disputation] admitted the following three main charges: errors, blasphemies in Deum and the *stultitiae*. They denied the charges of: *blasphemiae in Christum* and *blasphemiae contra Christianos*.' The rabbis (i.e., Yeḥiel and Judah) admitted nothing, except in the trivial sense of agreeing that the Talmudic passages were correctly quoted. If they had admitted that the Talmud contains blasphemies and obscenities, this would have been a betrayal of Judaism. Isadore Loeb's remarks on this matter[12] are worth quoting:

> Le Talmud est un livre profondement religieux, c'est le plus singulier des contre-sens que de lui attribuer des intentions de blasphème contre Dieu ou contre les règles de la morale. Mais le Talmud est de son temps et de son pays, il n'a pas le même tour d'imagination que nous ni les mêmes pudeurs. Il reste, en partie, une espèce de code, et tous les codes du monde ont, pour la précision crue du langage, des immunités spéciales. Tous les arguments de cette espèce sont, du reste, tirés de cette partie du Talmud qu'on appelle l'Aggada, et à laquelle les juges de 1240 n'ont absolument rien compris. L'Aggada, ce sont ces jeux où se complaisait et se délassait, après l'étude serieuse, l'imagination des docteurs et où elle se donnait pleine carrière. Aller prendre au serieux et traiter gravement ces contes merveilleux, ces légendes, toutes ces inventions folles, mais souvent délicates et poétiques, des rabbins de Babylone, c'est commettre la plus lourde bévue. Il faut s'en amuser avec les docteurs, elles sont le charme et la récréation du Talmud.

2

The Barcelona Disputation, 1263

When we move from the Paris Disputation to the Barcelona Disputation, we find ourselves breathing a different atmosphere. Here we have a debate, rather than an inquisition. It would be wrong to overstress this point, for even in Barcelona, the discussion was far from being held on equal terms. There was always the possibility of violence below the surface of urbanity. Naḥmanides, the Jewish participant, despite all the guarantees of safety that were given him, was pursued later by the Dominicans (because of the account which he wrote of the disputation) and was lucky to escape with his life. From the first, Naḥmanides was most reluctant to take part, because of the danger to himself and to the Jewish population generally, since the non-Jewish population was liable to be roused to violence. Even during the course of the disputation he made a serious attempt to have it discontinued, because of warnings and threats which had been made.

Nevertheless, the tone of the Christian attack is here much more conciliatory than in Paris. There are no threats of confiscation or burning of the Talmud depending on the result.[1] The object is not to convict, but to win over. There are many reasons for this, ranging from the religio-political situation in Spain to the character of Dominican missionary activity in the school of Raymund de Peñaforte, the aged scholar and missionary (later canonised) who set the tone of the debate though he did not himself participate in it as a disputant, preferring to give this role to the convert from Judaism, Pablo Christiani.

The last three centuries in Spain before the Barcelona Disputation are known as the Golden Age for the Jews, because they were allowed to develop their literature and culture in comparative freedom. The reason for this is that, in Spain, the Christian states during this period had to contend with the power of Islam. During the course of the protracted reconquest in which the Christians gradually drove the Moors out of Spain, the Jews were needed by both sides. The Christian rulers in this period (*c.* 1000–1230) were more concerned to consolidate their conquests than to promote schemes of religious unification. They found the Jews most useful as an educated administrative middle-class through whom the newly conquered areas could be settled. At the same time, the position of the Jews remained always precarious, as aliens and religious outcasts, who posed no collective threat to the regime, however high individuals among them might rise in the court hierarchy. Jews became powerful in Spanish courts in the same way as Greek freedmen became powerful in the courts of Roman emperors: because they were without a power base, and had cultural qualities which were needed.

Anti-Jewish legislation was always theoretically in force throughout the period, but during the reconquest it was virtually ignored. King James of Aragon, who convened and acted as chairman at the disputation, is an example. He played a distinguished part in the reconquest (earning the sobriquet 'James the Conqueror') and relied heavily on Jews in his administrative posts. When he received missives from the Pope instructing him to dismiss his Jewish administrators, he handed on the instructions to some of his subject towns, but ignored them himself. Yet the very fact that the disputation was held was a sign that the age of toleration and symbiosis (with its extraordinary flowering of Jewish achievement in poetry, philosophy, law, grammar and science) was coming to an end. The Jews, as happened so frequently in various regions of Europe, had taught their pupils too well, and were about to be ejected ignominiously and brutally as superfluous. Christian Europe, now master in its house, was entering on its own period of cultural flowering, which produced many great figures, but also produced the Inquisition, the massacre of the Albigensians, the sack of Constantinople, and the systematic persecution and degradation of the Jews.

Meanwhile, the Jews of Spain escaped some of the manifestations of gathering Christian power. The massacres of Jews during the Crusades (including the Albigensian Crusade) in France and Germany passed them by. There were occasional outbreaks of violence against them, but on the whole they lived in prosperous, settled communities (*aljamas*). When the Dominicans moved against them, by calling their most famous rabbi, Moses ben

Naḥman, to a disputation, they did so in the guise of courtesy and persuasion, rather than denunciation as in Paris.

The new approach was to attempt to prove the truth of Christianity from the Jewish writings, including the Talmud. It was nothing new, of course, to prove Christianity from the Old Testament, which was the main source of Christian proofs, and had been a battleground for disputing Christians and Jews ever since the early Christian centuries. The Barcelona Disputation went over some of this old ground; for example, the 'Shiloh' text (Genesis, 49: 10), and the prophecies of Daniel, and the Suffering Servant passage of Isaiah. What was new was the adducing of Talmudic and Midrashic texts, both for their own sakes, and as part of the exegesis of Biblical passages. This shows a much friendlier attitude towards the Jewish post-Biblical canonical literature than had been shown at Paris. There the virulent anti-Talmudic attitude of the main Christian disputant, Nicholas Donin, sprang from his previous hostility to the Talmud while still a Jew, under the influence of Karaism. Donin had persuaded the Pope that the Talmud was wholly pernicious work, which ought to be expunged from the memory of man. Raymund de Peñaforte, however, had a much more civilised approach, towards both Jews and Muslims. He understood that in order to produce genuine conversions, he must enter into the culture and minds of his prospective converts. Accordingly, he set up academies where Dominican monks were set to work to study the Jewish and Muslim classics. This provided the first impulse for the study of Hebrew and Arabic at the universities, sanctioned by the Council of Vienne in 1311. In the study of the Talmud, Peñaforte was helped by the accession of Jewish converts to Christianity, some of them learned in the Talmud. One of these was Pablo Christiani, who took the main Christian role at Barcelona. Raymund Martini, the pupil of Raymund de Peñaforte, was the greatest Christian student of the Talmud and Midrash.

But the Talmud was studied not only as a guide to the Jewish mind, but as a source of Christian truth. The beginning of this line of thought is in the Barcelona Disputation, and it was further developed in Raymund Martini's work *Pugio Fidei,* written about twenty years later. Various Aggadic passages, collected from Talmud and Midrash, were thought to support Christian doctrines, especially the divinity of the Messiah, his suffering on the Cross, the date of his advent, and his promulgation of a new Law.

Naḥmanides immediately challenged the rationale of this contention. Why should the Talmud be thought to contain Christian doctrine? Why did the rabbis of the Talmud remain Jews, if they were the purveyors of Christian ideas? Pablo Christiani brushed aside this question as an evasion. From other sources, however, we see that the theory behind the Christian arguments from the Talmud was that the Talmud does contain early material uncontaminated by later Jewish opposition to Christianity. The Jews of the time of Jesus possessed traditions, other than the words of Scripture, bearing on the nature of the coming Messiah. This material they perversely refused to heed, and in compiling the Talmud, overlaid it with masses of other material in an opposite sense, but patient excavation can uncover the authentic earliest layer. This is an enterprise very similar to that of certain modern Christian students of the Talmud.

It must certainly be said in favour of this approach that there are certain aspects of Aggadah of both Talmud and Midrash which tended to be ignored by medieval Jews because they were felt to be something of a handicap in Jewish-Christian controversy. A good example (raised by Pablo Christiani at Barcelona) is afforded by the Aggadic material interpreting the Suffering Servant of Isaiah as the Messiah, rather than as Israel in general. Naḥmanides, in the disputation, did not deny the existence of such an interpretation in Midrashic sources, but said he preferred the alternative interpretation that the passage refers to the sufferings of the people Israel, the servant of mankind. Naḥmanides added that even if one accepts the Messianic interpretation, the passage has little application to Jesus, since it refers to sufferings but not to death at the hands of enemies. To the Christian scholars who had found the Messianic reference in the Midrash with great joy, this seemed an evasion. Any Midrashic interpretation, it seemed to them, should be accepted without further argument by Jews. They did not attempt to cope with the fact of contradictory interpretations existing in the Midrash. They themselves, as Christians, were entitled to accept part of the Midrash and reject the rest (this was of the essence of their method), but Jews were not entitled to a selective method. They must accept everything. The Jewish view that the Midrash gives a wealth of alternative explanations, not always consistent with each other, and that some may be taken literally, some allegorically, and some regarded as mere playful fancies, was somehow too sophisticated for their Christian opponents, especially when complicated by the view (put forward by Naḥmanides in the disputation in relation to King David and the Messiah) that a Biblical passage may sometimes carry double or multiple meanings simultaneously.

The modern view of the Suffering Servant passage, interpreted as referring to the Messiah, is that this interpretation is not found in the earliest Aggadic material, which regards the Messiah as a happy, triumphant figure. It was not until the defeat of the Bar Kokhba rebellion (135 CE) and the resulting miseries of the Jewish people, that the idea of a suffering Messiah entered Jewish thought and was reflected in Aggadah. This development may even have been influenced by Christianity—an ironic thought, when these Midrashim were to be used later to prove that Christian ideas of a suffering Messiah were derived from an early stratum of Judaism. A similar irony is to be found in the Renaissance interest in Jewish mysticism. Scholars like Pico della Mirandola, who discovered Christian doctrines in the Zohar, thus confirming the ancient origin of the doctrine of the Trinity and the Incarnation, were not aware that the Zohar was partly the result of gnostic, neo-Platonic, Albigensian and Christian influences on Judaism. Christian scholars tended to ascribe an awesome antiquity to Jewish works which were really of comparatively recent origin. (The above line of argument was not available, of course, to the Jews of the Middle Ages, since they too ascribed great antiquity to the works in question.) Jewish scholars, on the other hand, lacked an historical view altogether. They accepted all Aggadic material (in the recognised collections) as equally ancient. The Christian scholars were, in a sense, pioneers of an historical approach to the Aggadah, though their analysis, on a modern view, was topsy-turvy; they regarded the latest material as the earliest.

Similar considerations apply to some of the alleged Midrashic material included by Raymund Martini in the *Pugio Fidei.* Some of this material, of a markedly mystical or gnostic character, is not found in any Jewish collection of Midrashim, and controversy has raged about whether these are 'forged Midrashim', or whether Martini had access to Midrashic collections which are now lost.[2] Certainly, Martini was capable of misunderstanding Midrashic material, or of quoting it misleadingly out of context. It is doubtful, however, that he would have invented any. He probably took his mystical Midrashim, which seemed to support Christian doctrines of Godhead, from collections, such as those of Moses ha-Darshan (eleventh century) which drew on apocryphal or gnostic sources. The Midrashim were a vast, heterogeneous literature, covering many centuries in time, and derived from many sources, some of them medieval. Christian scholars, such as Martini, exaggerated their antiquity and made no attempt to distinguish between early and late Midrashim, except by the tendentious test that those which seemed to support Christianity must be ipso facto earlier and more authentic.

In the light of the above considerations, we may weigh the question of how far the Aggadic portions of the Talmud were regarded as authoritative and canonical by the Jews. This proved a highly important question in the disputations. The question of the status of the Aggadah had been raised in the Paris Disputation, where Rabbi Yeḥiel declared that he was not obliged to answer any questions based on Aggadic passages, since they were not authoritative 'for any practical decision'. This particular formula, expressing the inferior status of the Aggadah, was traditional since Geonic times. Some of the Geonim, in fact, had expressed themselves even more forthrightly about the Aggadah, declaring roundly that some Aggadic material was foolish. Even in the Talmud itself, some passages critical of the Aggadah can be found.[3] Much more common, however, was the view that the Aggadah was not exactly inferior to the Halakhah, but on a different plane, employing different criteria, and requiring a different kind of sensibility. For example, the famous legalist Rabbi Akiva, so brilliant in the intricacies of Halakhah, was roundly reproved when he ventured clumsily into the more imaginative and intuitive region of the Aggadah, and was told to go back to his usual studies (b San., 67b).

There is no need, therefore, to argue that Rabbi Yeḥiel at Paris, Naḥmanides at Barcelona, and the rabbis at Tortosa, were insincere when they dismissed Aggadic citations as unauthoritative. Many scholars, both Christian and Jewish, have expressed amazement at this, in view of the enormous respect shown by Naḥmanides, for example, in his writings on the Bible, for the Aggadic commentaries. Moreover, Naḥmanides was a great adherent of the Kabbalah, the mystical, theosophic doctrine which was making headway in Spain and Provence, and was soon to produce the Zohar; and this doctrine, which claimed to be the expression of the deepest truths of Judaism, found its chief inspiration in the Aggadah. But the point is that, precisely because of its profundity, the Aggadah could not be quoted in support of hard-and-fast doctrine. It would be like quoting a Keats sonnet in support of a theorem in geometry. The kind of truth to be found in the Aggadah was poetic, analogical, subliminal. Its object was to create a mood, rather than to state a fact. One could not argue about an Aggadic passage, one could only respond to it. A good example of this is the Aggadah quoted by Pablo Christiani at Barcelona, to the effect that the Messiah was born on the very day that the Temple was destroyed (*Ekhah* R, 1: 51). Pablo Christiani thought he had scored a great point; here was the Jewish tradition stating that the Messiah, for whom the Jews were waiting, had come long ago, just as Christians believed. Naḥmanides gave some rationalistic replies to this: that the date of the destruction of the Temple was not the date of the birth of Jesus; that the birth of the Messiah was not the same thing as his advent; that the Messiah, like Methuselah, might live for a thousand years or more before entering on his specific mission. But Naḥmanides' main reply was simply, 'I do not believe this Aggadah.' He went on to explain that other Aggadic passages gave a different view: that the Messiah would not be born until near the time of Redemption; and that, not being able to believe the literal truth of two contradictory propositions, he preferred to accept the latter view as fact, while reserving the probability that the Aggadah quoted by Christiani had some non-literal meaning—that 'it has some other interpretation derived from the secrets of the Sages.' An Aggadah might be fact, or it might not be; it was a matter of individual judgement to decide which. If Naḥmanides had been asked what he thought was the esoteric meaning of the Aggadah whose literal meaning he rejected, he might well have volunteered a kabbalistic interpretation. The story, considered in full, is certainly moving and poetically suggestive. The telepathic utterances, both of the destruction of the Temple and of the birth of the Messiah, are made by a wandering Arab, interpreting the lowing of the cow with which a Jewish farmer is ploughing. At the first low, interpreted as signifying the destruction, he tells the farmer to unharness the cow; at the second lowing, signifying the birth, he tells him to harness it again. Here we have basic polarities of agriculture and nomadism, destruction and rebirth. At the destruction of the Temple, the desert returns, and the cow is unharnessed; but the adventure of agriculture immediately begins anew, as the Messiah is born. Hope is born at the point of greatest despair, order is renewed as all things return to chaos. Whether by the canons of Kabbalah or of modern literary analysis, the story is full of meaning. The birth of the Messiah, in this story, is the beginning of new hope, not the fulfilment of all things. The emergence of the Jews from a nomadic past and the recrudescence of bare essentials at the moment of deepest crisis are expressed with the greatest of narrative and symbolic economy. A literal interpretation deprives the story not only of its poetry, but of its truth.

If we look at the history of Jewish Biblical exegesis in this period, whether in the French school of Rashi and Rashbam (see Rashi on Gen., 3: 8 and Rashbam on Gen., 37: 2), or in the Spanish school of Ibn Ezra and David Kimḥi, we find that it is, in a sense, a struggle against the Aggadah, especially that of the Midrash. These commentators were all striving for what they called *peshat*, the literal meaning of the Biblical text. To this end, they developed the profound grammatical studies which were later utilised by the Christian Hebraists of the Renaissance. The Aggadic type of interpretation (which they called *derush*) was allowed its own validity but was carefully distinguished from the plain, literal meaning of the text, to which it was regarded as supplementary, existing on a different plane of meaning. Here they based their researches on the Talmudic axiom, 'A Biblical text never loses its literal meaning (b Shabb., 63a)—however many symbolic, legalistic, or simply fanciful interpretations are added to it. As Frank Talmage has pointed out,[4] this drive for literal meaning was to some extent stimulated, even in the earlier period of David Kimḥi, by the needs of Jewish-Christian controversy. But it was also something perennial in Judaism, which was brought out into sharper emphasis by the need to answer Christian controversialists who blurred the distinction and tension, characteristic in Jewish exegesis, between literal and symbolic meaning.

Not that Aggadic passages were always to be regarded as symbolic. There was also a conflict, this time within the Jewish fold itself, between those who wished to allegorise away entirely the earthy folklore aspect of the Aggadah into frigid Aristotelian or Platonic conceptions, and those who wished to retain its warmth and reality. It was the followers of Maimonides (often going further than Maimonides himself would have ventured), who sought to spiritualise and conceptualise the Aggadah (in a style reminiscent of Philo's in relation to the Bible) to a point at which the representatives of the older, less philosophical, school rebelled. Judah Halevi, the greatest poet of the Golden Age, had protested that the Unmoved Mover of Aristotle was not to be confused with 'the God of Abraham, Isaac and Jacob'. This type of protest is to be found also in the work of Naḥmanides, defending the literal reality of Aggadic conceptions of the Earthly Paradise, the Messianic feast, the resurrection of the dead, the existence of evil spirits, against the allegorists. Naḥmanides, indeed, is a key figure, standing against the over-allegorisation of the Jewish philosophical school, on the one hand, and against the over-literal interpretations of the Christians on the other. The critique directed against the philosophical school was not so much a protest against symbolic interpretation as against a mechanical system of interpretation, based on categories external to Judaism. The critique directed against the Christians was a protest against a mechanical seizing on details, out of context, which might seem to confirm Christian dogmas.

So when the Jewish spokesmen at Paris, Barcelona and Tortosa said that they were not bound to accept the literal meaning of Aggadic statements, they were not expressing any contempt for the Aggadah, nor were they asserting an attitude which they did not genuinely believe. The Talmud, including its Aggadic elements, was held by them in the utmost reverence, as the repository of accumulated Jewish wisdom; but the wisdom was not necessarily on the surface. Moreover, since the Talmud is not an apodictic work, but consists of the opinions of named rabbis, who often disagree among themselves, there is nothing heretical in Judaism in regarding a given Talmudic view as worthy of attention, but peripheral or eccentric, if not downright wrong (and this applies in Halakhic matters too, where thousands of opinions are recorded which are overruled). Even the eccentric or overruled view is regarded as having a certain sanctity and as worthy of study, a contribution to the never-ending search for truth about the Torah. This might seem to make evasion too easy, as the Christian interlocutors Pablo Christiani and Geronimo protested. But the reply of Naḥmanides is that one must understand the style of the Aggadah in order to interpret it, and to know what in it was authoritative and what was not. And Christians would have appreciated such an attitude well enough in the part of their own tradition which corresponded to the Talmud; i.e., the writings of the Fathers, and the doctors of the canon law, where an opinion could be revered as in a sense authoritative even if it were overruled by an even greater authority, or if it were accepted in some sense other than the literal. Indeed, it was not that Christians were too stupid to understand the difference between the literal and the allegorical, for they themselves used just this distinction where it suited their doctrine; for example, in portions of the Old Testament where the Jews preferred a literal interpretation, and Christians preferred an allegorical interpretation (often enough taken from, or adapted from, the work of the Jewish-Hellenistic exegete Philo).

There can be little doubt, then, that Naḥmanides, the greatest Talmudic master of his age, had much the best of it in discussing Talmudic and Midrashic passages with Pablo Christiani, who, in his Jewish days, had reached no high level as a Talmudic student, and was in any case trying to play an unnatural Christian tune on a Jewish instrument. Naḥmanides' technique of argument was to adduce, from his vast knowledge, other passages similar to those quoted by Christiani, in order to show that the latter's inferences were inadmissible. For example, when Christiani argued from the fact that the Midrash interprets the expression 'the spirit of God' as referring to the Messiah to be conclusion that the Midrash regards the Messiah as pre-existent and divine, Naḥmanides merely pointed out that the Midrash elsewhere interprets the same expression as referring to Adam. When Christiani argued the Messiah's divinity from the Midrash's placing of the Messiah on God's right hand, Naḥmanides wanted to know what he made of the Midrash's placing of Abraham on God's left hand. These are typical examples of over-literalness produced by lack of familiarity with the general figurative style of the Midrash.

But there is also here a more fundamental point, relating to the difference between Judaism and Christianity. In Judaism, the Aggadah is subordinate whereas in Christianity, the Aggadah, or what corresponds to the Aggadah, is central. Christianity is an Aggadic religion. This difference accounts for the basic lack of rapprochement and mutual understanding in the disputations.

In Judaism, the centre is occupied by the Law, which regulates the behaviour of the community and the individual. It is in the sphere of law that the serious effort towards definition and precision occurs. Here it was that methods of formal logic and dialectic were developed in order to arrive at hard-and-fast solutions of any problems that arose. But there was no such logic or dialectic for dealing with matters which Christians would have called 'theological' (there is in fact no word for theology in Hebrew). Here the methods used by the Jews were literary, aphoristic, parabolic, intuitive. There was no real *argument* on such matters, for in this area contradictory propositions could both be true. Thus, in this poetic area, it could be true both that the Messiah was born at the time of the destruction of the Temple, and that he was yet to be born. Both statements could exist simultaneously in the yielding web of the Aggadah without arousing any pressing need for decision between the two views or the discovery of a mediating view. There was no urgency about discovering a solution (though it could be a matter of interest) because nobody's salvation hung on the issue. There were no theological dogmas which had to be refined and made precise in order to save one's soul from damning error. There was no religious *duty* to have a definite, precisely defined belief on such matters.

In Christianity, the situation was very different. To have correct, and precisely defined theological beliefs was a matter of the utmost urgency. Wars of theological factions could take place, on the question of whether the substance of the Son was similar *(homoiousios)* or identical *(homoousios)* to that of the Father. Heretics could be burnt at the stake for theological views which, in Judaism, would have been regarded as a matter of personal idiosyncrasy. In Judaism, on the other hand, someone might be excommunicated for holding the view that a particular kind of oven was not an object of ritual impurity (or rather, not for holding such a view but for refusing to bow to a majority decision of competent rabbis against it—see b BM, 59a). Such precisionism in matters of practice seemed to Christians ridiculous and unspiritual; but their own insistence on faith rather than works led to a precisionism in matters of belief which seemed equally ridiculous to the Jews. Jews might split hairs about 'the egg that was laid on a Festival', but Christians split hairs about the substance of the Son. People split hairs on things that they consider important: to Jews the important thing is how people act; to Christians, how they believe.

It is not surprising, therefore, that with such huge differences of outlook, Christians and Jews were often, in the disputations, talking at cross-purposes. Many of the matters discussed were to the Christians of life-and-death importance, but to the Jews of only peripheral interest. This applies in general to the Aggadah itself. Christians, studying the Aggadah, found in it things which seemed to go to the heart of religion, but were surprised to find the Jews wondering why they were making such a fuss about mere Aggadot, about which anyone was at liberty to think what he liked.

The best example of this kind of misunderstanding is the central topic of the Messiah itself. Naḥmanides, at one point in the disputation, begged leave to make a special statement about the Messiah, and the whole burden of this statement was that the Messiah was not as important to Jews as Christians seemed to think. Here again, Naḥmanides' sincerity has been doubted by many Christian scholars, and even by some modern Jewish scholars. But there is no reason to doubt his sincerity in the matter, which can be proved from the fact that he expresses the same point in other writings written for a Jewish audience and not under pressure of Jewish-Christian controversy. Indeed, the point is, in a way, obvious. For the whole point of controversy between Christians and Jews about the Messiah was whether he was to be a divine figure or not—in other words, the controversy was precisely about how important he was supposed to be. If, as Christians thought, the Messiah was divine, then his coming was for every human being the central and essential moment of all history, the moment that counted for every individual's personal salvation. For the Jews, the Messiah had quite a different significance. The essential struggle for salvation lay elsewhere; the Messiah was merely the reward, signifying that the struggle had proved successful. The Messiah did not solve the human dilemma; on the contrary, the appearance of the Messiah would show that the dilemma had already been solved. In Jewish-Christian controversy, of course, the question of the Messiah had to be a central focus of discussion; but that was because the Messiah, or Christ, was so important to Christians, not because he was so important to Jews. If Jews explained their religion to non-Christian inquirers (to the King of the Khazars, for example, as in Judah Halevi's *Khuzari)*, they did not begin with the Messiah as an essential Jewish doctrine. There were other far more important matters to explain first, such as the Exodus from Egypt and the Covenant on Mount Sinai.

Naḥmanides' contention that the Messiah is not of overwhelming importance in Judaism was based on the standpoint of the Talmud, which gives no support to any dogmatic view about the Messiah. It gives such a wide range of views on the subject that it is almost impossible, in Judaism, to hold a view about the Messiah that is heretical. The upshot is that the doctrine simply affords a general hope that history is moving towards an era of peace and justice, and that the struggles towards this end will not prove in vain. The character of this hope is political and social, not soteriological in the individual sense. Medieval Jewish thinkers differed amicably about whether to include the doctrine of the Messiah among the essential principles of Judaism (Maimonides included it, but Albo and Crescas did not). When Naḥmanides told King James that, for a Jew, life in the Exile might have more meaning than life under the Messiah, he was not indulging in posturing or paradox, but spelling out the saying of the Mishnah, 'Better is one hour of repentance and good works in this world than the whole life of the world to come' (M. Avot., 3: 17). In other words, there was more moral excellence in struggling towards a better world than in enjoying it once it had arrived.

This question of what level of importance to assign to the Messianic idea, in fact, underlies every matter discussed at the Barcelona Disputation. For example, it underlies the very interesting discussion that took place about the Christian doctrine of Original Sin. This might seem at first sight to be an independent point of theological difference between Christianity and Judaism. But it is intimately bound up with the status of the Messiah; for it is only if mankind is thought to be in a hopeless state of sin that a divine Messiah is needed to rescue mankind from an eternity of damnation. In Judaism, Naḥmanides stoutly maintained, there is no doctrine of Original Sin, in the Christian sense that Adam's guilt was inherited by his posterity. 'I did not inherit the sin of Adam any more than I inherited the sin of Pharaoh,' he said. Adam's sin was his own personal sin, and there is no such thing as inherited guilt. It was true, however, that mankind as a whole inherited the evil consequences of Adam's sin, namely, the curse of work and the curse of pain in childbirth; this is all that we can conclude from the Scriptural account. Consequently, mankind does not stand in fear of eternal damnation because of the sin of Adam, which has been sufficiently atoned for. There is thus no need for a divine Saviour to rescue mankind from a devil-dominated earth. Here again, the Jewish Messiah occupies a far smaller place in the scheme of things, being a reward, not a necessity.

It might be said the Pablo Christiani here missed an opportunity, because, despite Naḥmanides' sweeping disavowal of Original Sin, the Talmud does contain the assertion of something very like a doctrine of Original Sin. Ironically, this passage was quoted at the Paris Disputation by Nicholas Donin, but not as a confirmation of the Christian doctrine of Original Sin, rather as an example of the obscenity and stupidity of the Talmud. The Talmudic passage in question (b Av. Zar., 22b) is that which asserts that Eve had sexual intercourse with the serpent, and that, as a result, an 'impurity' *(zohama)* was injected into mankind; and that the Children of Israel were purified from this taint when they received the Law on Mount Sinai. (Some translate *zohama* as 'lasciviousness' rather than as 'impurity'.) This was attacked as obscene, because of the allegation of intercourse between Eve and the serpent, and as objectionable also because of the alleged taint remaining with those peoples which did not receive the Law. On the first point, modern Freudian analysis would see not obscenity but insight into the subliminal motivations of the Eden story. On the second point, there is some irony in the indignation expressed by Christians at the division of mankind into those purged of Original Sin and those still affected by it—a division very characteristic of Christianity, only in a much more extreme form, since those outside the Church were regarded as eternally damned. But the real point to be made is that this expression of the idea of Original Sin in the Talmud is not a *doctrine*. It is the stray idea of an individual rabbi, and has no doctrinal force. It is a piece of Aggadah, and as such has entered the Jewish tradition as a facet of the truth. Those Christians, whether in medieval or modern times, who have tried to validate Christianity from the Talmud, have tended to overlook the fact that while most of the doctrines of Christianity can be found somewhere in the Talmud, they are found in a very different perspective. Ideas which are central and essential in Christianity are, in Judaism, peripheral and inessential, and therefore, in the total perspective, very different in meaning.

The chief example of this, of course, is the doctrine of the Messiah itself; and the Barcelona Disputation is probably best understood as the thrashing-out of the difference of status of the Messiah-idea in Christianity and Judaism. Another very important aspect of this clash is the simple question with which the disputation began, 'Has the Messiah come, or is he still to come?' This is not a mere question of historical fact, but a question of philosophical approach.

One of Naḥmanides' greatest moments in the disputation was when he challenged the Christians' belief that they were living in the Messianic era, and that Christendom was the realisation of the Messianic ideal, the kingdom of God on earth. 'From the days of Jesus until now, the whole world has been full of violence and plundering.' Yet, according to the prophet, the advent of the Messiah would bring an era when 'they shall beat their swords into ploughshares . . . nation shall not lift up sword against nation, neither shall they learn war any more'. The Christians, however, were not greatly affected by this argument, because, as Pablo Christiani had explained, the great things wrought by the advent of the Messiah, Jesus, had all occurred not on the crude visible, political, social level, but in the area of the spirit. In a region beyond human ken, great things had happened: hell had been harrowed. On earth, the possibility of salvation had been opened, and a great institution, the Church, had been founded to develop this possibility, and this institution had clearly been blessed by God, as was shown by its success.

To Naḥmanides, on the other hand, all these great happenings were non-happenings. It was easy, he said, to talk of the overcoming of the forces of evil in some unverifiable region of the cosmos; but this did not amount to much when the forces of evil were clearly still rampant on earth. The coming of the Messiah ought to make some visible difference; and all the texts upon which Jews relied, both in the Bible and the Talmud, stated plainly that the coming of the Messiah would bring about many striking differences on the plane of visible reality: the redemption of the people of Israel, and the inauguration of an era of peace throughout the world. As for the alleged realisation of the kingdom of God in the form of the Christian Church, centred on the Pope in Rome, Naḥmanides could see in this only a continuation of the might of the Roman Empire, with its familiar accompaniments of warring and oppression.

The Christians contending that the Messiah had come, and the Jews insisting that he had not yet come, were thus arguing about an essential point of difference between the two faiths: the nature of salvation. To Jews, salvation was a social, political concept, involving the radical betterment of the whole of human society. Short of this, there could be no Messianic era. To Christians, salvation was a matter of the rescue of the individual soul from damnation. Human history did not enter into their concept of salvation. The function of the Messiah was to rescue humanity from history.

There was a sense, then, in which the Messiah was *more* important to Jews than to Christians; for to Jews, the Messiah was still a goal. To Christians, the Messiah had already happened. They did not have to devote their energies to bring about his coming. There was a certain complacency in this attitude, a complacency inherent in the view that Christendom was the fulfilment of the Old Testament prophecies. Judaism remained a Messianic religion, because it was still unsatisfied, its picture of the possibilities of mankind and the earth remaining an aspiration. True, there was the concept of the Second Coming of Christ, which to some extent performed the function of a goal for Christians. But this was merely the crown or seal of the Christian triumph, which was thought of as already accomplished. The main event in history had already happened, and the remaining scenes (even though they had proved unexpectedly protracted) were simply the working-out of the finale.

Naḥmanides' contention that the Messiah was not a central part of the Jewish faith was thus both true and untrue. The idea of a Messianic era is inherent in Judaism, and is demanded by its quest for justice and unity. Yet the form such an era might take is not rigidly defined. It might not be centred on a single *person,* of kingly descent, at all. Indeed, it is not to be taken for granted that the Messianic era will ever actually happen, for it is not an automatic event, but depends on whether mankind, and especially Israel, have deserved it, as Naḥmanides eloquently explained in his work *The Book of Redemption.* The main object of the life of a Jew, therefore, is not to centre his thoughts on the Messiah or develop any personal devotion to him, but to fulfil God's law of justice, and thus help to make the world worthy of a Messianic era. It is the Christian exaltation of the Messiah into the object of a personal cult which marks its departure from Judaism, which regards this as the substitution of the symbol for the reality. Naḥmanides expressed this in the disputation by saying that the Messiah was not a 'principle' *('iqqar)* in Judaism, and that the main point of difference between Judaism and Christianity was the latter's exaggeration of the role of the Messiah by its doctrine of the Incarnation, which was completely unacceptable to Jews.

Naḥmanides' attack on the doctrine of the Incarnation is the most daring feature of his contribution to the disputation. 'The doctrine in which you believe, the foundation of your faith, cannot be accepted by reason, nature affords no ground for it, nor have the prophets ever expressed it.' Only life-long indoctrination, Naḥmanides tells the king in a personal address, could induce any rational person to believe such a doctrine: namely, that God Himself was born from a human womb, lived on earth and was executed, and then 'returned to His original place'. The question inevitably arises whether Naḥmanides really voiced this strong criticism, which would have seemed plain blasphemy to his Christian hearers at the disputation, or whether this is an example of embroidery. The expression is certainly strong; yet it avoids the strongest expression. The real point of difference between Judaism and Christianity was not so much a question of rationality of belief, as Naḥmanides here seems to say, as a question of idolatry. The worship of Jesus as the Incarnation of God was, to the Jews, a clear infringement of the First Commandment. But Naḥmanides does not accuse the doctrine of the Incarnation of being idolatrous, only of being incomprehensible. This element of restraint suggests that this may be, after all, a true representation of what Naḥmanides actually said. The fact that he addressed himself at this point directly to the king is also a detail that makes for the credibility of the narrative. It was the king who had personally guaranteed that Naḥmanides would be allowed to speak his mind and would not be victimised for frankness.

Did Naḥmanides mean that the main point at issue between Jews and Christians was not whether Jesus was the Messiah, but whether he was God? If so, the implication would be that Jews would have no fundamental objection to the view that Jesus was a *human* Messiah. After all, throughout Jewish history there had been messianic movements, and there was no heresy, in Jewish eyes, in believing that a certain man was the Messiah, even if this view later turned out to be mistaken, as proved by events. Even people who refused to be convinced by events might be accommodated within the fold of Judaism; for example, the Ebionites for some years were regarded as good Jews, even though they awaited the return of the human Messiah, Jesus. The Talmudic rabbi who expressed the opinion that King Hezekiah had been the Messiah was not regarded as a heretic, though his opinion was regarded as eccentric. So Naḥmanides was correct in saying that the question which the Christians thought so fundamental, whether or not the Messiah prophesied in the Scriptures had come, was not really so important for the Jews. The important thing was that neither the Messiah nor any other man should be worshipped as God. After all, the title 'Messiah' was not even regarded by the Jews as exclusive to one man. Every king of the House of David had the title 'Messiah'. It was certainly Naḥmanides' view that there would one day be a final Messiah who would wind up history and put an end to all tribulations. But there was no great tension about this view. It was not a view for which he would be prepared to die; nor would he want to excommunicate someone who held a different view about the way in which history would culminate. He did object strongly, however, to the view that the final Messiah had come, not to change the world but to function as an object of worship.

Different Views of the Vikuaḥ *of Naḥmanides*

In the foregoing discussion, the *Vikuaḥ,* Naḥmanides' own account of the Barcelona Disputation, has been taken seriously as a truthful and profound representation of the issues at stake in Jewish-Christian confrontation. Note must be taken, however, of other views which do not rate the *Vikuaḥ* so highly.

In assessing the value of Naḥmanides' account, one has to compare it with the Christian account, which is an official document, prepared by the Dominicans and ratified by King James of Aragon himself as a correct account, in testimony of which the royal seal was affixed. This document gives a very different picture of the tone and upshot of the disputation from that found in Naḥmanides' version. According to the Christian account, Naḥmanides was thoroughly defeated. He was reduced to silence on some points, caught out in obvious inconsistencies, made admissions which he retracted, and finally fled from the scene in confusion, rather than face a further questioning by a 'small group', as he had promised, after the end of the disputation.

There can be no doubt that the brief and badly composed Christian document is a travesty of the disputation. The items of discussion have been compressed and jumbled to a point at which the succession of the argument and the relevance of the topics is often unintelligible. For example, a discussion of the Trinity is introduced into the disputation, though irrelevant to the subject-matter laid down in the beginning of the document itself. Naḥmanides' account explains that the Trinity was not discussed in the disputation itself but in the debate which took place eight days after the disputation, when the king and his court visited the synagogue. The Christian document introduces without explanation a discussion on whether Naḥmanides was entitled to call himself 'Rabbi'. The Jewish account sets this discussion in its context, namely, the general question of whether any rule or jurisdiction remains among the Jews, a question relevant to the Christian contention that Genesis, 49: 10 prophesies the end of such rule among the Jews on the advent of the Messiah ('Shiloh'). Many such puzzling details in the Christian account are made intelligible only by consulting the Jewish account, which sets them into a logical, ordered narrative of the discussion. At the same time, there is a remarkable correspondence between the two accounts in the actual topics and passages from Scripture and Talmud that were discussed, so that we clearly have two accounts of the same event, one confused and the other well-ordered.

The Christian account also contains some obvious misrepresentations of Naḥmanides' arguments, blunting and simplifying them in a naive way. For example, Naḥmanides' explanation of the figurative, non-literal status of many Aggadic passages comes out as: 'he said publicly that he did not believe in the authorities which were cited against him, though they were in ancient, authoritative books of the Jews, because, as he said, they were sermons, in which their teachers, for the sake of exhorting the people, often lied'. When Naḥmanides agreed that the Suffering Servant of Isaiah was taken to be the Messiah in some Talmudic interpretations, this was reported as a complete admission of the Christian case. This is the technique, used in the Paris Disputation, of representing any formal agreement as to the verbal correctness of a citation as a 'confession' of the truth of the Christian interpretation of the passage in question.

The Jewish account is thus much preferable to the Christian one, but the question still remains how far the Jewish account is to be believed. Though very far from being as crudely partisan as the Christian account, it may still contain certain aspects which may be questioned. When the Christian scholar Heinrich Denifle championed the Christian account as the truth, denouncing Naḥmanides (and the Jewish historian Graetz) as a liar, he was well and sufficiently answered by the Jewish scholar Isadore Loeb.[5] But once the battle for the superior truth of the Jewish account was won, Jewish scholars turned their attention to the possible deficiencies of the Jewish account too. Here they have had some just things to say, but have also, in their search for painful objectivity, sometimes succumbed to the pleasures of masochism. There is a false notion of objectivity which sees it as always lying midway between two extremes of opinion. Yet the truth often lies much nearer to one extreme than the other, and a mechanical steering for a midway position may be a falsification.

The views of three scholars, who have given particular attention to the Barcelona Disputation, need to be considered: Yitzhak Baer, Cecil Roth and Martin A. Cohen.

Yitzhak Baer. This fine scholar's work is indispensable for the study of the period. In his article, 'On the Disputations of R. Yeḥiel of Paris and R. Moses ben Naḥman', he confirms and deepens Loeb's criticism of the Christian account, but at the same time puts some probing questions against the Jewish account. While he considers that Naḥmanides gives an accurate account of his replies about the Scriptural and Talmudic texts cited, he doubts whether the sarcastic and daringly attacking remarks were ever made. He doubts also whether the speech on the relative unimportance of the Messiah in Judaism was really made at such length and with such freedom. He expresses even stronger doubt about Naḥmanides' account, at the end of his narrative, of the debate about the Trinity which took place in the synagogue eight days after the disputation. Baer finds it incredible that Naḥmanides' arguments could have silenced such a concourse of ecclesiastics, including the renowned scholar Raymund de Peñaforte.

Baer thinks too that Naḥmanides exaggerates his own share in the drawing-up of the agenda of the disputation. How could he have proposed at the start that the main topic should be the Messiah, when later he insisted that the Messiah is not fundamental to Judaism? Baer suggests, on the contrary, that the topic of the Messiah and the method of controversy (by examining Talmudic and Midrashic passages) were forced upon Naḥmanides, who would really have preferred to discuss more general, philosophical topics, and kept trying, unsuccessfully, to turn the discussion in their direction. The Christians, however, refused to allow the discussion of any topics which would 'put the certitude of the Christian faith into dispute', and strictly confined the discussion to alleged proofs of Christianity in the Jewish writings. In his account, however, Baer argues, Naḥmanides gave an impression of a wide-ranging debate covering philosophical points of disagreement between Judaism and Christianity. In particular, he misrepresents the final topic of the agenda (the fourth in the Christian account, and the third in the Jewish) which is correctly stated in the Christian account as: 'That the ceremonial law ceased and had to cease on the advent of the Messiah', but incorrectly stated by Naḥmanides as: 'Whether Jews or Christians practise the true religion'. Whereas Loeb saw these formulations as more or less equivalent, Baer sees them as very different, the Christian formulation being much more confined in its scope and susceptible of discussion by way of citing Aggadic passages (as we find in Raymund Martini's *Pugio Fidei)* purporting to show that the ceremonial law would cease on the advent of the Messiah. Moreover, Baer argues, Naḥmanides gives the impression that this final item of the agenda was actually covered in the disputation, whereas in fact it was never reached, since the king decided to end the disputation because of the danger of public disturbances.

Further, Baer argues that Naḥmanides was not entirely sincere in some of the arguments which he used in the disputation. He spoke more disrespectfully of the Aggadah than he really felt; for in reality, as we learn from his other works, he regarded it as full of profound meaning. In general, he adopted a rationalistic stance towards Christianity which he was far from adopting towards Judaism. Baer particularly wonders at Naḥmanides' words in relation to the Trinity: 'It is obvious that a person cannot believe what he does not know.' Baer comments: 'Does not all Naḥmanides' teaching, from beginning to end, contradict these words?'

Baer even suggests that the Talmudic quotation affixed to the beginning of the *Vikuaḥ*, in which the disciples of Jesus are refuted in a punning, jesting dialogue, was put there deliberately by Naḥmanides in order to hint to his Jewish readers that they should not take too seriously some of the arguments which he was forced to use in Christian-Jewish controversy.

Baer thus concludes that the *Vikuaḥ*, though a much better guide to the historical facts of the disputation than the Christian account, is still, like the Christian account, a work of propaganda, not a factual account in the modern sense. It exaggerates the range of the discussion and the freedom of action given to Naḥmanides in choosing the topics to be discussed. Moreover, even where correctly reported, discussion does not always represent his genuine thought, but was a disguise, to some extent, adopted for the occasion.

Baer thus takes issue with Isadore Loeb for defending the truthfulness of Naḥmanides' account too uncritically, and also for not taking some of the points of discussion seriously enough.

Baer seems to be presenting a balanced, objective picture, worthy of a truly scientific historian. Yet some of his points are of very doubtful weight. That Naḥmanides did say some sharp, daring things in the disputation is proved by the aftermath. When his account of the disputation was published (having been written at the request of the Bishop of Gerona), Naḥmanides was pursued by the Dominicans for having published 'blasphemies'. There is extant a letter-patent of James I, dated 12 April 1265 at Barcelona, in which the king describes how he handled this complaint of the Dominicans. Naḥmanides (called here by the name Bonastrug de Porta[6]) was summoned before the king and a court of ecclesiastics to answer the charge, and replied that in his disputation with Pablo (Paulus) he had been given permission by the king himself to say 'everything that he wished'. As for the composition of the book, Naḥmanides pleaded that he had written it only on the request of the Bishop of Gerona. Nevertheless, it was for the composition of the book that the king pronounced the mild sentence of two years' banishment—a sentence with which the Dominicans were by no means satisfied. What is significant is that the charges of the Dominicans on this occasion did not include any reference to any misrepresentation of the discussion. They did not allege that Naḥmanides had imported into his account 'blasphemies' which he did not pronounce at the disputation itself. On the contrary, the indictment states explicitly that the same blasphemies appeared both in the disputation and in the book *(quod in Domini nostri vituperium et tocius fidei catholice dixerat quedam verba et etiam de eisdem librum fecerat).* It was only later (in 1266), when the Dominicans, still pursuing Naḥmanides, brought the Pope into the matter, that the accusation of 'lying' was first heard, though even here it is not clear whether the 'lies' were about the events of the disputation, or were rather in the assertions made at the disputation itself, and repeated in the book.

It seems, then, that Baer has not allowed sufficiently for the provocative character of Naḥmanides' remarks at the disputation. If he was confined, more or less, to answering questions about certain Aggadic passages, and did not launch out into disquisitions about the shortcomings of Christianity, it is hard to see why he should have been accused of 'blasphemy'. The letter-patent of the king, furthermore, gives complete confirmation of Naḥmanides' statement that he was given special permission by the king to speak freely, a circumstance which would otherwise certainly have been strongly doubted by cautious historians.

As for the contradiction which Baer alleges between Naḥmanides' choice of the Messiah as the main topic of debate and his later assertion that the Messiah is not a basic element of Judaism, this 'contradiction' is merely a confusion of thought on Baer's part. The Messiah had to be the centre of the *discussion* because he was central in Christianity, even though he was not central in Judaism. To give an analogy, suppose that a new religion had been founded centred on the Jewish institution of *matzah* (unleavened bread for Passover). Suppose the adherents of the new religion asserted that there was evidence in the Talmud supporting this huge importance assigned to *matzah,* and its central role in religion. A disputation between Jews and the adherents of the new religion would have to be about *matzah* and nothing else, even though the Jews would inevitably protest that *matzah* was to them a relatively unimportant concept. Indeed, the content of the discussion would be precisely on the question, 'How important is *matzah?*—just as the Barcelona Disputation was mainly on the question, 'How important is the Messiah?' It would hardly seem necessary to labour this obvious point, were it not that Baer's confusion has been repeated by other scholars.

It is therefore perfectly possible that Naḥmanides, asked to propose an agenda for the disputation, chose the subject of the Messiah, even though he did not regard the Messiah as basic to Judaism. Otherwise, it would have been impossible to find a common subject of interest to talk about, since this was the aspect of Judaism with which Christians were mainly concerned and which they had made the centre of their religion. It should be mentioned, however, that Naḥmanides does not say that he alone chose this topic, but that it was agreed between the two parties. All that Naḥmanides says that he stipulated was that only topics of central importance should be discussed; by which he meant, presumably, that questions of religious practice, such as the appointed days of sabbaths and festivals, or the question of prohibited foods, should be excluded from the discussion. It certainly does not seem unlikely that Naḥmanides had some say in the choice of agenda. As for the difference here between the Jewish account and the Christian account (which says that the agenda was drawn up by Pablo Christiani), of which Denifle made much, it hardly seems worth discussion, as Loeb remarked (but Baer disagrees, seeing great significance in both the alleged overestimation of Naḥmanides' role, and the alleged improbability of his choice of such an agenda).

More important is Baer's contention that Naḥmanides disguised his real views, or 'did not reveal his full mind'. There was certainly some element of this at the Paris Disputation, where it is hard to believe that Rabbi Yeḥiel really thought that the Christian Jesus is nowhere mentioned in the Talmud. There, however, more was at stake. Rabbi Yeḥiel can hardly be blamed for some dissimulation, when the cartloads of Talmud volumes were waiting to be burned. To expect the entire Talmudic literature to be free of hostile remarks about Christianity (when Christian literature teemed with vituperation against Jews and Judaism) was an unreasonable demand which did not deserve a completely frank response. But in the Barcelona Disputation, there was no such pressure. There was nothing to prevent Naḥmanides from saying what he really thought. For example, instead of saying that the Aggadah is not authoritative, he could simply have argued about the interpretation of each individual Aggadah as it came up in discussion. In fact, he *did* use this tactic, as well as saying that the Aggadah was not authoritative. In every case, he provided two alternative arguments: (1) I do not accept this Aggadah as literally true; (2) even if one were to take it as literally true, it would not prove what you say it proves. Argument (2) would have been a sufficient answer in each case. Why then should he have included argument (1) unless he thought it both true and important?

What is true is that Naḥmanides was somewhat blunter in his expression of the subordinate, unauthoritative nature of the Aggadah than he would have been with a Jewish audience. This, however, was not dissimulation, but accommodation to the understanding of his audience, which could not be expected to understand the full subtlety of the Jewish attitude towards the Aggadah. It was hard to explain to an uninstructed audience that in the Jewish mind, the Aggadah was both belittled and exalted, that it was considered to be of no practical importance, and yet the repository of the profoundest truths to be found in Judaism. From which can one best expound Catholic doctrine: from Aquinas's *Summa*, or from Dante's *Divine Comedy?* Clearly, not from the poem—yet it contains a profounder statement of Catholicism than the *Summa.* To Naḥmanides, the Aggadah was a focus for personal meditation, a key to mysteries; but it was not something one could quote in disputations. To try to use it in this way was to misunderstand its nature, and this he attempted unavailingly to convey to his Christian hearers.

Baer complains of Loeb that he is too patronising to medieval disputants, considering that the whole discussion, to the modern scientific mind, is on a puerile level. Unfortunately, however, Baer too is infected with this attitude. He fails to appreciate the dialectical character of Naḥmanides' mind. The either/or approach which Baer employs in relation to the Aggadah appears also in his discussion of Naḥmanides' 'rationalism'. Either Naḥmanides was a rationalist (as he 'pretended' to be at the disputation) or he was a mystic. The possibility which Baer overlooks is that he was both.

It was a commonplace of Jewish-Christian controversy that the Jews prided themselves on the superior rationality of their faith. This contention can be traced throughout the literature of Jewish polemics. When Naḥmanides criticised Christianity as irrational, he was not adopting some pose, but following in the footsteps of Sa'adiah, Maimonides, Judah Halevi, David Kimḥi and many others. Yet none of these thinkers contended that everything in Judaism could be justified by reason. What they did contend was that there was nothing in Judaism which could be *refuted* by reason; that there were no illogicalities or contradictions. Christianity, on the other hand, they contended, did contain such illogicalities and absurdities, particularly in the doctrines of the Trinity and the Incarnation, where a proposition was stated only to be contradicted, and where even the laws of arithmetic were flouted. Baer's statement about Naḥmanides that 'all his ways were ways of faith' ignores the whole rationalistic side of his personality: the strenuous logic of his Talmudic writings, his study of Maimonides, whom he criticised, to be sure, but from whom he learnt a great deal. Naḥmanides even held that it was a rational thing to believe that Judaism contained elements which were beyond the scope of human reason: why should God's message be entirely intelligible in purely human terms? Yet human reason, limited as it was, nevertheless was a God-given gift, and partook of the nature of God's own reason. It was therefore impossible for the human reason to be wrong in something which it saw clearly, such as the elementary laws of logic; and therefore, no statement could be divinely inspired if it contravened those laws. Naḥmanides' love of reason is evident in everything he wrote, even his writings on mysticism. His passionate insistence on reason in the disputation, and his attack on the doctrine of Incarnation on the ground of its irrationality, are perfectly in accordance with his general outlook.[7]

As for his statement, at which Baer is so astonished—'A person cannot believe what he does not know'—this must be taken in the context of the argument. Naḥmanides has just criticised the doctrine of the Trinity as containing logical errors. He is told that even the angels cannot understand the Trinity. In that case, says Naḥmanides, the angels cannot believe in the Trinity. No one can believe something which is logically refutable. Naḥmanides is *not* saying that logic is our only source of knowledge. He believed that knowledge could be obtained by hearsay, or by revelation, which is a kind of authoritative hearsay, validated by proofs of the divine origin of what is transmitted, or even by direct mystical experience. But all these methods of obtaining knowledge have their own criteria, by which one is entitled to say, 'I know.' If these criteria have not been fulfilled, one cannot say, 'I know,' and therefore one cannot say, 'I believe.' Baer unhistorically ascribes to Naḥmanides a modern definition of 'belief' which makes it weaker than 'knowledge'. To Naḥmanides 'belief' meant to assert firmly, and loyally uphold, something which one knew to be true.

Baer also, in his desire to be 'objective', even supports Denifle in his denigration of Naḥmanides' account of the debate in the synagogue about the Trinity. Baer writes: 'Denifle is after all reliable in matters touching the doctrine of the Trinity and the interpretations of it which he found in the works of the scholastics; and he judges that Naḥmanides' arguments on the matter are nonsense [*unverstand*].' Denifle's actual criticism is as follows: 'Naḥmanides writes that he raised an objection against the Christian doctrine of the Trinity from the necessity of a Quaternity: *deus, sapientia, voluntas, potentia* [God, wisdom, will, power]. And that the last three are accidents. To this nonsense, the only answer that he received was that the Trinity was the highest mystery, which surmounted even the understanding of the angels. "But is it not true," answered the Jew, "that no one believes what he does not know? Therefore the angels too do not believe in the Trinity." After such a childish reply, according to Naḥmanides' account, all present were so baffled that they could not say another word.'

This is a complete travesty of Naḥmanides' argument, which is in fact a formidable one. Raymund de Peñaforte had argued in the synagogue that the Trinity could be understood in terms of the attributes wisdom, will and power. To this Naḥmanides replied, in effect, that any attempt to explain the Trinity in terms of attributes must fail, since this would destroy the separateness of the three Persons of the Trinity and reduce them to one Person with attributes. And, continued Naḥmanides, even if one were to overlook this point, why should one stop at three attributes? Why should wisdom, will and power be regarded as the only candidates for the position of important attributes of God? If we have a Trinity of attributes, we can just as easily have a Quaternity, by adding the attribute of substance. (Denifle here misunderstands Naḥmanides by using the word *deus* as a translation of Naḥmanides' suggested fourth attribute. Naḥmanides' phrase is *davar she-hu 'eloah*, which means 'a divine substance'.) Why not go on to have a Quinternity, by adding the attribute of 'life', which is surely just as essential to God as wisdom?[8] In fact, Naḥmanides, by his two arguments against an attributional theory of the Trinity, argued that on this theory, neither the separateness nor the threeness of the Trinity could be preserved. Both these arguments, as it happens, have been urged against the attributional theory by Christian writers, too. Denifle is thus wide of the mark in calling Naḥmanides' arguments nonsensical and childish.

Denifle also misrepresents Naḥmanides when he says that the latter referred to the three divine attributes of wisdom, will and power as 'accidents'. On the contrary, Naḥmanides said distinctly, 'wisdom, in the Creator, is not an accidental quality.' Naḥmanides argues that precisely because wisdom, will and power are *not* accidental properties, but essential attributes, they cannot be separated from the being of God Himself and made into separate Persons. On the other hand, he argues, if they *were* accidental properties, and thus separable in imagination from the being in which they inhere, this would make them far too fleeting and ephemeral qualities to be elevated to the status of divine Persons. (The king, who had argued less professionally than Peñaforte, from the analogy of wine, with its properties of colour, taste and smell, had laid himself open to this easy refutation.)

Of course, Peñaforte was at this point not without the possibility of a reply. He could have answered that the argument from the wisdom, will and power of God was not intended as a proof of the Trinity, but merely as an imperfect analogy, showing how it is possible for unity to exist in multiplicity. This type of analogy, taken from the faculties of the human soul, had been used previously by Augustine and other theologians, and had always been accompanied by the warning that the analogy was not complete. All that such analogies were intended to show was that the doctrine of the Trinity was not absurd, because the human psyche shows, by analogy, that personality is a mysterious phenomenon involving paradoxes of unity in multiplicity. The attributional argument was thus essentially a defensive argument, not intended to convince anyone of the truth or logical necessity of the doctrine of the Trinity, but to defend it from the charge of being illogical and absurd.

But it is important to note that, contrary to Denifle's assertion, Naḥmanides does not claim, in his account, that he reduced his Christian opponents to silence in the debate on the Trinity in the synagogue. He says that the companions of Pablo Christiani 'made him keep silent.' In other words, Christiani was most willing to continue the argument, but was persuaded not to do so by his 'companions' (who included Raymund de Peñaforte). Why they decided not to continue the argument is a matter for speculation; but it was certainly not for want of something to say, as Naḥmanides makes clear. There is only one occasion in his account where Naḥmanides states that his opponent was reduced to silence, and that was after Pablo's discomfiture over the quotation from Maimonides which he was unable to find (but see p. 133). Naḥmanides' account is in fact singularly free from the kind of exaggerated expressions of triumph which were usual in such accounts. Denifle's assertion, therefore, that Naḥmanides frequently claims to have silenced his opponent *('Auf seine blödesten Entgegnungen lässt Nachmani den Gegner Pablo Christiani verstummen')* is false.

Baer's attempt to arrive at a 'balanced' judgement on Naḥmanides' account of the disputation is thus seriously misleading. He underestimates Naḥmanides' sincerity and intelligence. Though it must be conceded that Naḥmanides did not convey his full mind on the Aggadah, this was only in the sense that it was necessary for him to simplify the matter in order to make himself intelligible to a non-Jewish audience. On the question of Naḥmanides' arguments on the Trinity, Baer is too ready to accept that this is Denifle's 'one strong point'. As for Baer's suggestion that Naḥmanides included, at the start of his work, a quotation from the Talmud as a hint that his arguments were not intended entirely seriously, reasons will be given on a later page for the view that this Talmudic quotation did not form part of Naḥmanides' original composition (see pp. 97–101).

Cecil Roth. The essay on the Barcelona Disputation by Cecil Roth is also an attempt to avoid the atmosphere of contention and Jewish-Christian polemics which characterised the essays of Heinrich Denifle and Isadore Loeb. Roth thus adopts a dispassionate tone, and tries to hold the honours fairly even between Naḥmanides and Pablo Christiani (or Pablo Christia, as he calls him[9]). Yet he remarks, 'From the human and literary point of view, certainly, the Hebrew document is far superior to its Latin counterpart.' He calls Naḥmanides' account of the disputation 'a human document, enlivened by occasional flashes of humour, by demonstrations of courage beyond the ordinary, and by glimpses of an attractive personality.' He concludes, however, 'it is impossible to think of the outcome of the controversy in terms of success or failure. The two adversaries were setting out from entirely different premises, and in the shadow-battle which resulted both tilted as it were at phantoms, without really getting to blows. For discussions on the application of Biblical verses and the significance of Talmudic legends affected the validity of neither faith.'

In his desire to be even-handed, however, Roth sometimes falsifies the issues. For example, at the start of the disputation, Pablo Christiani having announced that he intended to prove the truth of Christianity from the Talmud, Naḥmanides inquired why the rabbis who composed the Talmud remained Jews, if they were witnesses to the truth of Christianity. This was a fundamental objection to Pablo Christiani's whole method of argument, and required an answer (which could no doubt have been furnished by someone capable of constructing a theory of the strata of redaction in the Talmud). Pablo, however, could only answer, 'These long-winded statements are intended to circumvent the disputation.' Roth observes that long-windedness 'indeed seems to have been the Rabbi's failing'—a remark which he later reinforces by saying that Naḥmanides 'seems to have indulged in a prolixity that did his cause no good.' This is not even-handedness but unfairness. Pablo Christiani's taunt, made out of inability to reply sensibly to the point, is treated as if it were a legitimate argument. Actually, long-windedness was not a fault of Naḥmanides. In all his writings, including the *Vikuaḥ*, he makes his points with admirable succinctness. His pregnant brevity in his Halakhic writings was a byword, and led to the composition of works of methodology for interpreting him.[10] What can be said with truth is that he reported his own remarks at the disputation more fully than those of his opponent, which sometimes makes Pablo seem rather terse in comparison. This is a natural and probably unavoidable tendency in reporting a controversy in which one has taken part.

Roth repeats Baer's confusion about the alleged contradiction between Naḥmanides' assertion of the subordinate role of the Messiah in Judaism and his choice of the subject of the Messiah as the central topic of the disputation. He follows Baer, too, in doubting whether Naḥmanides could have discussed the Trinity successfully against eminent scholastics, whose more telling arguments, he thinks, must have been omitted from Naḥmanides' account.

In general, Roth gives a good résumé of the course of the debate (with a few questionable readjustments), but softens the impact of dramatic blows and startling pronouncements. To him, there is no real confrontation between Judaism and Christianity, only a 'shadow-battle'.

At the same time, there is good sense in the following remarks of Roth's:

> It is preposterous to expect from these records of seven centuries ago a standard of veracity that one so seldom encounters, or even (it may be) demonstrates, in similar circumstances today. There can therefore be no doubt that each writer recorded to some extent not only what was

> said, but also what he wished had been said; that a muttered repartee to which perhaps no attention was paid is represented as having triumphantly clinched an argument; that failure to answer some point because it was not heard, or because it was considered unimportant, was construed as a reduction to silence.

Yet on the much-mooted question of who won the Barcelona Disputation, it needs to be said that Naḥmanides never claimed, in any crude sense, to have won. The impression he gives is of one vainly trying to put over notions which were mostly unintelligible to his opponents, who certainly did not admit defeat, or even suffer any diminution of confidence in their opinions. Naḥmanides certainly claims the victory in the sense that his arguments were superior; but that is a matter for the judgement of posterity. It is only in the Christian account that we find the claim that their side had a palpable, crushing victory, with the Jewish participant reduced to silence and exposed to the contempt of his own co-religionists. This is a false claim: neither side convinced the other. Nevertheless, this is a very different thing from saying, as Roth seems to want to say, that neither side was more convincing than the other. It would after all be very strange if the greatest Talmudist of his generation could not produce convincing arguments on a Talmudic matter. Naḥmanides (except when he spoke about the Trinity) was on his own ground, and had all the advantage in the area of combat chosen by his opponents.

Martin A. Cohen. A much more radical criticism of Naḥmanides' account of the disputation has been put forward in an essay by Martin A. Cohen. He praises the literary quality of the account, as opposed to the 'terse, cold language' of the Christian protocol, but considers that we should be on our guard against accepting the Jewish account as reliable: 'The only danger which besets the reader of Naḥmanides' account is that the dazzling realism of his narrative, contrasted with the pall [*sic*] and laconism [*sic*] of the Christian version, will blind him to its numerous shortcomings, and impede him from using this text cautiously in reconstructing the . . . events.'

Cohen argues that, in effect, Naḥmanides lost the disputation. Reading between the lines of Naḥmanides' account, and supplementing it from the Christian account at certain points, Cohen concludes that Naḥmanides was outmanoeuvred by Pablo Christiani, who had made a study of Naḥmanides' own works and opinions, and chose his arguments accordingly. Pablo Christiani (whom Cohen calls Paul Christian) knew that Naḥmanides had sympathised mainly with the anti-Maimunists in the great Maimonides controversy of the 1230s, that he was an anti-rationalist and mystic who utilised Aggadic literature as the basis of his theosophic system. Pablo was thus on good ground in confronting Naḥmanides with Aggadic passages which supported the Christian idea of the Messiah as a supernatural being, and also as one who was already in existence. It was only in 'a move of desperation' that Naḥmanides denied the authority of the Aggadah and pretended to be a rationalist.

Cohen argues that Naḥmanides did not have any say in the agenda of the disputation, which was carefully arranged by the Dominicans to suit their purposes. Naḥmanides was given very little freedom of manoeuvre, and was never allowed to take the offensive. By weighting the procedure against Naḥmanides and by cleverly choosing issues that would put him at a disadvantage, the Dominicans ensured that Naḥmanides was 'vanquished'. Further, Cohen finds that, as a result, Naḥmanides was frequently caught out in confusions and contradictions, as well as denying his previous opinions.

Cohen then considers the historical question of the reasons for the setting-up of the disputation by the Dominicans with the sanction and co-operation of the king. He concludes that the king was using the rising power of the Dominicans to counteract the pressure against him from the high nobility with whom, at the time, he was almost at the point of civil war. A carefully staged triumph by the Dominicans in a disputation against the Jews would help in this political aim, since it would increase the prestige of the Dominicans and make them more powerful allies for the king. Naḥmanides himself co-operated in a measure in this manoeuvre, for he knew that the whole affair had been stage-managed as a Christian triumph, but took part in it in order to help the king, who promised in return to safeguard the interests of the Jews in his kingdom. The Jews themselves would be unimpressed by the Christian triumph, knowing the unfair conditions under which their rabbi had had to take part, so Naḥmanides could afford to undergo some humiliation for the sake of his community's future welfare. The incident during the course of the disputation when an attempt was made to put an early stop to the proceedings is explained by Cohen as arising from the alarm of the nobles and prelates at the possible increase in the power and prestige of the

Dominicans if the disputation were allowed to reach a successful conclusion. Cohen admits that evidence is lacking for some parts of this scenario, but submits that his theory makes better sense of the origin and course of the disputation than previous analyses, which saw the disputation as a mere dialectical exercise, ignored the political context, and took the *Vikuaḥ* at its face value as a record of a Jewish victory.

That part of Cohen's thesis which asserts that Naḥmanides was caught out in confusions and contradictions in his arguments may be safely rejected. The alleged confusions and contradictions do not exist, and arise from lack of comprehension on the part of Cohen himself. Moreover, Cohen systematically confuses the question of whether Naḥmanides succeeded in convincing his opponents with the question of whether his arguments were intrinsically correct. The frequent occasions during the disputation when an excellent argument of Naḥmanides failed to produce any impact on his opponents are taken as evidence of his defeat in the argument.

As an example of Cohen's method, the following may be quoted: 'Naḥmanides finally conceded that the rabbinic tradition supported Paul's claim that the Messiah had been born, but he tried to save his day by insisting that though he had been born, he had as yet not come. He sought desperately to explain the Messiah's longevity on the analogy of the long-lived antediluvian worthies mentioned in the Bible, but succeeded in convincing no one that the Messiah appeared on earth more than a millennium before but had as yet not revealed himself.' Naḥmanides never at any point 'conceded' that the Messiah had been born; he stated repeatedly that he did not believe this. But on the other hand, he was not irreconcilably opposed to the view that he *had* been born. The literal interpretation of the Aggadic passage which spoke of the birth of the Messiah at the time of the destruction of the Temple was a possible, if unlikely, interpretation, and he was prepared to argue on the hypothesis of its literal truth. This style of argument ('I do not believe proposition A, but even if it were true, it does not support your argument') was apparently too subtle for the Christians of the thirteenth century, and it is too subtle for Dr Cohen, too. The Christian protocol says: 'defeated by irrefutable proofs and authorities, he conceded that Christ, or Messiah, was born 1,000 years ago'; and Dr Cohen, echoing their incomprehension, says, 'Naḥmanides finally conceded that the rabbinic tradition supported Paul's claim that the Messiah had been born.'

As for Naḥmanides' contention that the Messiah, even if born, had not yet 'come', there is nothing 'desperate' about such an argument. After all, the Jews had long believed something very similar about Elijah: that, born over 2,000 years before, he was still alive and would eventually take a leading role in the Messianic age. The question whether the Messiah had been born or not was not very important, since he had clearly not yet embarked upon his Messianic mission. Pablo Christiani's attempt to make capital out of the fact that a stray Midrash, if literally interpreted, stated that the Messiah had been born was, just as Naḥmanides argued, a very feeble argument for Christianity, especially if applied to Jesus, who was born seventy years before the destruction of the Temple.

Cohen goes on to say: 'In the next session of the debate Naḥmanides, who had had time to think matters over, first declared that the Messiah had been living in the Garden of Eden. Little did he realise that even this statement would cost him dearly in subsequent discussion. Then Naḥmanides proceeded to contradict himself and to deny categorically that he believed the Messiah had come, and he strove to no avail to turn the discussion to a consideration of Jesus' qualifications for the Messiahship.' It is hardly necessary to comment on this in detail, but it should be noted how the assertion that Naḥmanides 'contradicted himself' slides into the different plane of assertion that he 'strove to no avail' to convince his opponents. Naḥmanides did not in the least contradict himself, but it is quite true that he strove to no avail. Pablo Christiani thought that he had accomplished something very important by 'proving' that the Messiah was already in existence, according to one Jewish opinion. When Naḥmanides asked what relevance this had to Jesus, he was told that this question was inadmissible as the topic of discussion was merely whether the Messiah was already in existence. Cohen seems to think that this was a very clever tactic, which defeated Naḥmanides. Yet it defeated him only in the sense that he was ruled out of order for no good reason. Pablo's tactics were to 'prove' something quite unimportant and trivial, which had no real bearing on the Christian claims for Jesus, and then act as if he had achieved a great victory. Here again, Cohen accepts the style of argument of the Christian protocol, which hails every 'admission' of Naḥmanides as acceptance of major principles of Christianity with which they were in no way logically connected.

It would be tedious to go through all Cohen's confusions and misunderstandings, of which the above is a fair specimen. His contention that Naḥmanides adopted an attitude towards the Aggadah which was the reverse of his true view is similar to the contention of Baer. Cohen attempts to bolster his case by an account of the relation between the Kabbalah, of which Naḥmanides was a great adherent, and the Aggadah. 'Again and again we find evidence among the friends and foes of the thirteenth-century Kabbalah of the indispensable role which the Aggadah, accepted literally, played among them.' Undoubtedly, the Aggadah was very important to Kabbalists, but it is far from true that the Aggadah was always 'accepted literally' by them. It was more a question of the style of non-literalist interpretation adopted. A Maimunist might interpret an Aggadah allegorically in terms of Aristotelian philosophy, while a Kabbalist would interpret the same Aggadah allegorically (or rather symbolically) in terms of theosophy. True, there were *some* Aggadic passages which Naḥmanides and other Kabbalists would interpret literally, rejecting rationalist allegorical interpretations. These were passages relating to the Garden of Eden, hell, and other similar topics. On the other hand, there were many Aggadic passages which would be interpreted literally by rationalists and symbolically by Kabbalists; so the division between the two groups (which was not as clear-cut as Cohen represents) was not on the matter of literalism.

The whole question of the relations between rationalism, Kabbalism, and Aggadah, is much more complex than Cohen thinks. There was a Kabbalistic type of rationalism, of which Naḥmanides was himself a representative, in which reason itself was regarded mystically, as an emanation of the divine. This was a view almost demanded by the requirement, acknowledged by Kabbalists, and particularly by Naḥmanides, that Jews should study the Talmud and the Halakhah, with all its strict logic and rationalistic methods.

Thus there was no reason for Naḥmanides to abjure his previous views when he declared that he did not accept the literal truth of some Aggadic passage. At the same time, he was careful to point out, even when discussing the matter with Christians, that a passage whose literal meaning he rejected might have 'some other interpretation derived from the secrets of the Sages [*misitrei ha-ḥakhamim*]'. This latter phrase would include, for Naḥmanides, the concepts of the Kabbalah. When dealing with an Aggadic passage, Naḥmanides felt himself to have great liberty of interpretation, including even the option of declaring the passage in question to be without value (though this latter option would be rarely exercised, since so many modes of interpretation existed by which it might be rescued).

As for Cohen's thesis about the political context of the disputation, this is tenable. It may well be that in acceding to the Dominicans' request for a disputation, the king was playing some devious political game, by which he hoped to gain the support of the Pope against his rebellious noblemen. Shortly after the disputation, however, we find the king at loggerheads with the Dominicans, but Cohen's explanation is that he had fallen out with them meanwhile.

Cohen's further thesis, that Naḥmanides himself co-operated knowingly with the king's plans in return for promises of good treatment of the Jews of Aragon, is mere fantasy. There was no need to secure Naḥmanides' co-operation, since he was compelled to obey the summons. Moreover, Naḥmanides did his best not to co-operate, for he tried to have the disputation discontinued after the third day. Cohen ingeniously copes with this difficulty by saying that Naḥmanides was loyally revealing to the king the attempts which were being made to discontinue the disputation—and had no desire to discontinue it himself! This kind of move belongs to a double-agent thriller, not to reality.

In attacking the idea that the disputation was a 'Jewish victory', Cohen is attacking a phantom. It is only in the eyes of posterity that it appears in this light. At the time, as Cohen correctly says, the whole affair was stage-managed to appear to be a Christian victory. Naḥmanides' best arguments were brushed aside as irrelevant, his request to put questions to his opponent was refused, as was his request to give an exposition of the Suffering Servant passage. But all this is plain from Naḥmanides' own account. He makes no pretence of having won a victory in the sense of having nonplussed his opponent or induced him to confess defeat. The picture he presents is of a kind of bear-baiting, in which the Jew is harassed into meaningless 'admissions' which are then invested with spurious meaning. The aims and atmosphere of the Christian side of the disputation are conveyed admirably by the Christian protocol, which claims a complete victory.

Even within this context, Naḥmanides managed a few small hits when, despite all the apparatus of procedure favouring the Christian side, Pablo Christiani was made to look rather foolish. One of these was Pablo's failure to find the passage in Maimonides about the death of the Messiah. Naḥmanides enjoyed Pablo's discomfiture over this, though he was well aware that the passage does exist in Maimonides' works, though not where his adversary was looking for it. Naḥmanides was entitled to this tiny triumph, in view of the fact that Pablo, if he had found the passage he was looking for, was going to use it quite illegitimately to 'prove' something about the death of Jesus. To say that the Messiah would be mortal (i.e., would eventually die of old age) was not at all the same thing as saying that he would be crucified. Moreover, Naḥmanides himself had made it clear that he too thought that the Messiah would probably be mortal in Maimonides' sense. So Naḥmanides would not have been in the least dismayed if Pablo *had* found the passage in question. It was a welcome relief, however, from the necessity of parrying Pablo's foolish misinterpretations to see him failing even in the elementary task of finding the passage which he wished to misinterpret. Yet even this moment of comic relief is understood by Cohen in a sense derogatory of Naḥmanides.[11]

The attempts by Baer, Roth and Cohen to diminish the stature of Naḥmanides in the Barcelona Disputation must be judged to have failed. Despite the unequal conditions of debate (which were nevertheless fairer than in any of the other disputations), Naḥmanides managed to make some far-reaching statements of the Jewish standpoint *vis-à-vis* Christianity. While his opponent, Pablo Christiani, sought to confine the discussion to trivial points, so that he could catch out Naḥmanides in 'admissions' the importance and relevance of which he could then exaggerate, Naḥmanides continually sought to turn the discussion to matters of real importance, in which the fundamental differences between Judaism and Christianity could be displayed. Thus Naḥmanides produced formulations, on the status of the Messiah in Judaism, on the nature of the Messianic era, on the Jewish attitude towards the Christian doctrine of Original Sin, on the place of reason in religion, on the relation between Aggadah and Halakhah, which proved of fundamental importance for later Jewish thinkers. That he was able to do so much in such unpromising circumstances is evidence of his outstanding character and courage. Not all his arguments were the best he could have used, as he must have realised after the disputation was over; yet he chose to record them all, just as they occurred in the hurly-burly of debate. When one considers that he was debating not with the peace of mind necessary for clarity of thought, but in fear of persecution by the dreaded Dominicans, and with anxiety of possible mob action against his people, it is extraordinary that he was able to argue with such coolness and humour. One of the chief Christian arguments used against him was that God had deserted the Jews; that they no longer had sovereign power and were serfs in a foreign land; that Christendom, on the other hand, was a great world force, glorying in power and wealth, clearly enjoying the favour of God. This argument came strangely from adherents of a religion which claimed to prize suffering and humiliation as the lot of the saints and saviours of mankind. Naḥmanides demonstrated in his own person that Jewish morale despite adversity was still high.

The literary qualities of the *Vikuaḥ*, Naḥmanides' own account of a unique historical event, have been appreciated to some extent by all who have written about it. Its vividness and drive put it into a class by itself in the literature of religious polemic. It eschews all pettiness, strives for actuality, gives a sense of great issues, yet also of personalities and social pressures. Yet the true status of this work as a classic is obscured if the significance of the encounter it records is belittled. This was no battle of pygmies, fought over dead issues. One of the greatest figures of Jewish history, at a climactic moment in human history, was called upon to make a statement, not in tranquillity but in the heat of controversy. Naḥmanides, who would otherwise speak to us only from his learned writings, here speaks to us as a living person, and also as the embodiment of Jewish culture, tradition and values. It is not 'objectivity', but falsification, to reduce the significance of the occasion.

3

The *Vikuaḥ:* Textual Considerations

The first printed publication of the *Vikuaḥ* was in the compilation *Tela Ignea Satanae* ('Fiery Darts of Satan') by J. C. Wagenseil (1681, Altdorf). The subtitle of Wagenseil's compilation is sufficient indication of its author's motives: *Arcani et horribiles Judaeorum adversus Christum Deum et Christianam religionem libri* ('The secret and horrifying books of the Jews against the divine Christ and the Christian religion'). Wagenseil also included a Latin translation of the *Vikuaḥ*. The Hebrew text from which he worked was a very imperfect one, being full of inauthentic additions, some of them taken from the *Vikuaḥ* of Yeḥiel of Paris, and some being the work of a German-Jewish editor. Wagenseil was aware of the imperfection of his text, and tried to emend it, without much success. Many later misapprehensions about the Barcelona Disputation were due to uncritical acceptance of Wagenseil's text. For example, Denifle based his remarks on this text, and therefore laboured under the impression that Naḥmanides was very abusive of Pablo Christiani in his account, introducing his speeches by opprobrious epithets. All this, however, was found to be absent in the better texts.

A much better text was the Constantinople edition of 1710 (included with other disputations under the title *Milḥemet Ḥovah* by an unknown editor). This text was used by Moses Steinschneider as the basis of his scientific edition (1860, Stettin/Berlin). He also made use of two MSS which he discovered, MS Leiden and MS Saraval. Later editors, R. Margoliouth (*c.* 1925, Lemberg), J. D. Eisenstein (1928, New York) and H. D. Chavel (1964, Jerusalem), all based their work on Steinschneider's edition.

The question still remains how near Steinschneider's edition is to the text as Naḥmanides wrote it. The lost MS on which the Constantinople edition, the MS Leiden and the MS Saraval were all based is regarded by Steinschneider as no older than 1600 (though his reasoning on this may be open to doubt, see p. 131). The most optimistic estimate is that our manuscript authority goes back to the fifteenth century; that is, two centuries after the composition of the work. In two centuries, many additions and alterations may have crept into the text.

The matter is complicated by the fact that the Hebrew version of the *Vikuaḥ* was not the only version composed by Naḥmanides. It is known that he originally composed his account of the disputation at the request of the Bishop of Gerona (see p. 98). Naḥmanides would not have written in Hebrew for the perusal of this churchman, but in Latin or Spanish (Catalan). The question about the Hebrew version, then, is not only whether it is as Naḥmanides wrote it, but also whether it tallies with the version, now lost, written for the Bishop. It is not even quite certain that Naḥmanides wrote the Hebrew version; it may be that he wrote only the non-Hebrew composition, which was then translated into Hebrew by another hand. There are in fact many possibilities about the relationship between the Hebrew and non-Hebrew versions, and their order of composition.

The aim of the present translation and commentary is to recover the original account written by Naḥmanides, not merely to translate the text as edited by Steinschneider, invaluable and indispensable as that edition is. The following is a summary of the conclusions reached, and of the principles used to arrive at them:

(1) Naḥmanides wrote two versions of the *Vikuaḥ*, one in Latin (or Catalan) for the Bishop, and one in Hebrew for his fellow Jews.

(2) Certain passages in our version did not exist in the original composition of Naḥmanides, in either the Hebrew or the non-Hebrew version. These are passages which are gratuitously polemical and go beyond the subject-matter of the disputation. There are three passages in question, the main one being the opening of the disputation (see especially pp. 97–101 and p. 117 for the full argument on this matter, especially the relevance of the charges made against the *Vikuaḥ* by the Dominicans in their indictment of 1265, and their silence on the passages in question).

(3) The Hebrew version of the *Vikuaḥ* shows signs of lack of revision and haste of composition. The evidence for this (which can be distinguished easily from copyists' errors and additions) lies in the tendency to random inaccuracy in quotations from Bible and Talmud (these would have been corrected, if anything, by an

officious copyist); verses are sometimes run together (see especially the note on p. 136), Talmudic phrases are slightly misquoted, and slight motiveless errors are made in Biblical quotations. These errors can be attributed to Naḥmanides himself, and to the probable fact that he brought out his Hebrew version in haste, and did not have the opportunity to revise it. These errors, therefore, being a feature of the original text, do not require emendation. The full evidence of random inaccuracy in quotation can be seen in the reference column of Chavel's commentary on the *Vikuaḥ*.

(4) Certain misreadings have been introduced into the text by copyists who did not fully understand some of Naḥmanides' arguments. Examples can be found on p. 120 and p. 145. Here the criteria are (a) a loss of cogency in the argument, and (b) the possibility of restoration of cogency by a simple, plausible emendation.

(5) The usual corruptions have crept into the text through copyists' lapses of attention. Most of these have been pointed out by Steinschneider and subsequent editors.

4

Biographical Notes on the Chief Persons Present at Barcelona

Rabbi Moses ben Naḥman (Naḥmanides, Naḥmani, Ramban, Bonastrug da Porta, Moses Gerondi). Chief Spanish rabbi of his generation. Cousin of Jonah Gerondi, and teacher of Solomon b. Abraham Adret (Rashb'a). Born 1194 at Gerona. Made his living as a physician.

In 1232, he acted as mediator in the controversy over the philosophical works of Maimonides, attempting to effect a compromise.

Also in 1232, King James I of Aragon consulted him on an important communal matter, the jurisdiction of the powerful Alconstantini family over Catalonian Jewry. N. advised against confirming this family in office.

Distinguished himself as Halakhist (expert in Talmudic law) in his youth by writing critical works on Maimonides, and Zeraḥiah ha-Levi. Throughout his life, he wrote novelle and monographs on the Talmud which are regarded as essential to Talmudic studies, and had great influence on later scholars.

In his old age he wrote his famous Commentaries on the Pentateuch (Torah) and on Job, written in philosophical and theosophical style. Four of his sermons have been preserved, and also a number of poems and prayers, as well as miscellaneous works, including the *Vikuaḥ*.

1263: Took part in Barcelona Disputation, at command of James I.

1265: Brought to trial by Dominicans for publishing the *Vikuaḥ*, containing 'blasphemies'. Given a light punishment by the king, who protected him from further harassment.

1267: Letter from Pope Clement IV to James I demands heavy punishment for N.

1267: He emigrated to Palestine, at the age of 73. Found Jerusalem in ruins. Set up a Jewish community and academy *(yeshivah)*.

1268: Moved to Acre, as rabbi of the community, in succession to Yeḥiel of Paris, who had also emigrated to Palestine after the Paris Disputation.

1270: died in Acre.

One of his grandsons was Levi b. Gershom (Ralbag), one of the profoundest Jewish thinkers of the Middle Ages (otherwise known as Leo Hebraeus, or Gersonides).

Pablo Christiani (Paulus Christianus, Pablo Christia, Pau Christia). Jewish name not known (Paul was a name commonly adopted by Jewish converts to Christianity). Pupil of Rabbi Eliezer of Tarascon. Native of Montpellier. After conversion, joined Dominicans, and preached conversionist sermons in Provence. Employed by Raymund de Peñaforte to teach Hebrew to Dominicans engaged in missionary activities to Jews. Sponsored by Louis IX of France to preach in Provence. It was on Pablo's advice that Louis IX enforced the wearing of the 'Jew-badge', 1269.

After the Barcelona Disputation, 1263, Pablo toured Jewish communities of Aragon preaching compulsory sermons in the synagogues. He had the special encouragement and support of the Pope, who wrote to James I of Aragon commending Pablo's abilities and services (1267) in the matter of the censorship of the Talmud.

Died in Taormina, Sicily, about 1274.

Raymund de Peñaforte c. 1180–1275. Canonised 1601.

1230: Appointed confessor to Pope Gregory IX, who gave him the task of collecting the papal decretal letters into one volume, known as *Decretales Gregorii IX*, an important source of canon law.

1232: Established Inquisition in Aragon.

1238: Appointed Master General of the Dominican Order. Codified the constitutions of the order. Resigned as general in 1240, to devote himself to missionary work among Moslems and Jews. Influenced Raymund Martini. Also influenced Thomas Aquinas to write *Summa Contra Gentiles*.

1264: Headed commission to examine the Talmud for 'blasphemy'.

1265: Took part in trial of Naḥmanides for publishing his account.

James I of Aragon (Jaime el Conquistador, James the Conqueror) 1208–76. Married Yolande, daughter of Andrew II of Hungary, 1234 (repudiating his former wife).

Conquered Balearic Islands, 1230–35.

Conquered Moorish State of Valencia, 1238.

Maintained liberal policy towards the Jews, whom he sought to attract to his kingdom, and employed to garrison frontier strongholds. Employed Jews as high officials, including Judah de la Cavalleria, bailiff of the province of Valencia, and Benveniste de Porta, bailiff of Barcelona. Nevertheless, under the influence of Raymund de Peñaforte, his confessor, he issued anti-Jewish legislation, but was vacillating in implementing these laws.

He was a man of huge stature and great physical strength. He alternated between periods of laxity and opportunism, and periods of religious fervour and superstition. He had many mistresses and many illegitimate children, whom he treated generously, to the disapproval of the Church. His worst quarrel with the Church, however, was when he cut out the tongue of the Bishop of Gerona (the predecessor of the bishop who requested Naḥmanides to write his account of the Barcelona Disputation). Previously, James had incurred Papal denunciation when he repudiated his first wife on grounds of consanguinity—an affair curiously similar to that of Henry VIII of England. James wrote an autobiography which is regarded as a literary classic.

5

The Tortosa Disputation, 1413–14

In terms of scale and splendour, the greatest of the disputations was that of Tortosa. Instead of lasting for a few days, this one lasted for a period of twenty-one months, with a total of sixty-nine sessions. Instead of being commemorated, on the Christian side, by a brief communiqué, it was the subject of voluminous 'protocols', or minutes, kept session by session by the papal notary, and comprising over 600 pages in the edition of Pacios Lopez (1957). On the Jewish side, however, it gave rise to a much shorter account, by Bonastruc Desmaîtres, one of the participants, covering only the first five sessions (translated in this book) and another even more fragmentary account.

While the Barcelona Disputation took place under the chairmanship of a king, the Tortosa Disputation was chaired by a pope, Benedict XIII. Instead of calling for one rabbi to represent the Jewish case, Benedict summoned representatives of all the communities of Aragon and Catalonia, and aimed at nothing less than the complete conversion of the Jews of these areas. The occasion was organised most lavishly, with seventy seats for cardinals, archbishops and bishops, and accommodation at the sessions for nearly a thousand Church dignitaries of the papal court.

The Tortosa Disputation presents countless interesting aspects, historical, theological and personal. To deal with it in full would require a large volume in itself. Yet as far as the larger issues of Jewish-Christian confrontation were concerned, it added little to the Barcelona Disputation. The arguments advanced there were advanced again, with more elaboration on the Christian side, since the Christian spokesman Geronimo (Hieronymus) de Santa Fe (formerly, as a Jew, Joshua Halorki) was a more sophisticated man, and more deeply versed in Jewish learning, than Pablo Christiani. On the Jewish side, the speakers were chiefly influenced by Naḥmanides, to whom they frequently referred. This is not to say that the Jewish speakers at Tortosa had nothing of their own to say. They did deepen in some respects the standpoints laid down in general outline by Naḥmanides. At certain moments in the disputation, the Jewish voices rang out clearly and courageously, enunciating essential Jewish positions. Yet, on the whole, the Tortosa Disputation, despite its splendour, was a much smaller occasion than the Barcelona Disputation. The drama and nobility of Barcelona were lacking.

There were many good reasons for this. The conditions under which the Tortosa Disputation was held were conditions of terror. As the Jewish account makes clear, the Jewish delegates were in constant fear for their lives. Not many years before, in 1391, the position of the Jews in Spain had suffered a blow from which it never recovered. A wholesale persecution and massacre of the Jews took place, beginning in Castile, and then spreading to Aragon and Catalonia. These massacres were fomented by Christian religious enthusiasts, who worked on the superstition of the peasants and artisans. Famous Jewish communities, including that of Gerona, the birthplace of Naḥmanides, were destroyed. The response of secular authorities responsible for law and order was sluggish and apathetic. The Jews were no longer so necessary to the kings and aristocracy of Spain. Their function as bourgeoisie and bureaucracy had been taken over by others. The way was open to the fanatics of the Church who for centuries had been restrained only by the opportunism of the kings from laying hands on the Jews and dragging them to death or baptism.

The crisis of 1391 passed over, but the climate had changed. Many important leaders had been killed. Many Jews, forced into baptism, now faced death at the hands of the Inquisition if they sought to return to the Jewish fold, as did any Jews who encouraged them to return. (Though canon law deprecated conversion of Jews by force, once they had been so converted, their conversion was regarded as legally valid, and any attempt to repudiate it was regarded as apostasy punishable by the Inquisition.)

Even more recently another crisis had occurred for the Jews of Spain. The sinister fanatic Vincent (Vicente) Ferrer (later canonised), surrounded by bands of flagellants, roused the mob to anti-Jewish fervour. He achieved such influence over the kings of Spain that he was able to persuade them to pass anti-Jewish laws, abolishing Jewish rights and reducing them to the status of pariahs. The chief object, however, was to dragoon the Jews into being converted to Christianity. Vincent Ferrer was so powerful that he was even a king-maker; he had the deciding voice in the election of Ferdinand to the throne of Aragon in 1412. Consequently, Ferdinand put no bar in the way of Vincent Ferrer's activities, and acquiesced in anti-Jewish legislation, and in the harrying of *conversos*, one of Ferrer's chief interests.

Vincent Ferrer was in the background of the Tortosa Disputation, for it was he who had converted Geronimo (Joshua Halorki) to Christianity. And he was in the background in another way too; for while the Tortosa Disputation was going on, Vincent Ferrer was making a tour of the towns from which the rabbis summoned to the disputation had been withdrawn, terrifying the leaderless communities and trying to bully them into conversion. Though he professed to be opposed to forcible conversion, Vincent Ferrer's visits were always accompanied by mob risings against the Jews.

It was in this atmosphere of fear for themselves, their families and their communities that the rabbis took part in the Tortosa Disputation. Rabbi Astruk Halevi, one of the leading Jewish participants, expressed this as follows (as recorded in the Latin 'protocols' of the Disputation):

> Even if we pleaded complete ignorance, no decision should be made against us in this Disputation. For though Aristotle said that ignorance does not excuse sin, he said this only about inexcusable ignorance. But such ignorance as ours has many excuses. We are away from our homes; our resources have diminished and are almost entirely destroyed; huge damage is resulting in our communities from our absence; we do not know the fate of our wives and children; we have inadequate maintenance here and even lack food, and are put to extraordinary expenses. Why should people suffering such woes be held accountable for their arguments, when contending with Geronimo and others who are in the greatest prosperity and luxury?

To this complaint of Rabbi Astruk, Geronimo gave a reply:

> A teacher, from whom others ought to derive an example, should show fortitude, which is to sustain the attacks of adversity. Whence it follows that the virtuous man does not fail in tribulations, as Aristotle says in his Ethics, and Solomon in his Proverbs, chapter 12, 'The righteous man will not be moved for ever.' You, Rabbi Astruch, since you regard yourself as a teacher, ought to be an example to others of fortitude, and ought not to be moved by thoughts of your wife, or by any other tribulation. And even if, by reason of unspirituality, you

become affected by such things, this effect should be of short duration, since sensuality ought to be defeated by reason, which indeed becomes purer in adversity than in prosperity.

With such a background of recent disaster, of gathering danger and of sinking status, it is hardly surprising that the spirit of the Tortosa rabbis was not so high as that of Naḥmanides at Barcelona. There is none of the joy in combat and in the defence of well-beloved doctrines that we can sense in Naḥmanides' replies. There is only the weary defence of people baited beyond endurance. One of the techniques of the Christian side was to wear down the Jewish opposition by repetition and long-drawn-out tactics. Several times, when the Jews were accused of prevarication *(variatio)*, the Pope gave orders that the whole disputation was to start again from the beginning. The tactics that at Barcelona were reserved for the Christian account drawn up after the disputation was over were here brought into the debate itself. Thus if the rabbis said that *some* people take literally the Midrashic statement that the Messiah had come, this was hailed as a full admission that the Messiah had come, despite the rabbis' repeated assertion that they did not themselves subscribe to this interpretation.

In the circumstances, it was amazing how much spirit the rabbis (some of whom were not much inferior in gifts to Naḥmanides himself) retained. Occasionally, they could not help flashing out a retort which showed their calibre. For example, when Pope Benedict expatiated on the irrationality of the Jewish belief (which, by the way, none of the rabbis present shared, as they had taken some pains to point out) that the Messiah had been in existence, in the Garden of Eden, for over 1,300 years, waiting for the time of his earthly advent, Rabbi Astruk could not resist pointing out that Christians believed many extraordinary things about *their* Messiah, so they could hardly complain if some Jews believed one extraordinary thing about their own. Such was the fury of the Pope at this retort that the whole Jewish party feared for their lives.

One feature of the Jewish case at Tortosa shows clearly the lowered tone of Jewish morale. This was the plea for *toleration*, based on the alleged futility of rational argument on matters of religious faith. Naḥmanides' great pride is in what he regards as the superior rationality of Judaism to Christianity, which he is prepared to argue in a robust and fundamental manner. He does not ask for tender regard for his religious susceptibilities, which might be injured by searching fundamental inquiry. At the Tortosa

Disputation we hear a plea for toleration which is in some respects anti-rational and obscurantist, but in other respects remarkably similar to modern notions of the inviolability of separate religious traditions. Rabbi Astruk is again the spokesman of this attitude:

> I say that all disputation about a principle of religion is prohibited, so that a man may not depart from the principles of his religion. It seems that only science should be made the subject of dispute and argument; but religion and belief ought to be consigned willingly to faith, not argument, so that he may not retreat from it. When we say, 'We do not know,' and cease disputing, we are doing what is right for every religious adherent. . . . Further, we do not say absolutely that we do not know any more; we mean that our previous arguments were sufficient to reply to the questions raised by Master Geronimo, and that at present we do not know any more. Therefore, with regard to this kind of ignorance we should not be regarded as defeated at all: firstly, because our declaration is due to faith, to which we are asserting our loyalty; secondly, because knowing more is not necessary for us with regard to the questions raised.

Rabbi Astruk is saying here that religious disputation can be carried only so far. Eventually, the disputants must come to a point where there is nothing more to say, because bedrock principles of faith have been reached on one or both sides which are too axiomatic to be questioned. At this point, it is necessary to say, 'I do not know anything more.' Rabbi Astruk may have been saying merely that when one has repeated a valid argument so many times without producing conviction in one's hearer, there is no point in going on repeating it. This was a sound attitude in a debate where the Christian side kept on repeating the same points *ad nauseam*, treating the Jewish replies as evidence of obduracy or incomprehension. But in his despair, and desire to bring the disputation to an end, Rabbi Astruk had to find some more polite way of putting the matter. The way he found was to enunciate a theory of religious autonomy; that each religion had basic principles which were beyond the reach of argument. Even apparent confutation in argument, he asserted, proved nothing: 'A Christian living in the land of the Saracens may be defeated by the arguments of a pagan or Saracen, but it does not follow that his faith has been refuted, only that he himself is lacking in knowledge.' The unspoken corollary was that the Jews had given up any expectation of refuting Christianity, which was also ultimately a matter of irrefutable faith. Implied was a theory of toleration, by which religions should live side by side, without presuming to criticise each other, until the day when God would show his hand by fulfilling the expectations of one religion or another.

This is an attitude which appeals to modern relativists and ethnicists, but it opened the way to a charge of irrationality. Astruk was pleading for an end to Christian interference in Jewish religious life; but it seemed that he was saying that Jews were not open to argument. Geronimo immediately took the opportunity offered. In his most effective speech of the whole disputation, he proclaimed the rationality of religious belief, and the need to argue out one's most fundamental articles of faith. The tables had been turned; it was now the Christians who championed reason, and the Jews who championed blind faith. 'Anyone who supports a religion,' asserted Geronimo, 'if he has the position of leader, ought to give his reasons for holding his belief. . . From what the Jew says, it would follow that a person holding a good faith should never inform another person who holds an erroneous faith, and so lead him back from error to the true faith, since such information cannot be given without having disputes.' Naḥmanides would have agreed with every word of this. Yet the rationalist stance now taken by Geronimo is hardly consistent with the declaration made by the Pope at the start, 'I have not sent for you in order to prove which of our two religions is true; for it is perfectly known to me that my religion is true and that your religion has been superseded'; and where the Jews were constantly told that the purpose of the assembly was not disputation but instruction. The Jews were left to be thorough-going rationalists and open to all arguments, while the Christians argued from entrenched, unchallengeable positions.

Nevertheless, though Geronimo's eloquent plea for rationality was one-sided, the attempt of the Jews to escape so uncharacteristically into a doctrine of the irrationality of faith was a sign of decreased confidence. Even Astruk's celebrated retort, mentioned above, would not have been made by Naḥmanides. For it amounted to saying, 'Allow us to be irrational, since you are even more irrational.' The same decrease in confidence is shown in the repeated plea by the Jewish speakers of their own ignorance and incapacity, motivated as this was often enough by sheer weariness and desire to escape from the farcical proceedings, especially towards the end of the unbearably protracted disputation. But even at the beginning, the Jews had complained that they were not able to cope with Geronimo's syllogistic style of reasoning, with which they were not familiar. In the eras of Maimonides, Naḥmanides and Gersonides, a Jewish disputant would have been ashamed to make such a complaint. There was no area of philosophy or science in which the Jews were not leaders and masters. The last great medieval Jewish thinker, Ḥasdai Crescas, philosopher and halakhist, acute critic of Aristotle and Maimonides, had died in 1412, just a year before the Tortosa Disputation. If he had lived to take part in it, there would have been no plea of incapacity.

It was among the Christians now that intellectual confidence was to be found, based on the dominant Aristotelian and Averroist philosophy. Judaism was fighting a rearguard action against a flood of Christian missionary propaganda, but even more damaging was the growing conviction that the Jews were becoming a backward enclave in a Christian society of advancing culture. Many Jews at this period became converted to Christianity not out of religious conviction, but because by doing so they entered a community of wider intellectual and cultural opportunities—the first time in European history when this temptation presented itself. At the same time, there was much that was spurious in this confident, not to say complacent, Christian intellectuality. Scholastic philosophy had entered its most unproductive and bombastic phase; it was soon to encounter fundamental criticism from the thinkers of the Renaissance (criticism which had been anticipated by Ḥasdai Crescas, who had a direct influence on Pico della Mirandola, and thus eventually on Galileo).

In the Tortosa Disputation there are examples in plenty of scholasticism at its worst in the style of debate adopted by Geronimo, himself a good example of the new breed of opportunist Jewish renegades. Right at the beginning, Geronimo announced that his whole argument would take the form of a syllogism, as follows. *Major premise:* anyone who fulfilled the prophecies was the Messiah. *Minor premise:* Jesus fulfilled the prophecies. *Conclusion:* Jesus was the Messiah. All that now remained, declared Geronimo, was to demonstrate the minor premise. It was probably this fatuous syllogism which alarmed the Jews into making their complaint that Geronimo was using logical methods with which they were unfamiliar. Naḥmanides would have laughed at it.

There is thus some substance in the criticisms made (particularly by Isaac Abravanel, the Jewish leader and thinker of the time of the expulsion from Spain) of the calibre of the Jewish representatives at the Tortosa Disputation. But it would be wrong to lay much stress on this criticism. The shortcomings of the Jewish representatives were the product of their time, and the strains under which Spanish Jewry were suffering. They were not able to speak with the universal voice of a Maimonides or a Naḥmanides, yet they were well versed in Judaism itself, and when given the opportunity, gave excellent and courageous replies, some of which are superior in formulation to those of Naḥmanides. As Yitzhak Baer points out in his excellent chapter on the Tortosa Disputation, 'Men like Isaac Abravanel, who later criticised the Jewish arguments as feeble, had not read the actual records of the discussions, and drew their information from inadequate sources.'

The object of the disputation was defined by the Pope at the start: it was to prove the truth of Christian doctrines about the Messiah from certain passages in the Talmud. Geronimo drew out explicitly the two-tier theory of the Talmud which Pablo Christiani had only implied. If the Talmud contained Christian truths, how was it that it also contained many things contrary to Christianity? How was it also (as Naḥmanides had asked) that the rabbis who compiled the Talmud or are mentioned in it remained impervious to Christian belief? The answer was that the Talmud contained two strata, one authentic and ancient, containing true perceptions of the nature of the Messiah and also of the facts of his advent and suffering on the cross; and the other, a later encrustation, developed out of hatred of Christianity and stubborn refusal to acknowledge its truth.

Geronimo also developed an interesting theory about the several attitudes proper to Christians and Jews towards the two strata in the Talmud so postulated. His view was that Christians were permitted to distinguish between what was true and what false in the Talmud; but Jews were obliged to swallow everything in the Talmud whole, contradictions and all. They were not allowed to reject any part of the Talmud as inconsistent with their basic religious standpoints, or even to reinterpret such a passage in a way consistent with the general tenets of Judaism. At one point, Geronimo even threatened the Jews with a prosecution for heresy for not taking the Talmud seriously enough! It is extraordinary how Christian attitudes had changed since the Paris Disputation, where Jewish belief in the Talmud was declared to be heretical.

The Jewish speakers, however, were not inclined to accept Christian directions as to how to believe their own religion. They were able to point to many precedents to show that they were not required to accept the Aggadic portions of the Talmud literally. They also pointed out, more clearly than Naḥmanides, that the Talmud contains many opinions, belonging to different rabbis, and that since many of these opinions oppose each other, it is impossible to accept them all, except in the sense of giving them all respect. More clearly than Naḥmanides, too, they pointed to the poetic, figurative character of many Aggadic passages. Worth quoting in this connection are the remarks of the rabbi of the Tortosan Jewish community (not named in the *Shevet Yehudah* account, but in the shorter Hebrew account named as Solomon Maimon) who interposed to say (about the Midrashic saying that the Messiah was born on the day that the Temple was destroyed): 'The verse [on which this Midrash is based] comes to comfort them [the Jews] for the destruction of the Temple, and to say to them that they will yet return to their original state. . . . It means that on the day of the destruction of the Temple, the creation of the Messiah arose in the thought of God. . .' The delicate literary perception of this remark, which indeed penetrates the true meaning of the Midrash, lifts the discussion for a moment above the level of sectarian disagreement.

The Jewish scholars thus claimed the right to use their own judgement about any Aggadic passage that might be quoted, and refused the role thrust upon them of unquestioning acceptors of their literal meaning (though even the question of what *was* the literal meaning was not as clear-cut as Geronimo, and Pablo Christiani before him, wanted to assume). At Tortosa, the matter was complicated by the fact that Geronimo brought into discussion many alleged Midrashic passages, not adduced at Barcelona, to which the Jewish speakers denied any validity or genuineness. There were episodes which might have seemed comic, were it not for the harassment involved.

Geronimo, on one occasion, quoted a Christological passage, allegedly from a named reputable Midrash, but actually from Raymund Martini's *Pugio Fidei.* Rabbi Astruk declared the passage to be spurious, and produced a copy of the actual named text to prove his point. At this, Geronimo resorted to the farcical procedure of snatching the copy away from him and pretending to read out his alleged passage from it. At another session, Geronimo argued that when he produced a passage the existence of which was disputed, he was not obliged to prove the existence of the passage by bringing forward the text in which he claimed to have found it;

on the contrary, the obligation was on the Jewish participants to search their literature until they found the disputed passage—and if they could not find it, this was to be regarded as proof of their incompetence. This was not genuine disputation, but mere insolent torture. In fact, Geronimo never once produced a copy of a disputed text, though from time to time he promised that he would do so at the next session.

While the rabbis were required to show indiscriminate faith in every word of the Talmud and Midrash—even in alleged parts of them of which they had never heard—Geronimo, by his two-tier theory of the Talmud, felt himself able to use it in two diametrically opposed ways: to prove the truth of Christian doctrine, and also to show the depraved and blasphemous nature of Talmudic teaching.

The final sessions of the disputation were concerned with the second approach. All the accusations against the Talmud which had been made by Nicholas Donin at Paris in 1240 were brought out again, together with some extra charges added by Geronimo. Thus the marathon Tortosa Disputation was intended to comprise in itself the two functions of the two previous disputations: to exploit the Talmud for Christian purposes, and to condemn the Talmud as blasphemous, anti-Christian, and obscene. But the rabbis had had enough. They resorted to silence. Having had abundant proof in the earlier part of the disputation of the unfair methods of their opponent, and having been subjected to more and more contemptuous abuse as the disputation wore on, they refused to debate the passages of the Talmud now brought forward for condemnation. They could not, of course, give their real reasons for this refusal, so they issued a statement that they were unable to defend the Talmud, because of their own incapacity and ignorance, but were quite sure that more competent people would be able to answer all charges against the Talmud. By this they hoped to bring the disputation to an end. It had lasted for twenty-one months, with long adjournments during which the Jewish participants were not allowed to return home. For the final sessions, the venue of the discussions was changed from Tortosa to the village of San Mateo (largely because the position of the Pope, or rather anti-Pope, Benedict XIII, had become unsafe in Tortosa). The silence of the Jewish scholars was, of course, taken by the Christians as complete defeat. The Pope and the King of Aragon issued a joint declaration and ordinances condemning the Talmud and ordering its censorship, and at the same time bringing in new laws to reduce all Jews to pariah status. All over the kingdom, Jews were mercilessly harassed and many communities totally destroyed.

Yet there had been some earlier sessions where real dialogue took place, and the rabbis were able to put forward their views in a coherent and logical style. Some of the sessions on the Jewish theory of the Messiah were even valuable in clarifying the basic differences between Judaism and Christianity. These sessions bore fruit in the later writings of Jewish thinkers, especially in the *'Ikkarim* of Joseph Albo, who took a fairly prominent part in the disputation itself. Basing themselves on the standpoint of Naḥmanides at Barcelona, and also on the writings of Ḥasdai Crescas, the rabbis insisted that the whole debate between Christians and Jews on the subject of the Messiah was lopsided, since the Messiah was far less important in Judaism than in Christianity. While the Jews believed in the coming of the Messiah, they did not believe that the Messiah had anything to do with the saving of souls. Even if it were proved to them that the Messiah had already come (a point which to Christians was of such overwhelming importance), this would not matter tremendously, since the definition of 'Messiah' to Jews was so different. Joseph Albo himself jumped up at one point to say that the question of whether the Messiah had come or not was irrelevant to his belief in Judaism. To the Jews, the point of existence lay in the moral struggle within the psyche of each individual. This struggle was within the capacity of the individual to handle, with the help of the moral instruction contained in the Torah. No Saviour was required to rescue the individual from his predicament. As for the Messiah, his function was to mark that the struggle had proved a success, not only on the individual level, but on the level of society and the world community. There could be many Messiahs, to mark different stages in human development.

There was in fact some disagreement between the Jewish speakers on the question of the Messiah. Some said that belief in a coming Messiah was an essential tenet of Judaism, others that it was not. Geronimo tried to make capital out of this disagreement to show that the Jewish speakers were being dishonest or incompetent or both. But such a disagreement was perfectly allowable within the limits of Judaism. It was a significant pointer to the non-dogmatic nature of Judaism that such a disagreement could take place between rabbis of equal authority without any mutual accusations of heresy. Such a situation, of course, could not take place in Christianity, where doctrine was laid down by ecumenical councils, who pronounced anathema against any dissentients. In Judaism, there was no official body which could pronounce such decisions of orthodoxy; and in any case, opinions on such matters were held to be free. Geronimo would not acknowledge that the very nature of doctrinal belief was different in Judaism and in Christianity. He kept adducing, for example, the authority of Maimonides, who had laid down thirteen principles of faith for Judaism. But Maimonides, though highly respected, was not regarded by any rabbi as a final authority. Each of the rabbis at the disputation felt himself just as entitled to pronounce on what was essential to Judaism as Maimonides. Geronimo's attempt to equate the concept of 'belief' in Christianity and Judaism also came into his arguments about the status of the Aggadah. The Aggadah, he argued, *must* be more authoritative than the rabbis said, because it was only in the Aggadah that theological statements could be found. Where, he wanted to know, was Jewish theology to be found, if not in the Aggadah? The answer was that theology, in the Christian sense, was not to be found in Judaism at all. There was poetry, and theological speculation, but nothing whatever for which Jews would be prepared to burn people at the stake.

The Tortosa Disputation was thus not without sessions in which the Jewish speakers were allowed to speak clearly and directly on Jewish standpoints, and they took good advantage of these sessions to produce statements of permanent value. The disputation as a whole, however, despite its lavish scale and appearance of a significant encounter between Christianity and Judaism, was a painful and deplorable affair. While preserving, with some effort, an appearance of being concerned with peaceful persuasion, it was conducted in an atmosphere of fear and doom, with the wild bands of Vincent Ferrer roaming the countryside, and the populace being whipped up into anti-Jewish fervour. In this atmosphere, many Jews succumbed and accepted baptism, and were then brought into the hall of assembly at Tortosa to declare before the participant rabbis their acceptance of Christianity. After the disputation was over, even more numerous baptisms took place, some induced by promises of high office in the court of Aragon. Even Don Vidal, who acted as chief spokesman, or *arenga,* for the Jews in the early stages of the Tortosa Disputation, became converted to Christianity, and became a high official. The morale of the Jews of Spain had suffered a great blow, not because of any arguments put against their religion at Tortosa by the renegade Geronimo, but because of the general worsening of the Jewish position, combined with the inroads of Averroist scepticism, which made a cynical transition to a despised Christianity from a despised Judaism a matter of easy, calculated self-interest.

Even the material splendour of the Tortosa Disputation was, to some extent, a sham. Benedict XIII was not, as he pretended to be, the Pope of the Catholic Church, but only one of the three claimants to that office who were at that time scheming to overcome their rivals. Benedict no doubt saw the disputation as a means towards recognition as Pope. In the event, however, he failed. At the Council of Pisa, and then at the Council of Constance, his claim was repudiated. He never accepted these decisions, and until his death remained a mini-Pope, ensconced in his fortress of Peniscola, where he had his own college of cardinals. When he died in 1424, these cardinals formed a mini-schism of their own, setting up two rival claimants to Benedict's ludicrous little curia. So ended the Pope of the Tortosa Disputation.

Yet the alliance of Church and State against the Jews, shown in the co-operation of Benedict and King Ferdinand, now continued, with tragic results. It had been owing to the support of the kings, who needed their talent and energy, that the Jews of Spain had been able to build up their brilliant culture, despite the ever-present hostility of the Church. Now the Jews were needed no more in Spain; their pupils had learnt too well from them. The rest of their time in Spain, until their final cruel expulsion in 1492, was a story of mounting tragedy.

Over the proceedings at Tortosa, projected from a previous happier era, stands the figure of Naḥmanides, whose words were so often quoted by the rabbis who took part. Naḥmanides at Barcelona had been a man at bay, but his spirit had remained high, a Jew not yet bowed down by insult and oppression. The rabbis at Tortosa in a time of depression and humiliation, behaved with stoical courage which demands our admiration; but the great figure of medieval Jewish-Christian dialogue, a figure of hope as well as courage, remains Naḥmanides.

PART II

THE BARCELONA DISPUTATION: TEXTS

6

Introductory Note on the *Vikuaḥ*

The Beginning of the *Vikuaḥ*

The first paragraph of the *Vikuaḥ*, as printed in Steinschneider's edition, is as follows:

> We read in Sanhedrin, 'Our teachers have taught: Jesus had five disciples, Mat'ai, Nak'ai, Nezer, Buni and Todah. They brought Mat'ai and he said to them, "Shall Mat'ai be killed? Does not Scripture say, 'Mat'ai will come and be seen before God'?" They replied, "Yes, Mat'ai must be killed, for Scripture says, 'Mat'ai will die, and his name be lost'."
>
> 'Then they brought Nak'ai and he said to them, "Shall Nak'ai be killed? Does not Scripture say, 'And Nak'ai and the righteous shalt thou not kill'?" They replied, "Yes, Nak'ai must be killed, for Scripture says, 'In the secret places shall he kill Nak'ai'."
>
> 'Then they brought Nezer and he said to them, "Shall Nezer be killed? Does not Scripture say, 'And Nezer shall grow out his roots'?" They replied, "Yes, Nezer must be killed, for Scripture says, 'And thou art cast out of thy grave like an abominable Nezer'."
>
> 'Then they brought Buni and he said to them, "Shall Buni be killed? Does not Scripture say, 'Buni is my first-born, O Israel'?" They replied, "Yes, Buni must be killed, for Scripture says, 'Behold I will slay thy Buni, thy first-born'."
>
> 'Then they brought Todah, and he said to them, "Shall Todah be killed? Does not Scripture say, 'A Psalm for Todah'?" They replied, "Yes, Todah must be killed, for Scripture says, 'Whoever slaughters Todah glorifies me'."'
>
> And Rabbi Solomon [Rashi] wrote, 'They [the disciples of Jesus] were close to the Roman government, and that is why the Rabbis had to answer all their sophistical arguments.' So in the same way, I am writing down the words with which I replied to the perversity of Fray Paul, who disgraced his education in public before our lord the King and his wise men and advisers, may his glory be exalted and his kingdom raised.

The Talmudic passage cited purports to describe how the 'five disciples of Jesus' were executed by the Jewish authorities. As each one was led to his death, he tried to obtain mercy by quoting a Scriptural verse containing a pun on his own name. In each case, however, the authorities were able to cap the quotation by another in which the name of the condemned man was also punningly contained, but with a connotation of condemnation instead of acquittal. The whole passage is clearly a piece of fantasy, in questionable taste, intended as a counterblast to Christian propaganda. The date of composition of the passage can be put at about 250 CE.

It is strange that the authenticity of the passage as the opening of the *Vikuaḥ* has never been questioned. It is omitted from the present translation on the ground that it is highly doubtful whether it formed part of the work originally composed by Naḥmanides. The following are the reasons for this conclusion:

(1) Naḥmanides' account of the Barcelona Disputation was composed at the request of the Bishop of Gerona, Peter of Castellnou. The first version of the work, therefore, must have been either in Latin or Spanish (Catalan). It would have been read without delay both by the Bishop and by the leading Dominicans. It is highly unlikely, therefore, that Naḥmanides would have introduced into his account highly offensive and inflammatory matter which was extraneous to the subject-matter of the disputation.

(2) In 1263–64, the very year in which Naḥmanides composed the *Vikuaḥ*, an investigation was proceeding into anti-Christian passages of the Talmud, instituted by the Pope and the Dominicans of Spain, and supervised by some of Naḥmanides' antagonists in the disputation, namely, Raymund de Peñaforte, Raymund Martini and Arnold de Segarra. A year and a half of 'intensive effort on the part of the Jews' (Baer) finally led to the rescinding by James I of his original decrees ordering censorship and expurgation of the Talmud, but the campaign of the Dominicans against the Talmud continued. It is incredible that, in this delicate period, Naḥmanides would have deliberately exacerbated the conflict by beginning his work either in the non-Hebrew or the Hebrew version with one of the very Talmudic passages under discussion for censorship and expurgation.

(3) In the course of the disputation, Naḥmanides is careful to avoid direct reference to the fact (as he conceived it) that Jesus was executed by the Jews by judicial process. Instead, he refers to

Jesus' having 'been killed', and having been 'pursued by his enemies'. Yet here, at the start of the *Vikuaḥ,* he apparently refers with the utmost bluntness to the purported judicial execution of Jesus' closest disciples—though Christian tradition does not even accuse the Jews of this.

(4) The only relevance of the passage to the rest of the *Vikuaḥ* might be that, as Baer argues, the author wished to warn his readers not to take too seriously the arguments put forward on the Jewish side during the disputation. But if, as argued above (pp. 61–3), Naḥmanides was fully serious in all his arguments, the passage becomes positively irrelevant and misleading.

(5) When the Dominicans complained about Naḥmanides' account of the disputation, they stated explicitly (see p. 60) that the account contained blasphemies which had previously been uttered at the disputation itself. They did not complain that he had added further blasphemies in his written account. While it is dangerous to argue from silence, it seems very likely that an added offensive passage, inserted at the very start, would have excited special wrath. Moreover, Naḥmanides pleaded before the king in his own defence that he had only repeated in his account what he had said at the disputation, where the king had given him special permission to speak freely. If, however, he had had the temerity to add further 'blasphemous' material, this would surely have been too good an opportunity for the Dominicans to miss. Yet it is clear that the king upheld Naḥmanides' defence as to the actual 'blasphemies' uttered, and only sentenced him (lightly) for issuing the written account without permission of the king (even though he did so at the request of the Bishop of Gerona).

The conclusion seems inescapable that this passage did not exist in the first version of the work, written for the perusal of the Bishop of Gerona. The question now presents itself: when was the passage added? It is not known under what circumstances the Hebrew version of the *Vikuaḥ,* the only version now extant, was written. Did Naḥmanides write it himself, or was it a translation by another hand? Was it written at approximately the same time as the Spanish (Latin) version, or some years later? It is impossible to answer these questions with certainty, but there is some likelihood that the Hebrew version was written some years after the disputation, and was a translation by someone other than Naḥmanides. There are some indications in the Hebrew text that it may have been written by someone who, at times, did not fully understand Naḥmanides' argument. Naḥmanides left Spain for

Palestine in 1267, and in the interval between the publication of the Spanish (Latin) version and his departure for Palestine, he was much harassed by the Dominicans and had to make several public appearances before bodies of inquiry. It is possible, therefore, that he would have had neither the time nor the inclination to work on a Hebrew version of the work which was already causing him so much anxiety.

A tenable solution, therefore, is that the Hebrew version was made about ten to fifteen years after the disputation, at a time when pressure on the Talmud had somewhat relaxed, and when Naḥmanides himself was lying in his grave in Palestine.

On this view, it was the pious translator, whoever he was, who, being somewhat alarmed at the boldness of some of Naḥmanides' statements about the Aggadah, and thinking (like modern commentators) that he could not have meant them seriously, added for the benefit of Jewish readers, the passage about the jesting replies made to the disciples of Jesus.

On the other hand, the Hebrew style of the main body of the *Vikuaḥ* shows great affinities to the Hebrew style of Naḥmanides' other works, and is, in general, too lucid and lively to be the work of a journeyman translator. The most likely solution to our problem, then, is that Naḥmanides did write a Hebrew version of his account. This was probably not circulated until some years after his death, when it was edited by someone who added the opening passage, in order to excuse the great Naḥmanides both for condescending to bandy words with Christians, and for expressing himself with too great freedom about the Aggadah. The same editor made some errors of comprehension in transcribing Naḥmanides' text, and added two further short passages which show the same gratuitous and irrelevant polemicism as appears in the opening (see pp. 117 and 123).

But what about the possibility that Naḥmanides himself added the opening passage after himself translating his account of the disputation into Hebrew? The main reason for rejecting this possibility is that the added passage is out of keeping with the tone of the rest of the work. It belongs to an utterly different style of polemics—the kind of jeering interchange which is rare indeed in the Talmudic literature, but may have had its place at the level of popular morale-building. It is hard to believe that Naḥmanides, after composing a work of such cool rationality and lofty feeling, would have ruined its tone right at the start by adding such an introduction. Moreover, as argued above, an inquiry was going on at the time into anti-Christian aspects of the Talmud. The Hebrew version of the *Vikuaḥ* must have been scrutinised by Christian Hebraists such as Pablo Christiani and Raymund de Peñaforte; and Naḥmanides must have known that it would be subject to such scrutiny. How then could he have deliberately added such a passage, right at the beginning of his Hebrew version?

7

The *Vikuaḥ* of Nahmanides: Translation and Commentary

The Disputation (Translated from the Vikuaḥ *of Naḥmanides, edited by Steinschneider, 1860)*

Our lord the King commanded me to hold a Disputation with Fray Paul in his palace in his presence and in the presence of his counsellors in Barcelona. I replied, 'I will do as my lord the King commands if you will give me permission to speak as I wish.'* I was seeking thereby the permission of the King and the permission of Fray Raymon of Pennaforte and his associates who were there.

Fray Ramon of Pennaforte replied, 'Provided only that you do not speak disrespectfully.'

I said to them, 'I do not wish to have to submit to your judgement on that,* but to speak as I wish on the matter under dispute, just as you say all that you wish;* and I have enough understanding to speak with moderation on the matters of dispute just as you do, but let it be according to my own discretion.' So they all gave me permission to speak freely.

Upon this I replied, 'There is dispute between Gentiles and Jews on many points of religious practice in the two religions* which are

---

permission to speak as I wish For the independent confirmation that N. was given special permission to speak freely, see Introduction, p. 59.

I do not wish to have to submit to your judgement on that Not 'it is not my desire to be at variance with your rule' (Rankin).

just as you say all that you wish Not 'as you insist' (Rankin).

points of religious practice in the two religions Hebrew, *minhagei ha-torot.* Rankin ignores the plural and translates 'customs of the Law'. N. does not want to discuss differences of

not essential for religious belief. In this honoured court, I wish to dispute only on matters which are fundamental to the argument.'*

They all replied, 'You have spoken well.' And thus we agreed to speak first on the subject of the Messiah, whether he has already come as Christians believe, or whether he is yet to come as Jews believe. And after that, we would speak on whether the Messiah was truly divine, or entirely human, born from a man and a woman. And after that we would discuss whether the Jews still possess the true law, or whether the Christians practise it.*

Then Fray Paul opened and said that he would show from our Talmud that the Messiah about whom the prophets testified had already come.

I replied, 'Before we argue about this I should like you to instruct me by telling me how this is possible. For ever since Fray Paul went around in Provence* and in many other places, I have heard that he has been saying something like this, and I found it very surprising. Let him answer me this: does he wish to say that

---

religious practice, such as the observance of Sunday as opposed to Saturday as the day of rest. Christianity too has its 'Torah' containing *minhagim* (observances). This gives more point to N.'s remark than a translation referring *ha-torot* exclusively to Judaism (perhaps by detecting an allusion to the Written Law and the Oral Law).

fundamental to the argument Hebrew, *she-kol ha-din talui ba-hem.* Rankin translates, 'upon which religion as a whole depended': *din* never means 'religion', though the related word *dat* can have this meaning. Of the various meanings of *din,* the most relevant here is 'argument', though possibly what is meant is 'decision'.

whether the Jews still possess the true law or whether the Christians practise it The word translated here 'law' is *torah,* which can also be translated as 'religion'. The choice of meanings is of some consequence, since Baer (1930–31, p. 183) has argued that there is a significant difference here between the Jewish and the Christian account. The latter states this article of disputation as *quod legalia sive ceremonalia cessaverunt et cessare debuerunt post adventum dicti messie.* Baer argues that N. is here representing the point of disputation as more general than it really was, thus obscuring his subordinate role in the choice of agenda and the limited nature of the agenda. This depends, however, on translating *torah* as 'religion' rather than as 'law'. That it ought to be translated here as 'law' is shown by the expression 'practise' *(osim),* used in preference to 'believe' *(ma'aminim).* Also, the expression *maḥazikin,* meaning 'hold on to' or 'still possess', as applied to the Jews, shows that the question at issue is whether the Jewish legal and ceremonial provisions are still in force or have been abolished. Thus N.'s description of this article of disputation, rightly translated, is identical with that found in the Christian account.

since Fray Paul went around in Provence S. has *she-ha-melekh be-provinzia* ('that the king was in Provence'), which E. emends convincingly to *she-halakh be-provinzia.* Rankin's mistake, 'in the province' instead of 'Provence', has been pointed out by Roth and others. It was Louis IX of France who commissioned Pablo to travel round Provence giving missionary sermons.

the Sages of the Talmud were believers in Jesus' Messiahship, and that they believed that he was not merely human, but truly divine, as Christians think? Is it not a well-known thing in truth that the affair of Jesus took place in the time of the Second Temple, and he was born and killed before the destruction of the Temple, while the Sages of the Talmud, such as Rabbi Akiva and his associates, were after the Destruction? And those who composed the Mishnah, Rabbi and Rabbi Nathan,* were many years after the Destruction, and all the more so Rav Ashi, who composed the Talmud and wrote it down, for he lived about 400 years after the Destruction.* And if these Sages believed in the Messiahship of Jesus and that he and his faith and religion were true, and if they wrote the things from which Fray Paul says he will prove this, if so how did they remain in the original religion and practice of Judaism? For they were Jews and remained in the Jewish religion all their lives and died as Jews, they and their sons and their pupils who listened to all their words from their own mouths. Why did they not become converted to Christianity, as Fray Paul did when he understood from their sayings that Christianity is the true faith, and he went and became converted according to their words? Yet they and their pupils who took instruction from their mouths lived and died as Jews like us today. And they were the very ones who taught us the religion of Moses and of the Jews, for everything we do today is according to the Talmud, and according to the custom and practice which we have observed in the Sages of the Talmud from the day it was composed until now. For the whole purpose of the Talmud is only to teach us the practice of the Torah, and how our Fathers practised it in the time of the Temple* from the mouth of the prophets and from the mouth of Moses our teacher, on him be peace. And if they believed in Jesus and his religion, why did they

---

Rabbi Akiva . . . Rabbi and Rabbi Nathan Rabbi Akiva is mentioned here not merely as a notable rabbi, but as one who had an important role in the formation of the Mishnah; his compilation (known as 'Rabbi Akiva's Mishnah') was an important source for the Mishnah in its final form. Rabbi (i.e., Rabbi Judah the Prince) is regarded by most medieval writers as the redactor of the Mishnah as we have it, but one Talmudic passage (b BM, 86a) associates Rabbi Nathan with Rabbi in this work, and mention is also made of 'Rabbi Nathan's Mishnah'.

400 years after the Destruction MS Leiden: 'five hundred years after Jesus'.

and how our Fathers practised it in the time of the Temple Rankin (p. 180) misunderstands this and starts a new sentence: 'Just as in this regard when the sanctuary stood our forefathers were guided by the prophets . . .' The point is rather that the Talmud tells us how our ancestors carried out the behests of the prophets.

not do as Fray Paul has done, who understands their words better than they did themselves?'

Fray Paul answered, 'These long-winded statements* are intended to circumvent the Disputation. Nevertheless, whatever you say, you shall hear what I have to say.'

I said to the assembly, 'This is a clear proof* that he will say nothing of any substance; but I will listen to his words, since such is the King's wish.'

He began, 'Scripture says [Genesis, 49: 10], "The sceptre shall not depart from Judah . . . until Shiloh come." Shiloh is the Messiah, and the prophet says that Judah will always have power until the coming of the Messiah who goes forth from him. And if so, today when you have not a single sceptre or a single ruler, the Messiah who is of the seed of Judah and has the right of rulership must have come.'

I replied, 'The prophet does not mean that the kingdom of Judah would continue without any interruption, but that it would never pass away from him [Judah] and cease for ever. And he means that whenever Israel does have a royal ruler, he has to be a member of the tribe of Judah; and if their kingdom should lapse for a while because of sin, when it returns it must return to Judah. The proof of my words is that many years before Jesus the royal power lapsed from Israel, though not from Judah, and for many years the royal power lapsed both from Judah and from Israel. For in the seventy years of the Exile in Babylon, there was no kingdom at all either for Judah or for Israel, and in the time of the Second Temple, only Zerubbabel and his sons reigned for a limited time, and after that came 380 years until the Destruction* under the

---

these long-winded statements See Introduction, p. 67.

I said to the assembly, 'This is a clear proof . . .' Rankin (p. 181) gives this speech (including the introductory words *va-'omar aleyhem)* to Fray Paul. They make much more sense, however, as spoken by N., with the introductory words as not part of the speech. Note that the introductory verb is a *vav*-consecutive. N. uses this Biblical style, here and elsewhere in the *Vikuaḥ,* when he wants a special dramatic emphasis in introducing a speech.

and after that came 380 years until the Destruction Rankin translates: 'And so thereafter for 380 years the position remained unchanged until the laying waste of the Temple when the Hasmonean priestly dynasty with their satellites became kings.' This is wrong. The word *ḥurban* refers to the destruction of 70 CE, not to the 'desecration' of the time of Antiochus Epiphanes. Naḥmanides' point is that the House of Judah ceased *('amdu)* to provide kings in the period after Zerubbabel's dynasty, since any kings that appeared in this period were not of the stock of Judah but of the stock of Levi (Aaronite priests). Thus the

reign of the Hasmonean priests and their servants.* And it goes without saying that when the people went into exile there was no kingdom, for if there is no people, there is no king.'

Fray Paul replied,* 'In all those times, even though they did not have kings, they had rulers. For so it is explained in the Talmud [b Sanh., 5a]: " 'The sceptre shall not depart from Judah'—these are the Exilarchs of Babylonia who rule the people with a sceptre; '. . . and a ruler from between his feet'—these are the descendants of Hillel, who teach the Torah in public." And today you do not have the Ordination* [*semikhah*] which was known in the Talmud, and that form of rulership also has ceased, and there is no one among you today who can rightly be called "Rabbi". As for the fact that you are called "Maestro",* that is a mistake, and it is dishonest of you to use that name.'

---

alleged 'cessation' did not begin with the advent of Jesus but much earlier. The approximate figure of 380 years from the accession of Alexander the Great to the destruction of the Temple is taken from traditional Jewish sources, which give: Greek rule, 180 years; Hasmonean rule, 103 years; Herodian rule, 103 years; total, 386 years. Modern historians would reckon this period as 400 years (330 BCE to 70 CE). See *Seder 'Olam Rabbah*, ch. 30: 'Rabbi Yose says, "The Persian kingdom in the time of the Temple lasted 34 years; the Greek kingdom, 180 years; the Kingdom of the Hasmoneans, 103 years; the Herodian kingdom, 103 years." ' The traditional Jewish date for the destruction works out as 68 CE, not 70 CE.

the Hasmonean priests and their servants Not 'with their satellites' (Rankin). The reference is not to any contemporary subordinates of the Hasmonean kings, but to their successors the Herodian kings, since Herod I, by Talmudic tradition, was originally a slave or servant of the Hasmoneans (see b BB, 3b). So in N.'s commentary on Genesis, 49: 10, where he uses the same expression, 'their servants', explicitly to refer to the Herodians: 'God caused their servants to rule over them, and they destroyed them.' The whole comment on this verse should be consulted.

Fray Paul replied Paul is very confused here (see Roth, p. 125). He thinks that the Exilarchs ruled during the Babylonian captivity and the period of the Second Temple. They actually ruled after the destruction of 70 CE right up to the thirteenth century CE. If N. had taken up this point, he could have turned P.'s argument against him, showing that the rule of the Exilarchs lasted many centuries after the advent of Jesus. However, N. did not wish to pursue the point in this way, since his own argument is that the Exilarchs were not 'kings' or 'rulers' in the sense of Genesis, 49: 10, but only officials with very limited powers.

Ordination The ordination ceremony of laying-on of hands was practised only in Palestine (see b Sanh., 14a: 'There is no ordination outside the Land'). To mark this fact, Babylonian rabbis were called 'Rav' instead of 'Rabbi' (b Sanh., 13b). This, however, was a matter of form, showing respect to the Land of Israel, and did not affect the judicial powers of the Babylonian rabbis, so P.'s point is invalid.

As for the fact that you are called 'Maestro' Not 'whatever you yourself may be called nowadays' (Rankin).

I replied somewhat mockingly, 'This is not relevant to the Disputation, and even so, what you say is not true. For "Maestro" is not the equivalent of "Rabbi" but of "Rav", and the title "Rav" is used in the Talmud for teachers who did not have *semikhah* [b Sanh., 13b]. But I confess that I am not really a "Maestro" or even a first-rate Disciple.' I said this in the way of modesty.* I now returned to the subject and said to him, 'Let me inform you that our Teachers (on them be peace) did not mean to explain the verse as referring to anything but true kingship. The trouble is that you do not understand Halakhic [legal] matters; you just know a little about Aggadic matters, in which you have busied yourself. The topic raised by the Sages is this: according to the strict letter of the law, a person who acts as a single judge is not free from liability to pay damages* (if he makes a wrong legal decision) unless he has received a licence from the Prince or King. And the Sages decided that in the time of Exile, since there existed persons of royal descent who had been given a little authority by Gentile kings, such as the Exilarchs in Babylonia and the Nasi in Israel, they should be allowed to exercise this right of granting licence and ordination [b Sanh., 5a].* This custom was in force among the Sages of the Talmud for more than 400 years after the time of Jesus.* But it was not thereby the opinion of the Sages of the

---

in the way of modesty Not 'by way of correcting him' (Rankin). The expression here connotes self-discipline rather than the disciplining of others. See the previous use of the expression *be-derekh musar,* translated above as 'with moderation' (p. 102).

is not free from liability to pay damages Rankin translates: 'and exempt anyone from the payment of a penalty, unless authority to do so be received from the prince'. This is a misunderstanding. It is not a question of exempting a defendant from penalty, but of exempting the *judge* from penalty if he should judge incorrectly (see b Sanh., 5a: Said Rav, 'If a man wishes to act as judge without incurring penalty if he should err, he must obtain a licence from the Head of the Exile'). N.'s main point is that it was only for this limited purpose that the Exilarchs were regarded as having a kind of regal power; they were not real kings within the meaning of Genesis, 49: 10.

they should be allowed to exercise this right of granting licence and ordination Rankin, again nonsensically, 'there was a (special) bestowal of authority together with ordination'. The point is that the right of the monarch to licence judges descended to the Exilarchs (not, as Rankin thinks, that the Exilarchs themselves had the right to act as judges).

for more than 400 years after the time of Jesus 'In the year 670 for deeds, that is the year 119 of the fifth thousand [4119 AM], in the days of Hillel the son of Rabbi Judah the Prince [Judah III], the Sanhedrin was abolished in the Land of Israel, and experts ceased' (Naḥmanides in *Sefer ha-Zekhut* on Gittin, 4). The year 4119 AM is 359 CE, and according to N.'s reckoning the death of Jesus was about 100 BCE.

Talmud* that the verse meant that there would always be some kind of "sceptre" attached to the seed of Judah or some kind of "ruler" belonging to Judah, but that the prophet had promised to Judah the royal throne of Israel—a promise of full kingship. Nevertheless, as I have mentioned, this could be interrupted for a long period, for at the time of the Babylonian Exile, they had no "sceptre" or "ruler" at all. And in the time of the Second Temple, when the royal power was exercised by the priests and their servants, the tribe of Judah had no power whatever, not even that of an Exilarch or a Nasi, for all such power belonged to the priestly kings and their judges and officers, and to anyone to whom they chose to give it.'

Then Fray Peire de Genova* spoke: 'This is true, for Scripture only says that the "sceptre" will not cease altogether, but it leaves open the possibility of an interregnum [*vagare*, in the common tongue].'

But it was not thereby the opinion of the Sages of the Talmud N.'s argument at this point needs some clarification. The sentence beginning, 'But it is not the opinion of the Sages of the Talmud' is the source of the confusion, and probably needs emendation; e.g., *ki ein da'at ḥakhmei ha-talmud she-yihyeh tamid eizeh min shevet mizer'a Yehudah u-meḥokek asher liyhudah.*

It may be surprising, at first sight, that N. argues *against* the theory that the Exilarchs and Nasi fulfil the prophecy of Genesis, 49: 10, while Fray Paul argues *for* it. Here N. takes a different line from other Jewish apologists, who tried to argue that the sceptre had never fully departed from Judah and that any surviving form of Jewish self-rule, however limited, could count as a continuation of the sceptre or the ruler. N. takes the more subtle and more easily defensible line that the promise was not for a continuous sceptre, but only that the sceptre would return one day to Judah. Fray Paul thinks he has refuted this line by drawing attention to the Talmudic passage which sees the Exilarch and Nasi as a fulfilment of the prophecy of sceptre and ruler; to which N. replies that this Talmudic view is not adduced in support of the theory that the sceptre is continuous, but only in the limited Halakhic context of providing legal justification for the right of Exilarch and Nasi to license judges. Even if the Exilarch and Nasi do exemplify in a limited way the survival of the sceptre in Judah, this does not mean that the prophecy rules out the possibility that there may be other periods in Jewish history when there may be no vestige of sceptre whatever. Such sceptre-less periods have occurred frequently in the past, even in Biblical times, and the present period of Jewish powerlessness is only one more such period and does not prove in the least that the Messiah must have come.

For a detailed survey of Christian and Jewish arguments on the Shiloh prophecy, see A. Posnanski, 1904, *Schiloh . . . Geschichte der Messiaslehre.*

Fray Peire de Genova He was of the Franciscan Order, and some have seen in his intervention here on N.'s side an indication of the rivalry between Franciscans and Dominicans (see Cohen, p. 186). Later the same Peire de Genova took a leading part in the move to suspend the disputation (see p. 69), and again, he hastily withdrew, as here, when his support for N. became embarrassing.

I said to the King, 'See, Fray Peire has given his decision in accordance with my words.'

Said Fray Peire, 'I have not given such a decision; for the seventy years of the Babylonian Exile were a short time, and there were many who could remember the time of the First Temple, as it is written in the Book of Ezra. This may be called an interruption, or *vagare*. But now that you have remained in this state of powerlessness for a thousand years and more, it is a complete "passing-away" [of the "sceptre"].'

I said, 'Now you are going back on your words;* for there can be no "passing-away" in a thing that returns, and the words of the prophet make no distinction between a long time and a short time. Furthermore, the periods which I cited were long periods. Furthermore, our father Jacob, on him be peace, did not promise the "sceptre" and "ruler" to Judah for his own tribe only, but he gave him the royal power over the whole of Israel,* as it is written, "Judah, as for you, your brothers shall praise you" [Genesis, 49: 8], and, "For Judah prevailed over his brothers and the prince came from him" [I Chronicles, 5: 2]. Now Judah lost the kingdom of all Israel on the death of Solomon, as it is written, "There was none that followed the house of David except the tribe of Judah alone" [I Kings, 12: 20]. Thus it is plain that the prophet meant only that the "sceptre" would not pass away for good. And the truth is that in the time of exile the terms "passing-away" and "suspension" are entirely inappropriate, because it is not the kingdom of Judah that has passed away, but the people themselves that have ceased to exist as a people;* for the prophet did not promise Judah that Israel

---

Now you are going back on your words Rankin's 'You are now the recipient of our consolation and comfort' is meaningless. For the *hithpael* of the verb *naḥam* in the sense of 'to reconsider', see Jastrow, *Dictionary of the Targumim, etc.*, p. 895.

royal power over the whole of Israel N.'s point here is that although there continued to be kings of Judah after the split between the southern and northern kingdoms after the death of Solomon, this was in fact the breakdown of the promised rule of the House of David over all Israel. Thus the interregnum should be reckoned from this early date, making a very long *vagare* even before the time of Jesus, contrary to Fray Peire's argument that there were only short interruptions before the time of Jesus.

because it is not the kingdom of Judah that has passed away, but the people themselves that have ceased to exist as a people Literally, 'it is not from the side of Judah, but from the side of the people'. Rankin fails to understand, and offers a meaningless translation ('since the exile was the concern not only of Judah but of the people as a whole'). It should be borne in mind that N., throughout this argument, distinguishes between *Judah* and *Israel.* The 'sceptre' prophecy applies only to Judah (i.e., the tribe of Judah) and says only that the royal power will not pass away permanently from that tribe to some other tribe. When the

would never go into exile, so that he might be king over them without interruption.'*

Fray Paul now resumed, and argued that it is stated in the Talmud that the Messiah has already come. He cited the Aggadah* in the Midrash of *Lamentations* [II: 57]:* 'A certain man was ploughing and his cow lowed. An Arab passed by and said to him, "Jew, Jew, untie your cow, untie your plough, untie your coulter, for the Temple has been destroyed." He untied his cow, he untied his plough, he untied his coulter. The cow lowed a second time. The Arab said to him, "Tie up your cow, tie up your plough, tie up your coulter, for your Messiah has been born." '

I replied, 'I do not believe in this Aggadah,* but in any case, it supports my words.'

Then that man cried out, 'See how he denies the writings of the Jews!'

I said, 'In truth, I do not believe that the Messiah was born on the day of the Destruction, and this Aggadah is either not true, or has some other interpretation derived from the secrets of the Sages. Nevertheless, I will accept it in its literal meaning just as you quoted it, for it gives support to my argument. See, it says that on

---

royal power does not belong to *any* tribe (e.g., in the Exile), the concept of *hasarah* ('causing to pass away') of the 'sceptre' from Judah does not apply at all, since there is no 'sceptre' to pass away. The Christian interpretation, on the other hand, applies the 'sceptre' prophecy to the whole of Israel, not just to the tribe of Judah.

so that he might be king over them without interruption Not 'and this for the reason that he, Judah, might become ruler over them at any time' (Rankin). N.'s point is that the only way that Judah's kingship could be uninterrupted would be if Israel never experienced exile. This was never promised, and so an uninterrupted kingship for Judah was never promised either.

Aggadah N. uses in fact the Hebrew word *haggadah* in preference to the Aramaised form *'aggadah,* but in order to avoid confusion (since *Haggadah* has another meaning in connection with Passover), *Aggadah* is used here throughout as the designation of the non-legal portions of Talmud and Midrash. (The fully Aramaic form of the word is *'aggadet'a.*)

the Midrash of Lamentations N.'s citation is much abbreviated from the text of Lamentations Rabbah (Ekhah Rabbati). One detail omitted is that the birth of the Messiah, at the time of the destruction, is located at Bethlehem (in fulfilment of Micah, 5: 1). Some commentators have suggested that P. did mention this detail, in support of Jesus' claims, but that N. omitted this aspect as disturbing to Jewish readers. However, P. is arguing here that the birth of the Messiah has already occurred, irrespective of who the Messiah was. The location would have added little to his argument at this point.

I do not believe in this Aggadah For N.'s attitude towards the authority of the Aggadah, see Part I, pp. 44 ff.

the day of the Destruction of the Temple, after the Destruction took place but on the same day, the Messiah was born. If so, Jesus was not the Messiah as you contend, for he was born and was killed before the Destruction, and his birth was nearly 200 years before the Destruction* in fact, though according to your reckoning it was 73 years before the Destruction.' Then the man was put to silence.

Maestro Guillaume,* the King's justiciary, spoke up and said, 'The argument at present does not concern Jesus.* The question is whether the Messiah has come or not. You said that he has not come, but this book of yours says that he has come.'

I said to him, 'You choose to reply, as is the custom of you lawyers, with sophistical logical arguments; nevertheless, I shall answer you all in this matter. The Sages did not say that the Messiah had *come,* but that he had been *born.** On the day that Moses, our teacher, on him be peace, was born, he had not yet *come,* and he was not yet a saviour; it was not until he came to Pharaoh by the command of God and said to him, "Thus saith the Lord, Let my people go" [Exodus, 8: 1] that he had *come.* And so with the Messiah; when he comes to the Pope, and says to him by the command of God, "Let my people go," then he will have *come.* But so far, he has not come, and further, he is not yet the "Messiah" at all. For King David, on the day that he was born, was not yet a Messiah, but when Samuel anointed him, then he became a Messiah. And on the day that Elijah anoints the Messiah by God's command, he will be called "Messiah", and not before. And on the day that he comes, after that, to the Pope, to redeem us, then he will rightly be called one who has *come.*'

---

nearly 200 years before the Destruction N. is here accepting the testimony of the Talmud (b Sotah, 47a) that Jesus was a pupil of Rabbi Joshua ben Peraḥia, who lived *c.* 100 BCE, in the reign of Alexander Jannaeus. Evidently, then, N. does not follow the line of Rabbi Yeḥiel of Paris, who argued in the Paris Disputation that the Jesus of Sotah 47a was not the Jesus of the Christian faith, but some other Jesus.

Maestro Guillaume See F. Darwin Swift, 1894, *The Life and Times of James the First the Conqueror*, p. 171, for the role of the *justiciar* in the constitution of Aragon.

The argument at present does not concern Jesus Cohen argues (p. 168) that this line was the basis of Pablo Christiani's whole case; but that this is obscured in N.'s account, which often represents P. as saying 'Jesus' where he really said 'Messiah'. However, this cannot be correct, for there are many instances where P. argues specifically for Jesus as Messiah, e.g., his interpretation of the prophecies of Daniel.

the Sages did not say that the Messiah had come, but that he had been born See Part I, p. 71.

That man then argued, 'See, the passage beginning with the words, "Behold, my servant will prosper . . . " [Isaiah, 52: 13] relates the matter of the death of the Messiah, of his subjection, and of his being set among the wicked, just as happened with Jesus. Do you believe that that passage speaks of the Messiah?'

I said to him, 'According to the truly plain meaning* of the passage, it speaks only of the people of Israel in general,* for so the prophets call them continually, e.g., "Israel my servant" [Isaiah, 41: 8] and "Jacob my servant" [Isaiah 44: 1].'

Said Fray Paul, 'Yet I will show from the words of your own Sages that the passage speaks of the Messiah.'

I said to him, 'It is true that our Teachers, may their memory be for a blessing, in the Aggadic books, interpret the passage allegorically of the Messiah.* But they never said that the Messiah would be slain by the hand of his enemies.* You will never find in any

---

According to the truly plain meaning Hebrew, *ha-mashma'ut ha-'amiti.* Not 'real meaning' (Rankin). N. uses here *mashma'ut* (equivalent to the more frequent *peshat*), in contrast with the word *doreshim* ('interpret allegorically', not just 'interpret', as Rankin) used below. The plain meaning of the passage, he says, is concerned with Israel as a whole; but an allegorical interpretation *(derashah)* has been given by the rabbis by which the 'Servant' was interpreted as the Messiah.

it speaks only of the people of Israel in general N. does not claim that this interpretation can be found in the Talmudic or Midrashic sources at all. He derived it, probably, from the commentary of Rashi on Isaiah, where the 'Servant' is interpreted as 'the righteous ones of Jacob'. David Kimḥi interprets the sufferings of the Servant even more generally as referring to 'the exile of Israel'. The tendency of Jewish medieval commentators to employ this interpretation was no doubt influenced by a desire to counter the Christian interpretation of the Suffering Servant as referring to Jesus; but in fact the more general interpretation of the passage as referring to Israel or the righteous ones of Israel, had a long history. It is to be found in the Targumim, and it is referred to by Origen *(Contra Celsum,* I, 55): 'my Jewish opponent replied that these predictions bore reference to the whole people, regarded as one individual, and as being in a state of dispersion and suffering, in order that many proselytes might be gained'. It is also found in the late Midrash, Numbers Rabbah, which was probably not known to N., or he would have mentioned it as supporting his view. See Neubauer and Driver, *The 'Suffering Servant' of Isaiah* (which, however, is incomplete on the early sources), and Strack and Billerbeck, *Commentar zum Neuen Testament etc.*, I, p. 481. One Talmudic passage (b Sotah, 14a) refers the passage to Moses, and Saadia Gaon referred it to Jeremiah.

allegorically of the Messiah The Midrashic sources for the Messianic interpretation of the Suffering Servant are Yalqut Isaiah, 476, and Tanḥuma Toledot, 14. Earlier sources are the Targumim, which however do not interpret Isaiah, 53 as referring to a *suffering* Messiah, but expunge all traces of suffering from their translation. See W. D. Davies, *Paul and Rabbinic Judaism,* p. 275, on Targum Jonathan.

But they never said that the Messiah would be slain by the hand of his enemies In his commentary on the Suffering Servant passage, N. addresses himself especially to this

book of the literature of Israel, either in the Talmud or the Aggadic books, that the Messiah, son of David,* would ever be slain, or that he would be betrayed into the hands of his enemies, or that he would be buried among the wicked, for even your Messiah, whom you made for yourselves, was not buried among the wicked.* If you like, I will give you an excellent and detailed explanation of the passage in Isaiah. There is nothing there about the Messiah's being slain as happened with your Messiah.' But they did not want to hear it.*

That man resumed, and said, 'In the Talmud it is explained [b Sanh., 98a] that Rabbi Joshua ben Levi asked Elijah, "When will the Messiah come?" To which he replied, "Ask the Messiah himself." Said he, "Where is he?" Said Elijah, "At the gate of Rome among the sick people." He went there and found him and asked him certain questions. If so, he has come, and he is in Rome; that is, he is Jesus, who rules in Rome."'

---

question. He interprets the verses which Christians thought referred to the death of the Messiah ('as a lamb that is led to the slaughter', 'he was cut off out of the land of the living', 'they made his grave with the wicked') as referring to the Messiah's thoughts and his willingness to die in the cause of his mission, and N. declares that the end of the passage states explicitly that the Messiah will not die. In this commentary, N. does not abandon his view that the passage, in its literal sense, refers to the sufferings of Israel as a whole, but sets out to expound the passage in accordance with the allegorical interpretation found in the Midrash, showing that even in this Messianic interpretation, there is no support for Christian doctrine of a crucified Messiah.

Messiah, son of David N. is careful to say 'Messiah, son of David' here, in order to distinguish between him and Messiah, son of Joseph, who, it was held, would be slain in battle with the enemies of Israel shortly before the advent of Messiah, son of David (see b Sukk. 52a).

was not buried among the wicked i.e., though Jesus was executed among the wicked (the two thieves), he was not buried with them; so the Christian claim that the prophecy 'And they made his grave with the wicked' was fulfilled in Jesus is not justified (see Mark, 15: 27). The Hebrew here says merely 'was not buried'. N. could hardly have meant that Jesus was not buried at all. Rankin, who translates simply, 'was not buried', suggests 'This may be an allusion to the Christian doctrine of the resurrection of Jesus.' N. would hardly refer to the resurrection as a fact, and in any case, according to the Gospel story, Jesus was buried before he was resurrected. Rankin's alternative suggestion is that there is here a reference to a Jewish tradition, found in the Toledot Yeshu literature, 'that Jesus was taken down quickly from the tree, and thrown into a tomb in a certain garden full of vegetables, for fear lest their land should be polluted'. Being thrown into a tomb is hardly distinguishable from being buried.

But they did not want to hear it The explanation of the Suffering Servant passage which N. offered to give here in the disputation, but was refused, is to be found in his commentary on the passage *(hineh yaskil 'avdi)* printed after the *Vikuaḥ* in the Hebrew editions and translated in Driver and Neubauer, *The 'Suffering Servant' of Isaiah*, p. 78.

I replied, 'And is it not clear from this that he has not come? For Rabbi Joshua asked Elijah, "When will he come?" Furthermore, it is stated, "R. Joshua asked the Messiah himself, 'When will the Master come?' " If so, he has not yet come, though, according to the literal sense of these Aggadahs, he has been born; but I myself do not believe even that.'

Then our lord the King spoke up: 'If he was born on the day of the Destruction of the Temple, which was over 1,000 years ago, and he has still not come, how can he ever come? For it is not in the nature of a human being to live 1,000 years.'

I said to him, 'The conditions were that I would not dispute with you, and that you would not intervene in the debate. Nevertheless—among the ancients, there were Adam and Methuselah, who lived for nearly 1,000 years; and Elijah and Enoch lived even longer—for life is in the hands of God.'*

Said the King, 'And where is the Messiah today?'

Said I, 'This is not relevant to the Disputation, and I shall not answer you. But perhaps you will find him at the gates of Toledo, if you send one of your runners there.' I said this ironically.

Then they adjourned, and the King set a time to resume the Disputation on the coming Monday.*

On Monday, the King went to a cloister which was in the city, and all the people of the city assembed there, Gentiles and Jews. Also there, were the bishop, and all the priests, and the scholars of the Minorites and of the Preaching Friars.* That man then arose to speak.

However, I said to our lord the King, 'My lord, hear me.' But the King said to me, 'Let him speak first, for he is the challenger.'

Said I, 'Let me explain clearly my opinion on the Messiah, and then he can answer without perplexity.'

Elijah and Enoch lived even longer Enoch, who 'was not' (Genesis, 5: 24), became an angel (Metatron), according to some sources, though in general the Enoch legend is played down in the Talmud, and even, on occasion, deprecated (Genesis Rabbah, 25: 1). For N.'s argument in general, see Part I, p. 71.

for life is in the hands of God Not 'these are they who are alive with God' (Rankin).

the coming Monday Not 'the day after next' (Rankin). The dates of the disputation are correctly stated by Roth (correcting Loeb), as follows:

Friday 20 July 1263	first session
Monday 23 July	second session
Thursday 26 July	third session
Friday 27 July	fourth session
Saturday 4 August	encounter in synagogue

Minorites and of the Preaching Friars i.e., the Franciscans and the Dominicans.

So I rose up and said, ' "Hear, all you peoples" [Micah, 1: 2]. Fray Paul asked me whether the Messiah of whom the prophets spoke has come, and I said that he has not come. And he cited an Aggadic book in which it is stated that on the day that the Temple was destroyed, on that very day, the Messiah was born. And I said that I did not believe in this, but that it supported my words nevertheless. Now I shall explain to you why I said that I did not believe in this. Know that we Jews have three kinds of books: the first is the Bible, and we all believe in this with perfect faith; the second is called the Talmud, and it is an explication of the commandments of the Torah, for there are 613 commandments* in the Torah, and every single one of them is explicated in the Talmud, and we believe in this explication of the commandments; and we have also a third book* which is called the Midrash, which means "Sermons". This is just as if the bishop were to stand up and make a sermon, and one of his hearers liked it so much that he wrote it down. And as for this book, the Midrash, if anyone wants to believe in it, well and good, but if someone does not believe in it, there is no harm.* Now certain Sages of ours have written* that the Messiah will not be born until near the time of the End, when he will come to take us out of exile, and for that reason I do not believe in the part of this book that says that he was born on the day of the Destruction. Moreover, we call the Midrash a book of "Aggadah", which means "razionamiento",* that is to say, merely

---

613 commandments See b Makkot, 23b, where Rav Simlai is given as the authority for this enumeration. Various medieval scholars tried to provide a detailed list of the 613 commandments. For a full discussion, see A. H. Rabinowitz, 1967, *Taryag*, Jerusalem. N. himself was one of the chief contributors to discussion of this topic, in his *hassagot* on Maimonides' *Sefer ha-mitzvot*. See H. D. Chavel, 1964, *Taryag Precepts in the Works of Ramban*, Jerusalem.

a third book N. is simplifying here. The Midrashic literature consists of many books of different periods. N.'s desire to simplify the topic of the status of the Midrash is evident throughout this speech, and should not be confused with insincerity.

there is no harm Not 'no one will do him any harm' (Rankin).

certain Sages of ours have written There seems to be no explicit source for this statement, but it seems to be implied in the legend (Pesiqta Rabbati, 36: 1) that the soul of the Messiah is located under God's throne, together with the souls of 'the children of his generation', waiting to be born.

razionamiento An Italian word, meaning 'story'. *Haggadah* or *'aggada* comes from a verb meaning to 'relate'—whence the name Haggadah for the Passover evening service at which the story of the deliverance from Egypt is related. N.'s point is that the very name of *'aggadah* demonstrates the narrative, recreational nature of the Midrashic material, as opposed to the difficult argument and strong practical relevance of the Halakhah.

things that a man relates to his fellow. Nevertheless, I accept that Aggadah in its literal meaning just as you wish, for it is a clear proof that your Jesus was not the Messiah, as I said before, for Jesus was not born on the day of the Destruction. On the contrary, the whole affair of Jesus has passed by a long time before. Now you, our lord the King, asked a better question, raising the difficulty that it is unnatural for a man to live 1,000 years, and I shall make clearer now my answer to your question. Adam lived for 1,000 years, less 70; and it is clear from Scripture that he died through his sin, and if he had not sinned, he would have lived much longer, or perhaps for ever.* Whether Gentiles or Jews, we all believe that the sin and punishment of Adam will be abolished in the days of the Messiah. After the Messiah comes, it will be abolished from all of us, but in the case of the Messiah himself, it is totally abolished, so that it is quite fitting that the Messiah should live for 1,000 years, or 2,000 years, or even for ever,* as the Psalm says, "He asked life of Thee, Thou gavest it him" [Psalms, 21: 5]. So this point has now been explained clearly. You asked further, our lord the King, where the Messiah is at present. Scripture makes plain that Adam's location was the Garden of Eden on earth,* and because of his sin, it is said, "God sent him away from the Garden of Eden" [Genesis, 3: 23]. The Messiah, then, who is free from the punishment of Adam, must be there in the Garden of Eden, and so the Sages have said in the book of Aggadah which I mentioned.'*

---

perhaps for ever N. is not sure whether the fall of Adam brought death into the world, or whether Adam would have died eventually even if he had not eaten of the Tree of Knowledge. He discusses this matter in full in his commentary on Genesis, 2: 17, where he comes, on the whole, to the conclusion that Adam would have lived for ever.

or even for ever Here again, N. leaves open the question whether the Messiah will live for ever, or will eventually die. This question becomes the centre of discussion later in the disputation (see p. 130, and Part I, p. 74), where P. confuses it with the question of whether the Messiah is to die by crucifixion.

Garden of Eden on earth A similar phrase is used in the Latin account of the disputation: *in paradiso terrestri.* It was a common medieval belief, both among Christians and Jews, that the Garden of Eden still existed somewhere on earth (Dante places it, together with Purgatory, in the Antipodes). N., on the basis of Aggadic statements, believed that this was so. (See J. Sarachek, *The Doctrine of the Messiah in Medieval Jewish Literature*, p. 190.) N.'s views on the earthly paradise can be found in his comment on Genesis, 3: 22, and in *Sha'ar ha-gemul.*

the book of Aggadah which I mentioned See Derekh Eretz Zutta, ch. 1. But see also p. 129.

Said the King, 'But have you not said, in that Aggadah, that he is in Rome?'

I said to him, 'I did not say that he was permanently in Rome, but that he appeared in Rome on a certain day, for Elijah told that Sage that he would find him there on that particular day, and he did appear there; and his appearance there was for the reason mentioned in the Aggadah, but I prefer not to mention it before such throngs of people.' The matter which I did not wish to reveal to them was what is said in the Aggadah: that the Messiah would remain in Rome until he brought about its ruin.* This is just as we find with Moses our teacher, on him be peace, that he grew in the household of Pharaoh until he called him to account and drowned all his people in the sea. Similarly, it is said, about Hiram, King of Tyre, 'Therefore have I brought forth a fire from the midst of thee which has devoured thee' [Ezekiel, 28: 18]; and Isaiah too said, 'Where the calf feeds, there he shall lie down and consume its branches' [Isaiah, 27: 10]; and in Pirqei Hekhaloth [6: 2] it is said, 'Until a man shall say to his fellow, "Here is Rome for you, and all that is in it, for one farthing," and he will reply, "I am not interested in it." ' But all this I said later to the King in private.

I asked further, 'Do you agree with my statement that the sin of Adam will be nullified in the time of the Messiah?'

Our lord the King, also Fray Paul, answered, 'Yes, but not in the way that you think. The fact is that all mankind entered Gehenna because of the punishment of Adam, but in the days of

---

what is said in the Aggadah: that the Messiah would remain in Rome until he brought about its ruin This saying does not appear in any extant Midrash. There seems to be some confusion of thought here, since the appearance of the Messiah in Rome 'on a certain day', while spending most of his time in the Garden of Eden, is not compatible with his remaining in Rome until its destruction. There are also other questions about this section of the *Vikuaḥ*, which cast some doubt on its authenticity. Would N. be likely to state in public that there were Aggadahs which he did not wish to reveal publicly? Would he reveal to the king, in private, Aggadahs relating to the overthrow of Christendom? The only private audience with the king at which this could have taken place is that which took place on the day after the disputation ended (see p. 146), and N. does not record that any further discussion of such matters took place then. Further, is it likely that N. would have included not very relevant matter about the destruction of Rome by the Messiah in the account of the disputation which he wrote in Spanish or Latin for the Bishop of Gerona? Surely there was enough said, of a bold nature, in the disputation itself, without adding further inflammatory matter which was not uttered at the disputation, and which he had therefore no permission from the king to express? This passage is clearly written for a Jewish readership only. It seems likely, therefore, that it was added to the Hebrew version of the disputation, either by N. himself, or (more likely) by the editor, whoever he was.

the Messiah Jesus, the punishment was nullified, and he led them forth from there.'*

I replied, 'They say in our land, "He who wishes to tell lies should cite evidence that is too far away to be checked."* Scripture mentions many punishments in connection with Adam and Eve: "Cursed is the ground for thy sake . . . thorns and thistles shall it grow for thee . . . in the sweat of thy brow shalt thou eat bread . . . for dust thou art, and to dust shalt thou return"; and about the woman, "In pain shalt thou bring forth children" [Genesis, 3]. And all this still holds at the present day too; so that in the era of your Messiah, nothing that can actually be observed and sensed has received atonement. But Gehenna, which is not mentioned in Genesis, has, according to you, received atonement, because this is a matter in which nobody can refute you.* "Send one of you" [Genesis, 42: 16] to Gehenna, and let him come back and tell us what is happening there! Moreover, God forbid that such doctrine should be true! For there is no punishment of Gehenna for the righteous,* arising from the sin of Adam their father. For my soul is no closer to the soul of Adam than to the soul of Pharaoh, and my soul will not enter Gehenna because of the sin of Pharaoh. The truth is that the punishments for the sin of Adam were physical, because my body is derived from Adam and Eve, and when it was decreed against them that they should be mortal,* their descendants became mortal by nature too for ever.'

---

he led them forth from there The reference is to the doctrine of the harrowing of hell, by which Jesus, during the three days before his resurrection, visited hell and rescued the souls of the righteous imprisoned there because of the sin of Adam. This was not included in articles of faith (except in the Church of England), but was firmly believed in the Middle Ages. (See the *Gospel of Nicodemus.)*

He who wishes to tell lies should cite evidence that is too far away to be checked Literally, 'should remove his witnesses afar'. This seems to have been a popular proverb. Rankin's translation, 'must get rid of the witnesses who testify against him', is wide of the mark. N.'s point is that a good liar does not lie about a matter for which witnesses are near at hand.

this is a matter in which nobody can refute you Rankin alters the punctuation and produces, 'In order then that no one may be able to contradict you on this point send one of your number to Gehenna that he may come back and report to you!' This somewhat obscures the point, which is that Gehenna has been chosen precisely because statements about it are unverifiable.

there is no punishment of Gehenna for the righteous For N.'s denial of the doctrine of Original Sin, see Introduction, p. 51.

that they should be mortal In his commentary on Genesis cited above, N. also considers possible the view that Adam would have been mortal even if he had not sinned. The argument here, however, does not depend on this point, because all N. is saying is that the punishment of Adam and his descendants was physical, not spiritual.

That man now stood up and said, 'I shall bring another proof that the time of the Messiah has already passed.'

However, I spoke myself: 'My lord King, hear me. The Messiah is not fundamental to our religion.* Why, you are worth more to me than the Messiah! You are a king, and he is a king. You are a Gentile king, and he is a Jewish king; for the Messiah is only a king of flesh and blood like you. When I serve my Creator in your territory in exile and in affliction and servitude and reproach of the peoples who "reproach us continually", my reward is great. For I am offering a sacrifice to God from my body, by which I shall be found more and more worthy of the life of the world to come. But when there will be a king of Israel of my religion ruling over all the peoples, and there will be no choice for me but to remain in the Jewish religion, my reward will not be so great.* No, the real point of difference between Jews and Christians lies in what you say about the fundamental matter of the deity; a doctrine which is distasteful indeed. You, our lord King, are a Christian and the son of a Christian, and you have listened all your life to priests who have filled your brain and the marrow of your bones with this doctrine, and it has settled with you,* because of that accustomed habit. But the doctrine in which you believe, and which is the foundation of your faith, cannot be accepted by the reason, and

---

The Messiah is not fundamental to our religion See Part I, pp. 49–55. In his work *Sefer ha-ge'ulah* (The Book of Redemption), N. goes even further, saying that belief in a world to come and in Heaven and hell, as well as belief in the coming of the Messiah, are not part of the essence of Judaism, though faith in them all is well-founded. Maimonides, though he included belief in the coming of the Messiah in his Thirteen Articles of Faith, says *(Melachim,* 12: 2): 'One should not spend too much time on inquiries on these topics [Messianic topics], and one should not regard them as fundamental [*'iqqar*], for they do not lead to either the love or the fear of God.'

religion The compound expression which is here translated by the one word 'religion' means literally 'law, truth and judgement', by which N. seeks to convey that Judaism is both a creed and a way of living in a just community. Rankin, evidently puzzled by this, produces: 'Religion and truth which for us Jews is the substance of religion'; taking the word *'iqqaro* with the previous word, instead of the subsequent word, as is necessary.

my reward will not be so great Not 'my gain would not be so much increased' (Rankin). N. no doubt has in mind here the saying of Mishnah Avot, 4: 17: 'Better is one hour of repentance and good works in this world than the whole life of the world to come.'

it has settled with you Reading *ve-yashav* instead of *ve-shav*. If, however, *ve-shav* is retained, the translation would be 'it recurs to you' (though the preposition *'etzel* seems a little inappropriate). Rankin wrongly reads this preposition as a verb *'atzilekha*, and translates, 'I would set you free again from that realm of habit and custom.' N. would not, in any case, suddenly switch to active proselytising of the king, which was unthinkable.

nature affords no ground for it, nor have the prophets ever expressed it. Nor can even the miraculous stretch as far as this* as I shall explain with full proofs in the right time and place, that the Creator of Heaven and earth resorted to the womb of a certain Jewess and grew there for nine months and was born as an infant, and afterwards grew up and was betrayed into the hands of his enemies who sentenced him to death and executed him, and that afterwards, as you say, he came to life and returned to his original place. The mind of a Jew, or any other person, cannot tolerate this;* and you speak your words entirely in vain, for this is the root of our controversy. Nevertheless, let us speak of the Messiah too, as this is your wish.'

Said Fray Paul, 'Will you believe, then, that he has come?'

Said I, 'No. On the contrary, I believe and know that he has not come; and so far there has never been any other man (leaving aside Jesus) who has claimed to be the Messiah (or has had that claim made for him)* in whose Messiahship it is possible for me to believe.* For the prophet says about the Messiah, "His rule shall

---

nor can even the miraculous stretch as far as this Hebrew, *gam ha-pel'e 'eyno yakhol le-hitpashet ba-davar ha-hu'*. Rankin translates, 'the miracle itself cannot be made intelligible'. H. H. Ben Sasson, however, translates, 'miracle also cannot extend to this' *(Enc. Jud.,* VI, p. 91), an ingenious translation of a difficult phrase. Further plausibility is given to this rendering by the contrast with the previous 'nature affords no ground for it'. The verb *pashat,* which has the derivative meaning 'to explain' (hence Rankin's rendering), has the more basic meaning 'to stretch', and the *hitpael* is more naturally understood as a reflexive, 'stretch itself', than as a passive.

the mind of a Jew . . . cannot tolerate this See Introduction, p. 54.

(or has had that claim made for him) Not 'nor will there ever be such who will say so concerning themselves' (Rankin). N. is obviously not predicting that the Messiah will *never* come. Rankin misunderstands the subject of the verb *she-yomeru,* which is impersonal.

so far there has never been any other man (leaving aside Jesus) . . . in whose Messiahship it is possible for me to believe All commentators have understood N. to say at this point that there has never been anyone apart from Jesus who claimed the Messiahship. However, N. could not have said this, since he knew of many such claimants in the past (e.g., Bar Kokhba, plainly mentioned in the Talmud, and discussed in the very chapter of Maimonides later cited in the disputation; also, N. himself discusses Rabbi Akiva's mistake in hailing Bar Kokhba as Messiah in his *Sefer ha-ge'ulah,* part 4). By omitting the word *'iy* ('not') in the second clause of the sentence, this impossible statement is removed, and N.'s meaning becomes clear. He is saying that he disbelieves in all past claimants, including and apart from Jesus; i.e., the fact that the world has undergone no Messianic change rules out not only Jesus but all other past claimants. The intrusion of 'not' ('in whose Messiahship it is not possible for me to believe') is probably due to the misunderstanding of a pious editor or copyist who thought that N. seemed to be saying that 'it is possible for me to believe', which was too shocking to be correct. In the Christian account, N. is represented also as saying

be from sea to sea, and from the River until the ends of the earth" [Psalms, 72: 8]. Jesus, however, never had any power, but in his lifetime he was fleeing from his enemies and hiding from them, and in the end he fell into their hands and could not save himself, so how could he save all Israel? Even after his death he did not have any rule, for the power of Rome is not because of him. Even before they believed in Jesus, the city of Rome was ruling over most of the world, and after they adopted faith in him, they lost many provinces; and now the worshippers of Mohammed have greater power than they. The prophet says that in the time of the Messiah, "They shall teach no more every man his neighbour, and every man his brother, saying, Know the Lord: for they shall all know me" [Jeremiah, 31: 34]; also, "The earth shall be full of the knowledge of the Lord, as the waters cover the sea" [Isaiah, 11: 9]; also, "They shall beat their swords into ploughshares . . . nation shall not lift up sword against nation, neither shall they learn war any more" [Isaiah, 2: 4]. Yet from the days of Jesus until now, the whole world has been full of violence and plundering, and the Christians are greater spillers of blood than all the rest of the peoples, and they are also practisers of adultery and incest.* And how hard it would be for you, my lord King, and for your knights, if they were not to learn war any more! Moreover, the prophet says about the Messiah, "He shall smite the earth with the rod of his mouth" [Isaiah, 11: 4]; and this is explained in the book of Aggadah which Fray Paul has in his hand, as follows [Midrash Tehillim, 2]: "If the King Messiah is told, 'A certain province has rebelled against you,' he will say, 'Let the locust come and destroy

---

that no one apart from Jesus had ever claimed to be the Messiah. This too is probably a misunderstanding of N.'s meaning, caused by his emphatic statement, 'There has never been any claimant to Messiahship, apart from Jesus . . . in whom I could possibly believe.' The first part was heard with delight (since it seemed to make the task of proving Jesus to be the Messiah much easier), and the conclusion of the sentence was ignored. N. would be much more likely to stress that there *had* been many other Messianic claimants apart from Jesus. Roth comments (1950, p. 129), 'Is is extraordinary that he did not recall the Messianic pretensions of Bar Kokhba, recorded in the Talmud, or more recent claimants such as those mentioned by Maimonides in his Epistle to the Yemen. This curious absence of historical perspective is characteristic, though, of the age rather than of the person.' But 'absence of historical perspective' does not explain the alleged ignoring of the well-known texts about Bar Kokhba in the Talmud. See p. 211 for a phrase in the Tortosa Disputation (Christian account) which gives more support to the above emendation.

practisers of adultery and incest Literally, 'uncoverers of nakednesses'. Not 'revealers likewise of indecencies' (Rankin). The expression, frequent in the Talmud, is derived from the Biblical 'thou shalt not uncover the nakedness of . . .' (e.g., Leviticus, 18: 6).

it'; or if he is told, 'A certain eparchy has rebelled,' he will say, 'Let wild beasts come and consume it.'" This did not happen with Jesus. As for you, his servants, you think it better to have horses clad in armour, and sometimes "even all this availeth you nothing" [Esther, 5: 13]. Now I shall bring you many other proofs from the words of the prophets.'

That man cried out, 'This is always his way, to make long-winded speeches. But I have a question to ask.'

Said the King to me, 'Be silent, for he is the questioner.' So I was silent.

Said Fray Paul, 'Your Sages have said about the Messiah that he is more honoured than the angels, and this is impossible unless it refers to Jesus, who was both Messiah and God Himself.' Then he cited what is said in an Aggadah: [Yalkut Isaiah, 476]: ' "My servant shall be exalted and lifted up and shall be very high" [Isaiah, 52: 13]: this means exalted above Abraham, lifted up above Moses, and higher than the ministering angels.'

I said to him, 'But our Sages say this continually about all righteous people, "Greater are the righteous than the ministering angels" [b Sanh., 93a]. And Moses our teacher said to the angel, "In the place where I sit,* you have no authority even to stand" [Sifre, Nitzavim, 305]. And about the whole community of Israel, the Sages said,* "More beloved is Israel than the ministering angels" [b Hullin 91b]. But the meaning of the author of this Aggadah is this: though Abraham our father (on him be peace) converted Gentiles and preached belief in God to the nations and debated against Nimrod without fear; and though Moses did even more than he, for he stood in his lowliness against Pharaoh, the great and wicked king, and showed him no favour in the great plagues with which he smote him, and brought out Israel from his hand; and though the ministering angels too were most zealous in the matter of redemption, as it is said, "there is none that holdeth with me against these except Michael your prince", and also, "and now I will return to fight with the prince of Persia" [Daniel, 10: 20–21]; yet the Messiah will do more than all of them, for "his

---

in the place where I sit Not 'where I have my dwelling' (Rankin). It is true that the verb *yashav* can have the meaning 'dwell' as well as 'sit', but here the meaning 'sit' is necessary, because of the opposition between 'stand' and 'sit'.

about the whole community of Israel, the Sages said Hebrew, *u-bi-khelal yisra'el 'ameru.* Rankin, not recognising the common expression *kelal yisra'el*, 'community of Israel', translates: 'and in general Israel avers'—taking Israel to be the subject of the verb *'ameru*, and translating *bi-khelal* as 'in general'!

heart will be lifted up in the ways of the Lord" [II Chronicles, 17: 6], and he will come and command the Pope and all the kings of the peoples in the name of God, "Let my people go, that they may serve me" [Exodus, 8: 16], and he will perform on them many great signs and wonders, and will not fear them in the least, and will stand against their city Rome until he reduces it to ruins.* And if you like, I will explain the whole passage.' But he did not so wish.

He then cited further an Aggadah which says about the Messiah that he prays for Israel that God may pardon them for their sins and accepted on himself sufferings, but said before God, 'I accept the sufferings on condition that the Resurrection of the Dead shall take place in my days; and not only for those who die in my era, but also for all those who have died from Adam onwards. And not only for those who died natural deaths, but also for those who were thrown into the sea and drowned, or who were eaten by wolves and other wild animals.' [See Pesiqta Rabbati 36: 1.]

'Now,' said Fray Paul, 'the sufferings which the Messiah undertook were the execution of Jesus, which he accepted of his own will.'

I said, 'Woe to him who has no shame! For Jesus did none of this. He did not bring back to life those who died from Adam onwards, and he did not do anything of all this. Moreover, this prayer shows that he is a man and not God, and that the power to bring the dead to life is not his. As for these sufferings, they are nothing but the pain that he feels because his coming is so long delayed and he sees his people in exile and "there is nought in the power of his hand" [Deuteronomy, 28: 32], and he sees that people who serve "them that are not God" [II Chronicles, 13: 9], and deny his Messiahship and set up another Messiah, are more honoured than his own people.'

He then resumed: 'Daniel said, "Seventy weeks* are decreed upon thy people and upon thy holy city, to finish the transgres-

---

will stand against their city Rome until he reduces it to ruins It seems hardly likely that N. would have said this, which seems needlessly provocative. Moreover, it does not tally with his previous reluctance to state publicly Midrashic sayings about the future destruction of Rome (see p. 117). It seems likely that this clause is an addition by the editor for the Jewish readership.

Daniel said, 'Seventy weeks . . .' The cryptic numerical calculations of Daniel, chapters 9 and 12, had long been a focus for 'reckoners of the End'. This topic of controversy between Jews and Christians can be traced back to the ninth century in the controversy of the convert to Judaism Bodo and Pablo Alvarez (see B. Blumenkranz, 1960, pp. 166 ff.).

sion, and to make an end of sin, and to forgive iniquity, and to bring in everlasting righteousness, and to seal vision and prophet, and to anoint the most holy" [Daniel, 9: 24]. The "seventy weeks" are weeks of years, meaning the 420 years that the Second Temple stood, together with the 70 years of the Babylonian Exile; and the "most holy" is Jesus.'

I said to him, 'But was not Jesus over thirty "weeks" before this time, by our reckoning, which is the truth, witnessed by his contemporaries who knew him and were personally acquainted with him? And even by your reckoning, he lived over ten "weeks" before the Destruction.'

Said he, 'That is so; but in the next verse, which says, "Know therefore and discern that from the going forth of the words to restore and build Jerusalem unto one anointed, a prince", the "anointed" and "prince" are Jesus.'

I said, 'This too is an obvious mistake. For Scripture divides up the seventy "weeks" which are mentioned, counting "seven weeks" [v. 25] until the "anointed prince", and then "sixty-two weeks" for the building of "broad place and moat", and then one "week" when "he shall make a firm covenant for many" [v. 27]; and so the number of "seventy weeks" is made complete. But Jesus, whom you call the "anointed prince" did not come at the end of "seven weeks", but after more than sixty "weeks", on your reckoning. But explain to me the whole scriptural passage, according to your theory, and I will return an answer; for you cannot explain it in any way in the world. Yet you are not ashamed to speak about something you know nothing of. But let me inform you that the "anointed prince" was Zerubbabel,* for he came at

---

the 'anointed prince' was Zerubbabel Zerubbabel was a leader of Davidic descent who was appointed governor of the Jews by the Persian king Darius after the return from the Babylonian Exile (see Ezra, 2: 2; 3: 2–13; 5: 1–2; Haggai, 1: 1 to 2: 9; Zechariah, 4: 9). N.'s statement that Zerubbabel came after 'seven weeks' is based on *Seder 'Olam,* chapters 27–8 (see also b Shabb., 145b and b Yoma, 54a), where the actual interval given is 52 years (reckoned as seven *complete* 'weeks'). See also Rashi on Daniel, 9: 24, where the same interval of 52 years is given, but the 'anointed prince' is identified as Cyrus (called 'Messiah' in Isaiah, 45: 1), not Zerubbabel. N. discusses this difference of opinion between himself and Rashi in *Sefer ha-ge'ulah,* Part 3. Pablo's attempt to identify the 'anointed prince' as Jesus is strange since, as N. points out, this prince was to appear only 'seven weeks' after the destruction of the First Temple. More suitable for Pablo's purpose was Daniel, 9: 26: 'And after threescore and two weeks shall an anointed one be cut off and be no more.' N. does not deal with this verse in the *Vikuaḥ,* nor does he report that P. mentioned it. Yet it would seem rather suitable for P. to cite, since it prophesies that a Messiah would be 'cut off' shortly before the destruction of the Second Temple—too shortly before, indeed, being

the time of the "seven weeks", as can be seen clearly from Scripture.'

Said he, 'But how could he be called "Messiah"?'

I replied, 'Even Cyrus was called "Messiah" [Isaiah, 45: 1], and of Abraham, Isaac and Jacob it is said, "Do not touch my Messiahs" [Psalms, 105: 15; I Chronicles, 16: 22]. And that is why* he is called "prince" (not "king"), for Zerubbabel's kingdom would not be exalted, though he himself would be honoured and exalted among his own people; similarly, we have "The princes of the peoples* will be gathered to the people of the God of Abraham" [Psalms, 47: 10]. And now I will explain to you the whole passage from Daniel, in a clear interpretation, if you and your associates here wish to learn, and have an understanding heart. I say before our lord King and "all the peoples" that no time is set for the coming of the Messiah in this passage, or in any of the words of Daniel, except at the end of the book. For it is clear in Scripture that, despite all that is said there in this passage and in other passages, he continued to pray* for knowledge of the time of the End; and finally, they told him the End-time in the verse that says, "And from the time that the continual burnt-offering shall be taken away, and the detestable thing that causeth appalment set up, there shall be a thousand two hundred and ninety days" [Daniel, 12: 11]. And now I shall explain, before the eyes of the peoples, the meaning of this verse, even though it may be hard to bear for the Jews who are here.* The verse says that from the time that the

---

only seven years before, but near enough for Christian calculators who associated the death of Jesus with the destruction of the Temple. There would be no need, however, for N. to suppress mention of this verse, if it was made, since Jewish commentators had their own interpretation of it. (see Rashi, ad loc., and N., *Sefer ha-ge'ulah*, Part 3). The 'anointed one' of this verse was identified as Agrippa II, the Jewish king at the time of the destruction of the Second Temple.

And that is why Not 'Besides' (Rankin).

The princes of the peoples N.'s point is that the word 'prince' signifies a minor leader, and thus cannot mean the Messiah. In the verse he quotes from the Psalms, the sole kingship of God is stressed—the kings of the peoples are therefore demoted to 'princes'. However, the Hebrew word for 'prince' differs in the two cases. In Daniel, 9: 25, the word is *nagid*, while in Psalms, 47: 10, it is *nadiv*. This seems a slight lapse on N.'s part. Rankin's attempt to explain the relevance of this verse from Psalms is beside the point. ('Z. though a prince of Persia was honoured by his own people and so in reality was an Israelite prince'; and 'in the world of the future . . . Z. will appear as a prince of Israel.')

continued to pray e.g., Daniel, 8: 15; 9: 2, etc.

I shall explain, before the eyes of the peoples . . . even though it may be hard to bear for the Jews who are here Rankin translates, '. . . even though this verse may be difficult for the

daily burnt-offering was removed until God will render desolate the abomination which removed it—and that is the people of Rome who destroyed the Temple*—will be 1,290 years; for the "days" which are mentioned here are years,* as in "for a year shall be his right of redemption" [Leviticus, 25: 29], or "from year to year" [Exodus, 13: 10, etc.], or "a year or ten months" [Genesis, 24: 55]. And then Daniel says, "Happy is he who waiteth and reacheth to 1,335 days" [v. 12], thus adding forty-five years. And the meaning is that at the first date the Messiah will come,* and he will cause the abomination, which worships that which is not God, to be desolate* and destroyed from the world; and after that he will gather the dispersed of Israel to the "Wilderness of the Peoples" [Ezekiel 20: 35] as Scripture says, "And I will bring her to the wilderness, and I will speak to her heart" [Hosea, 2: 14], and he will bring

---

Jews that are here present, I shall interpret it to the Gentiles'. N. does not mean any antithesis between Jews and Gentiles. The expression 'before the eyes of the peoples' simply means 'publicly', echoing 'all the peoples' two sentences before. (The expression has a Biblical ring, and therefore is used as a rhetorical device to draw attention to the importance of what he is about to say; see Psalms, 49: 2.) When N. says that his interpretation of the end of Daniel will be hard to bear for the Jews, he means that the coming of the Messiah, on his interpretation, will not be in the lifetime of his hearers, being 95 years hence.

until God will render desolate the abomination which removed it—and that is the people of Rome who destroyed the Temple Rankin misunderstands this completely, translating, 'until there shall be set up the one who makes desolate, namely the one who is the abomination that has removed the daily burnt offering'. N. interprets the infinitive *la-tet* not as 'to set up', but as 'to cause to be' or 'render', thus translating Daniel, 12: 11: 'to render desolate the abomination'.

the 'days' which are mentioned here are years The philological proofs which follow are rather shaky, as all of them involve the plural *yamim* (literally 'days') used to mean 'one year'. There is no instance to be found of the singular *yom* used to mean 'year' or of the plural *yamim* used to mean 'years'. If N. had merely said that 'days' are being used in a cryptic prophecy as a code word for 'years', he could have pointed out that his Christian opponent, Pablo Christiani, had been arguing this very thing in relation to Daniel, 9: 24 (when he took a 'week' to mean 'seven years'). As it is, N. laid himself open to philological refutation, which duly came. It is interesting that N. did not lay stress on philological 'proofs' when he came to write the *Sefer ha-ge'ulah,* but relied chiefly on citing the authority of *Seder 'Olam* and Sa'adiah Gaon for the symbolism of 'days' for 'years' in Daniel.

at the first date, the Messiah will come Not 'when the Messiah shall first come' (Rankin).

he will cause the abomination . . . to be desolate Rankin makes the same error as before: 'the abomination, which worships that which is not God, the one that makes desolate, shall be delivered up'. This requires the verb *yiten* to be read as *yutan (hophal),* and to be translated as 'he will be delivered up', a most unlikely sense, as well as a most unlikely reading.

Israel to their land, as did Moses our teacher, on him be peace, who was the first Redeemer; and this will take 45 years.* And after that, Israel will rest on their land and rejoice in the Lord their God and in "David their king" [Hosea, 3: 5], and happy is he who waits and reaches those good days. Now the present date is 1,195 years from the Destruction; so 95 years are lacking from the number given by Daniel. We may expect, then, that the Redeemer will come at that time, for this interpretation is firm, fitting and easy to believe.'

Fray Paul answered, 'But the Sages have said [Yalqut Hosea, 518] in an Aggadah, "What are those additional days? These are the forty-five days in which the Redeemer will be concealed. Just as Moses, the first Redeemer, revealed himself, and then was concealed from them, so the last Redeemer will reveal himself and then be concealed." Now in this Aggadah, the Sages have stated "days",* which shows that literal days are meant, not years.'

I replied, 'The Midrash simply quoted the expression which it found in the Scriptural passage* in Daniel, and therefore repeated the expression "forty-five days", though what is really meant is

---

and this will take 45 years N. is trying to explain why there will be a gap of 45 years between the coming of the Messiah and the final redemption. He finds the answer in Ezekiel's concept of the 'wilderness of the peoples', which is a kind of analogue, in Messianic times, of the wilderness of the time of Moses, where the people wandered for 40 years before being allowed to enter the Promised Land. (See also Yalqut Hosea, 518.) In *Sefer ha-ge'ulah*, N. explains that the Messiah who appears 1,290 years after the destruction (i.e., in 1358 CE) will be the Messiah son of Joseph, who will destroy Rome, but will be killed in the battle of Gog and Magog after a career of 40 years. Then the Messiah son of David will appear and complete the redemption (1403). It is interesting that N. does not mention the Messiah son of Joseph at all in the *Vikuaḥ*. The reason was probably that he knew that Pablo Christiani would seize the opportunity to point out that this Messiah was destined to die a violent death, which he would see as a confirmation of the destined crucifixion of Jesus. Though there is little in common between death in battle and crucifixion, Pablo would be sure to see an opportunity for wearisome argument—indeed later, he even argued that Maimonides' assertion that the Messiah would eventually die of old age was some sort of confirmation of the crucifixion. N. can be forgiven for wishing to avoid such an argument.

the Sages have stated 'days' Rankin: 'wherever these scholars mention the word "day", actual days are intended and not years'. This is incorrect. P. is referring only to the present occasion of the use of the word 'day', and not attempting to enunciate a general rule.

The Midrash simply quoted the expression which it found in the Scriptural passage Rankin is wide of the mark: 'The scriptural exposition [the Midrash] deals with the language of the text and notes that in this passage the 45 days signify that number of years. It thus follows the instructions of our teachers to "pay close attention to" [lit., hold on to] the language of the biblical verse.'

years. As the Rabbis say, "He has adopted the language of the Scriptural passage." '*

Said Fray Paul, 'There is no Jew in the world who will not agree that "day", in Hebrew [*yom*], means literally "day". But he changes the meanings of words just as he likes.'

So the King called out, and they brought in the first Jew that they found, and asked him, 'What is the meaning of the Hebrew word *yom*?'; to which he answered, 'Day.'

I, however, said, 'My lord King, this Jew is certainly a better judge of the matter than Fray Paul, but not better than I. The word *yom*, in Scripture, sometimes means "time", for example, "on the day [at the time] when I smote every first-born" [Numbers, 3: 13, etc.]. And in the plural *yamim* it can be used to mean "years",* and here Scripture uses it to refer to "years". And it was necessary [to use an unusual expression for "years"] because Scripture sought to conceal the matter,* as the angel said several times to Daniel, "Shut up the words, and seal the book, even to the time of the end: many shall run to and fro, and knowledge shall be increased" [Daniel, 12: 4]. But I am speaking on matters of wisdom to someone who does not know and does not understand, and it is fitting that fools should give judgement for him!'

Fray Arnol of Segura spoke up, 'See, Jerome has interpreted "days"* in this passage as meaning "days of the people".'

He has adopted the language of the Scriptural passage Aramaic, *lishn'a de-qer'a neqat*. There is no such expression, exactly, in the Talmud, so E. emends 'as the Rabbis say' to 'as the saying goes'. Chavel cites the expression *lishn'a de-'alm'a neqat* (e.g., b BM, 2a), which differs by only one word, but means something unrelated to what N. has in mind. There is, however, a Talmudic expression which means just what N. required, namely *teney lishn'a de-'urait'a* (see b Kidd., 2b). It seems that N. was thinking of this phrase, but confused it with the expression cited by Chavel. This is something he could have checked, and the fact that he did not do so is evidence of the hasty composition of the *Vikuaḥ* (see Part I, pp. 77–78).

the plural yamim *can be used to mean 'years'* See above, p. 126.

And it was necessary [to use an unusual expression for 'years'] because Scripture sought to conceal the matter It would have been better for N. to have relied on this argument, which is in fact correct, for there is every likelihood that the author of Daniel, in his cryptic prophecy, meant 'days' to stand for 'years'. As for the rabbinical saying quoted by P., he was undoubtedly correct in saying that here the interpretation is in terms of literal days; but in view of the latitude and variety of rabbinical interpretations of such topics, this was no bar to N.'s interpretation, for which he had the authority of the rabbinical *Seder 'Olam*, and also of Sa'adiah Gaon.

Jerome has interpreted 'days' . . . This comment does not appear in Jerome's commentary on Daniel, where, indeed, Jerome explicitly interprets the 'days' as literal days. Fray Arnol may have been referring to a comment of Jerome's on some other passage, and N. misunderstood him to be referring to a comment on the verse in Daniel, 12.

I rejoiced at his words, and said, 'You can see from Jerome's words that "days" here are not to be taken in their literal sense as in other passages, and that is why he felt it necessary to give an interpretation. And I think that his expression "days of the people" means "years" and arises from the people's expression, "It has been many days since a certain thing happened"; by which they mean many years.'

That man resumed, 'Their Sages have said that the Messiah entered the Garden of Eden, and it is stated there, in the Aggadah, "Why the Messiah?* Because he saw that his ancestors were idolaters,* and he separated himself from their way, and worshipped the Holy One, blessed be He, who hid him in the Garden of Eden." '

I laughed at him, and said, 'This proves my case, that he, being the descendant of idolaters, must be completely human. God reckoned it to him as merit that he separated from the ways of his ancestors and did not worship idols, as they did. Could this be said about the Deity Himself?' And I took the book which he was holding, and read out to them the Aggadah from its beginning, showing that it says that there were fourteen people who entered the Garden of Eden alive,* including Seraḥ the daughter of

---

Why the Messiah? Rankin does not understand that the quotation begins with these words, and produces: 'in the Aggadah the Messiah explains why'.

Because he saw that his ancestors were idolaters This particular Midrash is no longer extant, though it shows affinities with extant Aggadic passages. The explanation given for the inclusion of the Messiah among those who entered alive into the Garden of Eden seems inappropriate. It would be far more appropriate for any of the four proselytes included in the various lists: Eliezer, the servant of Abraham; Hiram, King of Tyre; Eved-Melekh the Ethiopian; and Bithiah, daughter of Pharaoh. Any of these could well be said to have seen that 'his ancestors were idolaters, and separated . . . from their way'. It is true that *some* of the Messiah's ancestors could be called idolaters (i.e., those kings of Judah who 'did evil in the eyes of the Lord', e.g., Ahaz and Menasseh). But the Messiah's ancestors also included the loyal kings David, Solomon, Jehoash, Amaziah, Azariah, Hezekiah; so it is odd that his ancestors should be called 'idolaters' in an unqualified way. It would seem, then, that the Midrash originally gave this as a reason for the inclusion of one of the proselytes, not of the Messiah.

fourteen people who entered the Garden of Eden alive Several sources are extant in which the people who enter the Garden of Eden alive are listed, but none of these sources quite tallies with the version given here. In Derekh Eretz Zutta, 1, nine people are listed, including the Messiah, Bithiah, and Seraḥ. Yalqut lists thirteen who 'did not taste death' (Yalq. Sh., II, 367): Enoch, Eliezer, Methuselah, Hiram, Eved-Melekh (see Jeremiah, 38: 7), Bithiah, Seraḥ, the three sons of Korah, Elijah, the Messiah, Rabbi Joshua ben Levi. According to the same source, nine entered the Garden of Eden alive: Enoch, Elijah, the Messiah, Eliezer, Eved-Melekh, Hiram, Ya'avetz (the grandson of Rabbi Judah the Prince), Seraḥ, Bithiah. If Ya'avetz is added to the previous list of thirteen, N.'s number of fourteen

Asher,* and Bithiah the daughter of Pharaoh.* 'And if the Messiah was Jesus, and he was God, as you think, he would not be with the women in the Garden of Eden, for God's "throne is in the heavens, and the earth is his footstool" [Isaiah, 66: 1]. God forbid such a thought! But it is as I said before; that he is staying in the Garden of Eden, the dwelling-place of Adam before he sinned; for that is the opinion expressed by the Sages in the books of Aggadah. So this has been explained.'

Then our lord the King stood up, and they all went.

On the following Thursday, our lord the King arranged the place for the Disputation in his palace, and ordered that it should be held in private.* We sat down near the entrance of the palace. Fray Paul began with vain words without meaning, and after that said, 'I shall cite a proof from their great Sage whose like has not been for the last 400 years,* and his name is Maestro Moses of Egypt. He says that the Messiah will die and his son and grandson will reign after him. So it is not as you said, that he would not die in the usual way of men.' And he asked that they should bring him the book of *Judges*.

---

is reached. Perhaps the lost Midrash gave this list as those who entered the Garden alive. Probably this Midrash, to which the *Vikuaḥ* gives us such interesting clues, contained also reasons for the selection of each of the fourteen people who entered the Garden of Eden alive. The Midrash was, however, in a somewhat corrupt textual state even at this time, since it assigns the wrong reason for the selection of the Messiah, as argued above.

Seraḥ the daughter of Asher She became a focus of legends because she was the only woman to be mentioned among those who 'descended to Egypt' (see Genesis, 46: 17). She was held to have survived the whole period of the exile and to have shown Moses where to find the bones of Joseph (b Sotah, 13a). She was even held to have survived to the time of King David, being the 'wise woman' who advised the surrender of Sheba ben Bichri to Joab (II Samuel, 20: 16–22). See Genesis R., 94: 9, and Targum Jonathan at Genesis, 46: 17.

Bithiah the daughter of Pharaoh Her name is found in I Chronicles, 4: 18, where she is described as the wife of Mered (identified in the Talmud with Caleb).

ordered that it should be held in private Roth (p. 132) translates wrongly, 'the King enjoined moderation'.

for the last 400 years The time span of 400 is something of a puzzle. Rankin sees here a reference to Sa'adia Gaon (born 892), who was 'the last great figure before Maimonides'. The interval, however, between the *floruit* of Sa'adia and that of Maimonides is about 250 years, not 400. Moreover, a natural understanding of the Hebrew ('there has been none like him for the last 400 years') is that 400 years have elapsed since the death of Maimonides. Loeb (1887, p. 10) takes this to be the meaning and assumes that Pablo Christiani was making a mistake: '*Pablo (p. 16 de la Relation) place Maimonides, qui était à peine mort depuis 60 ans, à 400 ans en arrière.*' Rankin (p. 168 n.) criticises this view, saying, 'Paolo was no fool, but a very competent person, and is not likely to have thought that the Maimonidean disputes were about a person who had died 400 years ago.' Rankin has a good point here, but unfortunately goes on to suggest that Loeb crassly misunderstands the

I said before them, 'It does not say so in that book.* But I admit that some of our Sages do say so, as I mentioned earlier. For the opinion of the books of Aggadah is that he was born on the day of the Destruction and that he will live for ever. But the opinion of those who take a more literal approach is that he will be born close to the time of the End, or Redemption, and he will live a long but finite life, and he will die in honour and bequeath his crown to his son. And I have already said that this is what I believe, and that "there is no difference between this world and the days of the Messiah* except deliverance from bondage to the kingdoms" [b Shabb., 151b].

Hebrew text. 'His error would appear to arise from thinking that *kemoto* ('his like') has to do with the word for *death.*' Loeb could not possibly have made such an elementary mistake; nor could Steinschneider, who also understood the figure of 400 to refer to the time since the death of Maimonides. Steinschneider, however, considers that the figure of '400 years' was added by the copyist, and he takes this as an indication of the date of the MS from which the Constantinople edition, the Leiden MS and the Saraval MS were all derived; i.e., about 1600 CE, 400 years after Maimonides. It seems strange, however, that a copyist should insert such an inappropriate figure into Pablo's speech, oblivious of a gap of over 300 years between himself and the time of Pablo. The best explanation seems to be an adaptation of that of Rankin: Pablo was saying simply that Maimonides was the greatest figure since the Geonic age, without specific reference to Sa'adia (the Geonic age is usually reckoned to have begun in 589 CE). If this explanation is correct, there is no need to place the source MS as late as 1600, though it is not likely to have been earlier than the fifteenth century (see Steinschneider's comments in 1858, *Catalogus codicum hebraeorum Bibliothecae Academiae Lugduno-Batavae,* Leipzig, p. 275).

It does not say so in that book N. does not deny that Maimonides held this opinion, only that it is not to be found in the Book *Judges (Shofetim,* a part of Maimonides' great code, *Mishneh Torah).* Maimonides does, however, express the opinion that the Messiah will be mortal elsewhere in his works: in his commentary on the Mishnah (Introduction to *Ḥeleq)* and in his *Ma'amar Teḥiyat ha-metim,* ch. 6: 'But the Messiah will die and his son and his son's son will reign in his stead. God has clearly declared his death in the words, "He shall not fail nor be crushed until he have set the right in the earth"—Isaiah, 42: 4. His kingdom will endure a very long time and the lives of men will be long also, because longevity is a consequence of the removal of sorrows and cares'—Introduction to *Ḥeleq;* 'If in the days of the Messiah or before him or after his death . . .'—*Ma'amar Teḥiyat ha-metim.* N.'s main point is that, as far as Judaism's teachings go, it is immaterial whether one holds that the Messiah is mortal or that he is immortal. Both views can be found in the sources. P. tries to utilise *both* views to support the claims of Christianity: the 'immortal' view to show that the Messiah is divine, and the 'mortal' view to show that the Messiah must die on the cross. N. answers that whether mortal or immortal, the Jewish Messiah does not conform to the Christian conception. If mortal, he dies not on the cross but after a long, prosperous reign. If immortal, he is not divine, but lives in the terrestrial Eden together with other privileged human beings such as Elijah, Seraḥ and Bithiah.

there is no difference between this world and the days of the Messiah This was the opinion of Mar Samuel, the third-century rationalistic Babylonian *'amora* (the Talmud reports that he was eminent in astronomy and medicine). He considered that there would be nothing

They brought the book which he had asked for, and he searched it but could not find what he had said was there. I took the book from his hand, and said, 'Listen to the words of the book which he cites.' And I read out to them from the beginning of the chapter: ' "The King Messiah will arise in the future for Israel and will build the Temple and gather the dispersed of Israel." '

Said Fray Arnol of Segura, 'He is lying in his teeth.'*

I said, 'Up to now, he was a great Sage with no one like him, and now, he is a liar?'

But the King rebuked him, and said, 'It is not fitting to dishonour Sages.'

I said to the King, 'He is not a liar, for I will prove from the Torah and from the prophets that all that he said was the truth. For it is the task of the Messiah to gather the "dispersed of Israel and the scattered ones of Judah" [Isaiah, 11: 12], that is, the twelve tribes. But your Messiah, Jesus, did not gather one man of them, and did not even live in the time of the Exile. It is also the task of the Messiah to build the Temple in Jerusalem, but Jesus did not carry out anything in connection with the Temple, either building or destruction. Also the Messiah will rule over the peoples, and Jesus did not rule even over himself.' Then I read out to them the passage* of Scripture beginning, 'And it shall come to pass when

---

miraculous about the Messianic age, but that it would be an age of peace and prosperity, when the Jews would regain their independence in their own land.

He is lying in his teeth This angry reaction had an unpleasant aftermath for the Jews, for when on 28 August 1263, the king, at the instigation of the Dominicans, issued a rescript ordering the censoring of the Talmud, orders were included to the Jews to surrender all copies of the section *Shofetim* of Maimonides' code which were to be publicly burnt. Cohen (p. 180) states incorrectly that 'the king ordered the seizure and burning of all the writings of Maimonides'. (See Denifle, 1887, document 3: *'omnes libros qui vocantur Soffrim* [*sic*], *compositos a quodam Iudeo, qui vocabatur Moyses filius Maymon egipciachus sive de Alcayra'.)* The reason given was that the section *Shofetim* contained blasphemies against Jesus Christ, a reference no doubt to the statement (in the subsection *Melakhim*, XI, 4) that Jesus and Muhammad were 'nothing else than a means for preparing the way for the king Messiah'. Though this particular passage did not enter into the disputation, attention would not have been focused on the contents of *Shofetim* had the altercation between N. and P. not taken place. P., therefore, took his revenge for his worsting by N. on this topic. Actually, the passage in *Shofetim* regarded as 'blasphemous' (and therefore regularly excised by Christian censors from this time on) showed a commendable toleration towards Christianity and Islam as a means for the spread of monotheism throughout the world.

Then I read out to them the passage . . . The reading of this passage and the application of the term 'thine enemies' to the Christians and of the term 'them that hate thee' to the Moslems do not seem to be authentic. The passage is irrelevant, for it contains no mention of the Messiah. This is a piece of gratuitous polemic in which N. would not have indulged at

all these things are come upon thee, the blessing and the curse which I have set before thee' and the end of the passage until 'and the Lord thy God will put these curses upon thine enemies and on them that hate thee, which persecuted thee' [Deuteronomy, 30: 1–7]. And I explained to them that the expression 'thine enemies' means the Christians, and the expression 'them that hate thee' means the Ishmaelites [Moslems], the two peoples who have persecuted us. And Fray Paul did not answer a word. So they adjourned the session.

On the next day, Friday, they arranged rows in the palace, and 'the King sat in his usual place, upon a seat by the wall'* [I Samuel, 20:25] on his throne. And the bishop was there, with many lords, including Gilles of Cervello and Peire of Berga, and many knights, and people from all quarters of the city, including some of the poor people.

Then I said to the King, 'I do not wish to continue the Disputation.'

Said the King, 'Why?'

I said, 'The Jewish community here is large,* and they have all sought to prevent me and have begged me to desist, for they are very much afraid of these men, the Preaching Friars, who cast fear on the world; and also the greatest and most honoured of the priesthood have sent to me to say that I should not continue. And also many knights from your own household, my lord King, have said to me that I was doing wrong to speak before them against their faith. Also Fray Peire of Genova, the scholar of the Minorites, has said to me that the matter is not good. Also people from various quarters of the city have said to some of the Jews that I should discontinue.' And though this was true, when they saw the King's wish, they all hesitated and said that I should continue after

---

the disputation. The passage was added to the Hebrew account, possibly by N., but more probably by the editor. It is even possible that the uncharacteristic 'And he did not answer a word' is also a later addition. It is the only occasion on which N. claims to have silenced his opponent, who, on the other hand, may have been somewhat dashed by his inability to find the passage in Maimonides (see Part I, p. 65).

the King sat in his usual place, upon a seat by the wall Rankin translates, 'by the place where was situated the recess with his throne', not recognising the Biblical reference to King Saul, which is somewhat pointed since it recalls the dangerousness of Saul to David.

The Jewish community here is large Hebrew, *rav ha-qahal be-k'an.* Roth and Cohen take it that the move to end the disputation came entirely from Christian sources. The word *qahal,* however, is more likely to denote the *aljama,* or Jewish community, of Barcelona, who had good reason to fear the Dominicans, the prime movers of the Inquisition.

all. There was long discussion over this, and in the end, I agreed to continue the Disputation, saying, 'Nevertheless, it is fair that for one day I should be the questioner and Fray Paul the answerer, since so far, he has questioned me and I have answered him for three days running.'

Said the King, 'Nevertheless, you answer him.'* So I agreed.

Fray Paul stood up and asked, 'Do you believe that the Messiah prophesied by the prophets will be both entirely human, and truly Divine?'

I said, 'At the beginning we laid down that we would speak first about whether the Messiah has come, as you assert and after that we would speak about whether he was Divine. But you have not proved that he has come, for I have refuted all the vain arguments which you have adduced. Thus I have won my case, because the onus of proof is on you, and this was your undertaking. And if you do not agree that I have won my case, I undertake to bring completer proofs in the matter, if you will listen to me. And after it has been made clear that your Jesus is not the Messiah, there will be no point in discussing whether the Messiah who will come to us in the future will be entirely human, or what he will be.'

Then the learned judges who were there said that my point was correct.

Said the King to me, 'Answer his question, nevertheless.'

I said, 'The truth is that the Messiah will come and he will be completely human, the son of a man and a woman from their intercourse just like myself; and he will be of the stock and seed of David, as it is written, "And there shall come forth a rod out of the stem of Jesse" [Isaiah, 11: 1], and also, "Until Shiloh shall come" [Genesis, 49: 10]—and *shiloh* means "his son", being connected with the word *shilyah* ["afterbirth"], for he will be born with an afterbirth like the rest of humanity. If he were born through the Spirit of God,* as you say, he would not be "of the stock of Jesse", and even if he lodged in the womb of a woman who was of the seed of David, he would not inherit the kingdom of David,

---

Said the King, 'Nevertheless, you answer him.' So I agreed Rankin translates wrongly: 'The King (consenting) said, "At any rate answer him (now). So I thanked him.' The king did not at all consent to N.'s request to change roles with Pablo Christiani.

shilyah [*'afterbirth'*] See Midrash Leqaḥ Tov on Genesis, 49: 10. The same etymology is given by David Kimḥi, and by ibn Ezra.

through the Spirit of God Literally, 'if he were the Spirit of God', and this ought perhaps to be the rendering, as N. may have reproduced Christian doctrine sketchily here. But see p. 140, where Fray Paul argues that the Messiah is the Spirit of God.

because daughters, with their progeny, do not inherit, according to the Torah, where there is a male, and there have always been male descendants from David.'

Said he, 'There is a Psalm* which says, "A psalm of David: the Lord said to my lord: Sit thou at my right hand" [Psalms, 110: 1]. And who is this whom King David calls "my lord", other than a Divine personage? And how could a human being sit at the right hand of God?'

Said the King, 'He asks well,* for if the Messiah were entirely human and literally of the seed of David, David would not call him "my lord". If I had a son or grandson who ruled over the whole world, even, I would not call him "my lord". I would rather wish him to call *me* "my lord", and kiss my hand, too.'

I turned my face to Fray Paul, and said, 'Are you the clever Jew who made this new discovery and became an apostate because of it? Are you the one who bade the King to assemble before you the sages of the Jews to hold a disputation over your discoveries? Do you think we have never heard this argument before? Is there a single priest or Christian child who will not raise this hard question to the Jews? This question is very antiquated.'*

Said the King, 'Nevertheless, give your answer on it.'

I said, 'Now hear me. King David was the poet who composed the Psalms by the Holy Spirit. He composed them so that they should be sung before the altar of the Lord, but he himself did not sing them there, and was not allowed to do so, for he was forbidden to do so by the law of the Torah. But he gave the Psalms to the Levites to sing; and so it is plainly stated in Chronicles [I Chronicles, 16: 7]. Consequently, he was forced to compose the psalm in a style which was suitable for a Levite to say.* If he had written, "The Lord said to me," the Levite would have been saying

---

Said he, 'There is a Psalm . . .' This is not a continuation of the previous argument (as Rankin represents by inserting, 'Here Fra Paulo interposed and said, "There is, however . . ." '), but a new argument. There is no 'Here' or 'interposed' or 'however' in the text.

Said the King, 'He asks well . . .' This intervention of the king is very much in character, for the king sees the matter as one of royal protocol.

This question is very antiquated N. is certainly correct in saying this, for the question is as old as the Gospels (see Luke, 20: 42: 'Thus David calls him "Lord"; how then can he be David's son?'), and had consequently always been used in Christian-Jewish controversy.

suitable for a Levite to say Kimḥi and ibn Ezra, however, prefer the explanation that this psalm was composed by one of the Levites (its superscription, 'A Psalm of David' being translated as 'A Psalm for David').

falsehood; but it was quite fitting for the Levite to say in the sanctuary, "The Lord said to my lord [i.e., David], Sit at my right hand." And the meaning of this "sitting" is that the Holy One, blessed be He, would guard him all his life* and save him and give him victory over his enemies. And so it was, for he lifted up his spear over 800 slaughtered at one time.* Is there any of these knights before you who could do the same in his might? And this is what is meant by "the right hand" of God. Similarly, it is written by David, "Thy right hand supports me" [Psalms, 18: 36]; and, "The right hand of the Lord does valiantly; the right hand of the Lord is exalted" [Psalms, 118: 15]; and it is written of Moses our teacher, on him be peace, "He causeth his glorious arm to go at the right hand of Moses" [Isaiah, 63: 12]; and Moses himself said about the downfall of Pharaoh, "Thy right hand, O Lord, dashes in pieces the enemy" [Exodus, 15: 6]. Also, Scripture in some places speaks in this way [of using the third person instead of the first person], "And Jephthah and Samuel"* [I Samuel, 12: 11], and

---

would guard him all his life E.'s emendation, 'with his right hand' *(biyemino* instead of *beyamav)*, is plausible. N. is suggesting (following Rashi) that 'sit at the right hand of God' should be translated 'to sit in peace because of the support of the right hand of God'. However, in the Talmud, R. Akiva, interpreting Daniel, 7: 9 ('thrones were placed'), said one was for God and one for David (b Sanh.; 38b and Hag., 14a), and was criticised for this by R. Jose the Galilean, who retorted, 'Akiva, how long will you go on profaning the Shekhinah?' Akiva may have been influenced by the psalm under discussion here to give his interpretation of Daniel, 7: 9. Elsewhere in the Talmud, however, this psalm is interpreted as referring to Abraham, not to David or the Messiah (see b Ned., 32b), and Rashi follows this interpretation.

800 slaughtered at one time See II Samuel, 23: 8 and 18; and I Chronicles, 11: 11. N. has strangely conflated these three verses into one compound statement (probably by a lapse of memory) with a result which could be endorsed by a modern textual critic. The question of errors of quotation in the disputation is interesting (for example, even the beginning of the psalm just discussed is wrongly quoted, the first two words being inverted). The heat of controversy, with its inevitable slight errors, seems to be preserved. Did N. lack time to check these quotations, or did he deliberately leave the errors in, to show that he had not tampered in any way with the notes of the debate which he took at the time? See Part I, p. 77.

And Jephthah and Samuel The Books of Samuel were held, in the Jewish tradition, to have been written by Samuel himself (see b BB, 15a, ref. to I Samuel, 28: 3). So the reference to Samuel in I Samuel, 12: 11 is regarded by N. as an example of a Scriptural writer referring to himself in the third person. Moreover, since the Pentateuch, or Torah, was held to have been written entirely by Moses, all references to Moses in the Pentateuch are similar examples. Consequently, David could have referred to himself in the third person as 'my lord'. This is an alternative explanation to that previously given by N., by which David wrote the psalm in a style suitable for recitation by a Levite. The sum of both arguments is that 'my Lord' is David himself, not someone greater than himself whom he is addressing.

"O wives of Lemech" [Genesis, 4: 23]; and, similarly, all the words of Moses our teacher in the Torah. But in this instance, he was forced to speak in this manner anyway, as I have observed. And know that the Psalms were composed by the Holy Spirit, and they apply to both David and to his son who will sit on his throne, that is, the Messiah;* for the things that happened to David partially will happen to the Messiah in full; for while the right hand of God would support David and give him victory over his enemies round about him, he would help the Messiah to such a point that he would make all the nations into his footstool—for they are all his enemies, for they have enslaved his people and denied his coming and his kingdom, and some of them have set up another Messiah. And it is fitting to sing this Psalm in the Temple in the days of David and also in the days of the Messiah his son, for it is all about the throne of David and his reign.'

Fray Paul answered, 'How can he say this thing? Their Sages say that this Psalm speaks of the Messiah, for the words must be interpreted in their literal sense that the Messiah is to sit at the right hand of God.' And he cited an Aggadah which says, 'In the time to come, the Holy One, blessed be He, will seat the Messiah on his right and Abraham on his left.'

I said, 'This is also as I said, for I have already said that the meaning is partly about David, but more essentially and fully about the Messiah.'* And I asked for the book, and he handed it to me.

And I said, 'See how he was misrepresenting the matter! This Aggadah says [Yalqut Tehillim, 869], "In time to come, the Holy One, blessed be He, will seat the Messiah on His right hand and Abraham on His left, and the face of Abraham will turn pale, and he will say, 'My descendant sits on the right of the Holy One, blessed be He, and I sit on his left,' but the Holy One, blessed be He, will comfort him." It is quite plain here that the Messiah is not

---

they apply to both David and to his son . . . the Messiah This argument does not contradict the previous one, for N.'s view is that David's reign prefigured that of the Messiah, and that the victories and glory of David are to be paralleled on a larger scale in the Messianic age.

partly about David, but more essentially and fully about the Messiah Rankin misunderstands this, and produces, 'as the view which I then expressed set aside all reference to David and in the main was wholly concerned with the Messiah himself'. He evidently misreads *qetzatah* ('part of it') as *qatzetah* ('cut off'). N. is repeating that the psalm deals with David *and* the Messiah, David's reign being a foreshadowing and partial realisation of the glory of the Messiah.

Divine,* and that Jesus is not the Messiah at all. For if he were Divine, Abraham would not feel ashamed because a Divine being received more honour than he; and his face would not grow pale or green at all. Moreover, he calls the Messiah "my descendant" [literally, "son of my son"], not "son of my daughter". But Jesus, according to your opinion, was not the "son of the son" of Abraham at all. And as for the Messiah's "sitting at the right hand of God", it is like Abraham's "sitting on the left hand of God"—they are both entirely human beings. Moreover, the Messiah cannot be Jesus, because the Aggadah says "in time to come", and the Sages were saying this about 500 years after Jesus' lifetime. But Fray Paul suppresses the beginning and the end* of the passage, and has no shame.'

Fray Paul resumed and brought a proof from a Midrash in which it is said [Yalqut Behuqotai, 672], ' "And I will walk among you" [Leviticus, 26: 12]: they told a parable about this verse. What is this like? It is like a king who went out to take a walk with his tenant in his garden, and the tenant sought to hide himself from him. Said the king to him, "Why do you hide yourself? I am like you." So in the future the Holy One, blessed be He, will walk* with the righteous in the Garden of Eden, and the righteous will see Him and tremble before Him. And He will say to them, "Why do you tremble before me? I am like you." Does this mean perhaps that the fear of me should not be on you at all?* No, for Scripture

---

It is quite plain here that the Messiah is not Divine N.'s argument above on Psalms, 110: 1 thus appears unnecessary. Since it is possible for David or the Messiah to sit at the right hand of God without thereby being divine, it was not necessary to argue that 'at the right hand' should be translated 'with the support of the right hand'. N. might reply, however, that he was giving a literal translation, while the Midrash is giving a fanciful, anthropomorphic interpretation, not to be taken literally, but still affording no grounds for the idea of a divine Messiah.

suppresses the beginning and the end Hebrew, *'okhel r'osho ve-sofo.* This is a difficult phrase which has defeated all commentators (Chavel confesses himself baffled). Rankin detaches the phrase and puts it at the head of the next paragraph, with the translation, 'But Fra Paolo, demolished utterly in debate, without being ashamed'. (This seems to depend on *'okhel* being read as the *pual 'ukhal,* an impossible construction in medieval Hebrew.) Literally, the sentence reads, 'But Fray Paul eats its head and its end and is not ashamed'; and the meaning, I suggest, is that Fray Paul suppresses ('swallows') the beginning and end of the Midrashic passage, and quotes only the middle, the only part that suits his purpose.

So in the future the Holy One . . . will walk Not '. . . the Holy One . . . is ready to walk' (Rankin). *'atid* is the regular expression for the future of the Last Days.

Does this mean perhaps that the fear of me should not be on you at all? Rankin produces here one of his worst confusions. He puts this sentence as belonging to God's speech, says, "And I shall be to you for a God, and you shall be to me for a people' [ibid.]." Now since God said, "I am like you," he must have become a man like them.'

I said, 'Everything that he cites, he cites against himself. For this is an event which will take place in the future, in the Garden of Eden. Jesus did not walk with the righteous in the Garden of Eden when he "became a man", but he was fleeing all his life before his enemies and pursuers. But this Midrash is a parable, as we can tell by its beginning, "They told a parable. What is it like?" Its meaning is that in this world, the righteous are not able to attain the true grade of prophecy, and they are not able to gaze at the brightness that is called "gloria",* as it is said, "I will make myself known to him in a vision" [Numbers, 12: 6]. Even Moses our teacher trembled at the beginning of his career as a prophet, as it is said, "And Moses hid his face, for he was afraid" [Exodus, 3: 6]. But in time to come, the souls of the righteous will be purified of all sin and all ugliness, and they will have permission to gaze through a bright glass,* as did Moses our teacher, on him be peace, of whom it is said, "God spoke to Moses face to face, as a man speaks to his fellow" [Exodus, 33: 11]. And the Sages used the expression "I am like you" in the way of parable, to mean that they should not tremble and be afraid, just as they would not be afraid of one another. And the same kind of language appears in Scrip-

---

translating it ' "Perchance you have no reverence for me?" ' Then he goes on, ' "But thanks be to God," said Fra Paulo, "the verse affirms: 'And I will be your God and ye shall be my people.' " ' The abbreviation *tl* does not stand for *todah la-'el* ('thanks be to God') but for *talmud lomar* ('there is a text which teaches'). The whole form of argument here (in which a statement is made, then a question takes the statement to an unacceptable extreme, then a Biblical text is cited to refute this extreme) is very common in Talmud and Midrash.

the brightness that is called 'gloria' N. translates here by the Latin word *gloria* the Talmudic word *ziv* ('brightness') often found in the expression *ziv ha-shekhinah* ('the brightness of the Divine Presence'); e.g., b Ber., 17a: 'In the future world there is no eating or drinking . . . but the righteous sit with their crowns on their heads feasting on the brightness of the Divine Presence, as it is said, "And they beheld God, and did eat and drink." ' N.'s point is that when God says, 'I am like you,' the meaning is not that God has descended to humanity, but that men have ascended to the highest grade of prophecy, when they are sufficiently like God to be able to gaze on His glory.

through a bright glass See b Sukk.; 45b and b Sanh.; 97b: 'But are those who see Him through a bright speculum so few?' The word used is *'ispaqlaria,* which is derived from Latin *specularia,* prob. indirectly through Gk. σπεκλάριον; see Samuel Krauss, 1898, vol. 2, p. 93. It is not certain whether the word means 'mirror' or 'window'. Paul's similar expression in I Corinthians, 11: 12 suggests that 'mirror' is preferable. God's glory cannot be seen direct even in Heaven, and the elect are divided into those who see His glory reflected in a bright mirror, and those who see it in a dark mirror.

ture: "as a man speaks to his fellow"; which does not mean that God became a man at the time when he was speaking to Moses. And this is a customary expression of the Sages, as is found in *Yelammedenu:** "If you do my commands, you will be like me." Similar is the language of Scripture: "And you shall be as God, knowing good and evil" [Genesis, 3: 5], and "Behold, the man is become as one of us" [Genesis, 3: 22], and "And he that is feeble among them at that day shall be as David; and the House of David shall be as God" [Zechariah, 12: 8]. This does not mean that they will be the same in form.'

That man resumed, and argued, 'It is said in *Bereshith Rabbah* [2: 4], " 'And the spirit of God hovered over the face of the waters' [Genesis, 1: 2]—this is the spirit of the Messiah." If so, the Messiah is not a man, but the spirit of God.'

I said, 'Woe to him who knows nothing, and thinks that he is wise and learned. It is also said there [8: 1]: " 'And the spirit of God hovered'—this is the spirit of Adam."* Does this really mean that Adam would be a Divine being? But someone who does not know "what is above or what is below"* in books, turns upside down the words of the living God. But the expounder of allegories who gave the allegorical explanation "This is the spirit of the Messiah," expounded the whole verse in terms of the Four Kingdoms, and said that the language of Scripture here provides hints of

---

Yelammedenu A term which includes many collections of Midrashim, including Midrash Tanḥuma, Deuteronomy Rabbah, Numbers Rabbah II, Exodus Rabbah II, and parts of Pesikta Rabbati, all of which frequently mention Rabbi Tanhuma, and use the introductory formula, *yelammedenu rabbenu.* Many medieval citations from *yelammedenu* are no longer traceable, including this one. Probably many books included under the term are no longer extant. For the problem of the works covered by the expression *yelammedenu,* see *Enc. Jud.,* 15, p. 794.

this is the spirit of Adam N. refers here to another section of Bereshit Rabbah, namely section VIII: 1: 'Rabbi Simeon ben Laqish said, "*And the spirit of God hovered* refers to the soul of Adam, as we read, *And the spirit of the Lord shall rest upon him*" [Isaiah, 11: 2].' It is interesting that the same Rabbi Simeon ben Laqish is quoted in the earlier passage as saying that *the spirit of God hovered* refers to the spirit of the Messiah (Gen. R., II; 4). The Aggadic interpretations are not regarded as mutually exclusive, the same verse being regarded as capable of varied and, in the literal sense, incompatible interpretations, even by the same teacher.

what is above or what is below Not 'what comes first and what follows later' (Rankin). The reference is to Mishnah, Hag., 12: 1: 'Whoever speculates on four things, it would have been better for him not to have come into the world: what is above, what is beneath, what is before, what is after.' This is a warning against mystical speculations. N.'s point is that for Fray Paul, even simple books are deep mysteries which he does not understand.

future events. He said, "'And the land was waste [*tohu*]'—this is Babylon, of whom it is said, 'I saw the land, and behold, it was waste [*tohu*]' [Jeremiah, 4: 23]; 'and void [*vohu*]'—this is Media, of whom it is said, 'And they hastened [*vayavhilu*] to fetch Haman' [Esther, 6: 14]; 'and darkness'—this is Greece, who darkened Israel's eyes with their harsh decrees; 'on the face of the deep'—this is the wicked kingdom [Rome]; 'and the spirit of God'—this is the spirit of the Messiah. By what merit* will his [the Messiah's] spirit hover over the face of the waters? By the merit of repentance, which is likened to water."* So we see that the Midrash causes to pass before us Four Kingdoms, of which the fourth is Rome; and finally introduces "the Spirit of God", which is the Messiah, a human being entirely, but full of wisdom and the Spirit of God—just like Bezalel, of whom it is said, "I will fill him with the Spirit of God" [Exodus, 31: 3], or Joshua, of whom it is said, "And Joshua the son of Nun was full of the spirit of wisdom" [Deuteronomy, 34: 9]. And so it is clear that the Midrash speaks of the Messiah of the future, who will come after the Fourth Kingdom. But I have not been able to explain to Fray Paul the style of the Midrash,* which consists of deriving hints from some nuance of the language* of the text, without arguing that these constitute the main meaning of the text. And there are similar comments in many passages of *Bereshith Rabbah;* e.g., the comment on the passage beginning, "And Jacob went out . . ."* [Genesis, 28: 10].' I said

---

By what merit Not 'to effect what benefit' (Rankin).

likened to water N. gives a somewhat abbreviated version of the passage in Gen. R., II: 4.

I have not been able to explain to Fray Paul the style of the Midrash Roth (p. 137) misunderstands this as a declaration to the reader that N. refrained from expounding the full meaning of the passage 'and its recondite, or even esoteric, implications'. N.'s point is his own inability to communicate to Fray Paul the correct way to regard the interpretations of the Midrash.

from some nuance of the language Hebrew, *mi-semakh (semekh) ha-lashon.* This expression is equivalent to the Aramaic *'asmakht'a,* used as a technical term in the Talmud to mean a 'hint' derived from a Biblical text; i.e., a nuance of the text which suggests a certain view, without being the main or literal meaning of the text. (For the rare form *semakh* or *semekh,* instead of the frequent *'asmakht'a,* see b Sefer Torah, 1a: *u-semakh liy min ha-miqr'a.*) Rankin misunderstands, and translates, 'allusions whose expounding requires the assistance of the knowledge of the language'. The root *samakh* (Aramaic, *semakh)* does mean 'to support', but it is the derivative meaning 'to support a view by quoting a Biblical text' which is relevant here.

the passage beginning, 'And Jacob went out . . .' It is not clear why N. gives this particular example. Chavel suggests that there is a link between the passage cited by Fray Paul (Gen. R., II: 4) and this passage, in that Jacob's dream was interpreted in the Midrash in terms of

this in order to show to them all that Fray Paul did not know how to read the book which he had cited, since he erred in the matter of understanding the style.

Now the King rose and the assembly too.

This is the content of all the discussions. I have not altered one thing in them, to my knowledge. Afterwards on the same day, I stood before our lord the King, and he said, 'Let the Disputation be discontinued;* for I have never seen a man who was in the wrong argue as well as you did.'* And I heard in the court that it was the wish of the King and the Preaching Friars to visit the synagogue on the Sabbath, so I was kept in the city for eight more days.* And when they came there on the following Sabbath, I gave a worthy and fitting reply to our lord the King, when he had given a lengthy speech* to prove that Jesus was the Messiah.

---

the Four Kingdoms. However, Genesis Rabbah itself does not give this interpretation of Jacob's dream (it is found in Tanḥuma, in Pirqei de R. Eliezer and Leviticus Rabbah). Yet N. specifically mentions Genesis Rabbah as the source of his example. (Though it is true, as C. points out, that N. uses the notion of the Four Kingdoms in his own commentary on Jacob's dream.) N. probably means simply that Genesis Rabbah on Jacob at Bethel gives many different interpretations based on nuances of the text, rather than on the literal meaning.

Let the Disputation be discontinued Hebrew, *yisha'er ha-vikuaḥ*. Not 'the debate still remains to be concluded' (Rankin).

as well as you did Hebrew, *ka-'asher 'asiti*, which means literally 'as I did', but this seems to be a lapse by N. into indirect speech rather than a case for emendation.

I was kept in the city for eight more days This is a very different story from that of the Christian account, which says that N. 'fled away and departed', adding, 'From this it is plain that he does not dare and is not able to defend his erroneous creed.' Loeb (1887, pp. 14–15) gives the best explanation of this discrepancy. When the disputation was discontinued, the last item on the agenda (whether the Jewish law was abrogated by the advent of Jesus) was left undiscussed. N., however, agreed to the request of the Dominicans that he would answer questions on this matter at a later date in the presence of the king. (Christian account: 'he had promised in the presence of the lord King and many others that he would answer questions on his faith and law to a small gathering'.) When, however, after the discussion in the synagogue described at the end of the *Vikuaḥ*, the king left Barcelona on protracted business, N. felt himself absolved from his promise and returned to his home in Gerona. The Dominicans chose to represent this as a flight. Such a flight would have been pointless, however, since N. could not run away from the king. Indeed, it appears that the promised discussion did eventually take place after all, for N.'s sermon *Torat Adonai Temimah* is addressed to the very issue of the deferred topic, and there is evidence that this sermon was preached before the king.

to our lord the King, when he had given a lengthy speech This is a unique event in the history of Jewish-Christian relations; the delivery of a sermon by a king in a Jewish synagogue. Conversionist sermons in synagogues by Dominican friars were common

I stood on my feet and said, 'The words of our lord the King are noble, exalted and honoured, since they go forth from the mouth of one who is more noble, exalted and honoured than anyone else in the world. But I will not give his words the praise of saying that they are true. For I have clear proofs, and arguments that shine like the sun, to show that the truth is not in accordance with his words, but it is not fitting for me to hold a controversy with him. One thing only I will say, about which I wonder very much. The things which the King says in our ears to induce us to believe in the Messiahship of Jesus were argued by Jesus himself to our forefathers, and he it was who took great trouble to urge it before them, yet they denied it with a complete and strong denial. He was a person who had greater knowledge and capability to prove his words than the King, according to your opinion that he was Divine. And if our forefathers, who saw him and knew him, did not listen to him, how shall we believe and listen to the voice of the King, who has no knowledge of the matter except through a remote report which he has heard from people who did not know Jesus and were not from his land like our forefathers, who knew him and were eye-witnesses?'*

Then Fray Ramon of Pennaforte* rose up and preached about the Trinity, and he said that it consisted of wisdom, will and

---

enough, but these were affairs of ignominy and compulsion, with no element of free interchange. On this occasion, however, the affair seems to have had the character of a ceremonial visit to the synagogue by the king, who showed respect to the Jewish community and allowed their rabbi to reply. Here James I showed more facets of his complex character: his love of argument, evincing itself both in his own venture into amateur theologising, and his willingness to hear a response; and the essential toleration shown in his respect for Jewish institutions.

and were eye-witnesses N.'s point here is that the refusal of Jesus' Jewish contemporaries to accept his Messianic claim is a strong argument against that claim, since they were in a much better position to assess it than anyone in later generations. N. is assuming that Jesus' claim took the form of claiming divine status. N. is not aware of the line of argument taken up by later Jewish scholars (from the fourteenth-century Profiat Duran) who argued, on the basis of New Testament analysis, that Jesus never claimed divine status, and that his Messianic claim was never rejected by his fellow-Jews, but was disproved by his failure to establish his throne as Davidic king against the Romans.

Fray Ramon of Pennaforte This is the only recorded occasion (apart from the brief exchange on p. 102) when a direct confrontation took place between Raymund de Peñaforte, one of the greatest figures in Christian scholasticism and canon law, and Naḥmanides, a great representative of Jewish scholasticism and of Jewish law, as well as of Jewish mysticism. The occasion is full of drama. (On Raymund de Peñaforte, see p. 80.)

power. And he said in the synagogue,* 'The Maestro too, in Gerona,* agreed in this matter to the words of Fray Paul.'

I stood on my feet and said, 'Hearken and listen to my voice, Jews and Gentiles. Fray Paul asked me in Gerona whether I believed in the Trinity. I said, "What is the Trinity? Does it mean that the Deity has three physical bodies such as those of human beings?" Said he, "No." "Does it mean, then, that the Deity has three refined entities, such as souls or angelic beings?" Said he, "No." "Does it mean one entity derived from three, as bodies are derived from the four elements?" Said he, "No." "If so, what is the Trinity?" Said he, "Wisdom, will and power." '* So I said, 'I

---

in the synagogue Rankin, perhaps regarding these words as redundant here, detaches them and inserts them in the following speech: 'in a synagogue in Gerona'. There does not seem to be sufficient justification for this emendation.

in Gerona This indicates that there had been a previous disputation between N. and P. on the subject of the Trinity. Chavel suggests that this earlier disputation is identical with that mentioned in ibn Verga's *Shevet Yehudah* in the course of the account of the Tortosa Disputation (see *Shevet Yehudah,* ed. Shohat, p. 102. See also p. 179). This account, however, says that this disputation took place before Don Pedro the Elder. Roth (1950), however, takes the view (p. 133) that *Shevet Yehudah* is actually quoting from the Barcelona Disputation, and that the argument quoted was omitted from our text of the *Vikuaḥ;* Roth therefore fits it in to his account of the Barcelona Disputation. The argument, however (about whether the Christians should be called 'Israel') does not fit into the topics discussed at Barcelona; but it does fit into the topic which was omitted, that of whether the Jewish law was abrogated at the advent of Jesus. The best solution seems to be that of Loeb (1887, p. 14): that this argument took place *after* the Barcelona Disputation, at the discussion mentioned above where the omitted topic was debated in a 'small gathering' before the king ('Don Pedro the Elder' being a mistake for James I). There were thus four occasions on which N. and P. met in disputation:

(1) At Gerona, before 1263, where they discussed the Trinity, which P. explained in terms of 'wisdom, will and power'.

(2) At the Barcelona Disputation, 1263.

(3) In the synagogue at Barcelona, eight days after the disputation, when the Trinity was discussed again.

(4) Some time later, probably at Barcelona, when the question of the abrogation of the Jewish law was discussed, and N. preached his sermon of the 'perfect law' in the presence of the king.

wisdom, will and power See Introduction, p. 64. This type of argument, based on the analogy of the faculties of the human psyche, can be traced back to the fourth-century theologian Marius Victorinus (see H. A. Wolfson, 1956, p. 361). Augustine too sponsored this type of argument for the Trinity; the three faculties which he selected for his analogy were memory *(memoria),* knowledge *(notitia)* and will *(voluntas).* The triad of wisdom, will and power is found as an important group of divine attributes in Jewish theology (e.g., Maimonides, *Guide,* I: 58). It would seem, therefore, that P. chose this triad of attributes as especially suitable for persuasion of Jews, and that Raymund de Peñaforte followed suit. The same triad is found in the Trinitarian theory of the twelfth-century Christian authors William of Saint Thiery and William of Conches. See D. J. Lasker, 1977, pp. 63–76.

agree that God is wise, and not foolish, that he wills, and is not inert,* that he is powerful, and not powerless; but the expression "Trinity" is a complete mistake, for wisdom, in the Creator, is not an accidental quality, but He and His wisdom are one,* And He and His will are one, and He and His power are one. Thus, wisdom, will and power are all one. And even if God did have accidental qualities, this would not make Him into a Trinity, but He would be one substance with three accidental properties. Our lord the King has expressed here an analogy which he was taught by those who err. He said that there were three things in wine—colour, taste and smell—yet wine is one thing. But this is a complete mistake; for the redness and the taste and the smell of the wine are three separate qualities, one of which may be found without the other—for there is red wine, and white wine, and wine of other colours, and similarly with taste and smell. Moreover, the redness is not the wine, nor is the taste or the smell, but the wine itself is the stuff that fills the vessel. So it is a material substance with three disconnected accidental properties which do not form any unity. And if we do mistakenly count in this way, then we are forced to assert a Quaternity; for the substance which is Deity,* as

---

that he wills, and is not inert Hebrew, *ḥafetz be-l'o hargashah*. This means literally, 'wills without sensation'. If so translated, it would refer to the 'impassibility' of God; that his will, unlike the human will, is not accompanied or acted on by emotions and outside stimuli. However, such an observation would be irrelevant here, where one would expect 'has will, and is not inert' on the analogy of 'is wise, and not foolish', 'has power, and is not weak' (cf. Maimonides, *Guide*, I: 58: 'we say of Him . . . that He is powerful and knowing and willing . . . to signify that He is neither powerless nor ignorant nor inattentive nor negligent'.). Further, the phrase 'without sensation' does not tally in *form* with the phrases 'and not foolish', 'and not powerless'. I suggest therefore the emendation *ve-l'o be-l'o hargashah*, 'and not inert' (lit. 'and not without feeling'). A would-be clever copyist could easily have made the error of omitting 'and not', importing a philosophical distinction which is here irrelevant, and not realising that in this context it is correct to ascribe 'feeling' to God; i.e., to say that He is an animate being. In any case, it is not part of N.'s theology to ascribe impassibility to God.

He and His wisdom are one Compare Maimonides, *Guide*, I: 50 (ed. Pines, p. 111): 'If however someone believes that He is one, but possesses a certain number of essential attributes, he says in his words that He is one, but believes Him in his thought to be many. This resembles what the Christians say: namely that He is one but also three, and that the three are one.' Here Maimonides goes further than N., by saying that God not only does not possess accidental properties, but does not even possess essential attributes, since in His case, the distinction between substance and attributes is invalid. N., on the other hand, is not interested here in carrying the argument so far. He merely points out that whereas in a human being, wisdom, etc., are accidental properties, in God they are essential properties, and therefore do not form a plurality, not being separable from His essence.

the substance which is Deity See Part I, p. 64.

well as its wisdom, will and power, ought to be reckoned, and they come to four. You ought even to go on to assert a Quinternity, for God is alive, and his life is as much a quality as His wisdom; so that His definition would be: living, wise, willing, powerful, and Deity itself, totalling five. But this is plain error.'

Then Fray Paul stood up and said that he believed in a perfect Unity, and together with it there is a Trinity, and that this is a matter so deep that even the angels and princes on high do not understand it.

I stood up and said, 'It is obvious that a person cannot believe what he does not know;* which means that the angels cannot believe in the Trinity.' And Fray Paul's companions made him keep silent.*

Then our lord the King stood up, and they descended from the Ark,* and they departed. And on the following day, I stood before our lord the King, and he said to me, 'Return to your city in life and peace.' And he gave me 300 dinars,* and I took my leave of him with great love. May God make me worthy* of the life of the World to Come. Amen.

---

it is obvious that a person cannot believe what he does not know For the charge that N. was insincere in saying this, see Part I, p. 63.

Fray Paul's companions made him keep silent See Part I, p. 65.

from the Ark The pulpit, as in modern synagogues, was situated just in front of the Ark containing the scrolls of the Law.

he gave me 300 dinars This gift has been confirmed from a document (Regné, 1910–19, no. 319), dated 25 February 1265, where the king acknowledges a debt of 300 solidi to a Jewish merchant who gave this sum at the king's direction to 'the Rabbi from Gerona'. The confirmation of this gift goes some way towards confirming also N.'s statement that the king admired the way in which N. performed his part in the disputation—a statement which some commentators have doubted, in view of the king's signature on the denigratory Christian account. However, it is quite probable that the king signed this account without even reading it (see Loeb, 1887, p. 13).

make me worthy Not 'make him worthy' (Rankin).

8

The Christian Account of the Barcelona Disputation

Translated from the Latin, edited by Y. Baer, *Tarbiz*, 2, 1930–1, pp. 185–7

In the year of the Lord 1263, on the 20th of July, in the presence of the lord King of Aragon, and many others, barons, prelates, and religious and military persons in the palace of the lord King at Barcelona, when Moses, called Master, a Jew, had been summoned from Gerona by the lord King himself at the instance of the Preaching Friars, and was present in that same place together with many other Jews who seemed and were believed by the other Jews to be experts, Brother Paulus, after discussion with the lord King and certain Friars of the Preaching and Minorite Orders who were present (not in order that the faith in the Lord Jesus Christ, which because of its certitude should not be put into dispute, should be drawn into the arena with the Jews as if it were a matter of doubt, but that the truth of that faith should become manifest in order to destroy the errors of the Jews and remove the confident faith of many Jews who, though they could not themselves defend their errors, said that the said Jewish Master could sufficiently reply to each and every point which was put to them) proposed to the said Jewish Master that he would prove, with the help of God, through writings accepted and authoritative among the Jews, the following things in order, namely: that the Messiah (of which the interpretation is 'Christ') whom the Jews expect, has undoubtedly come; further, that the Messiah himself, as had been prophesied, must be both God and man; further, that he truly suffered and died for the salvation of the human race; further, that legal or ceremonial matters ceased and had to cease after the coming of the said

Messiah. When therefore, the said Moses had been questioned whether he wished to reply to the aforesaid matters, he said and firmly asserted, 'Yes,' and that he would remain, if necessary, for this reason, in Barcelona for a day or a week or a month or even a year. And when it was proved to him that he ought not to be called 'Master', because no Jew ought to be called by this name since the time of the passion of Christ, he conceded this at least, that it was true for the last 800 years. Eventually it was put to him that when Brother Paul had come to Gerona to discuss with him matters which are relevant to salvation, and expounded diligently, among other things, the belief in the Holy Trinity, both as to the Unity of the Divine essence, and as to the Trinity of the Persons, as held by Christians, he [Moses] conceded that if Christians believed what had been expounded to him, they believed what in truth ought to be so held. And when this was repeated in the presence of the lord King, he did not deny it, but was silent, and so, by his silence, assented. Then in the palace of the lord King the said Jew was asked whether the Messiah who is called Christ had come; and when he answered with the assertion, 'No,' and added that Messiah and Christ are the same, and if it could be proved to him that the Messiah had come, then this ought to be believed about no other than him, to wit Jesus Christ, in whom Christians believe, since no other had come who dared to usurp this name, or had been believed to be the Christ, it was proved to him clearly both by the authority of the Law and the Prophets and by the Talmud, that Christ had in truth come, as Christians believe and preach. To this he was not able to reply. And defeated by irrefutable proofs and authorities, he conceded that Christ, or Messiah, was born 1,000 years ago in Bethlehem and later appeared to some people in Rome. And when he was asked where that Messiah is, whom the Jews declared to have been born and to have appeared at Rome, he said that he did not know. Afterwards, however, he said that he lived in the earthly Paradise with Elijah. But he said that though he had been born, nevertheless he had not yet come, because the Messiah is said to have come only when he assumes dominion over the Jews and frees them and the Jews follow him. Against this reply the authority of the Talmud was adduced, which says plainly that the Messiah will come to them even today, if they listen to his voice and do not harden their hearts, as it says in the Psalm: 'Today if you listen to his voice' [Psalms, 95: 7]. It was added, too, that for the Messiah to have been born among men is the same thing as for him to have come amongst men, and it cannot be otherwise understood. And to these things he was able to make no reply. Further, among the proofs put forward for the advent of the Messiah was adduced that one from Genesis: 'The sceptre shall not pass away from Judah' [Genesis, 49: 10]. Since, therefore, it is certain that in Judah there is neither sceptre nor leader, it is certain that the Messiah who was to be sent has come. To this he replied that the sceptre has not been taken away but is merely discontinued, as it also was in the time of the Babylonian Captivity. And it was proved to him that in Babylon they had the heads of the captivity with jurisdiction, but after the death of Christ they had neither leader nor prince nor the heads of captivity such as those attested by the prophet Daniel, nor prophet nor any kind of rule, as is manifestly plain today. By this, it is certain, that the Messiah has come to them. He, however, said that he would prove that they had the aforesaid heads after Christ, but he could show nothing about the aforesaid, and indeed admitted that they had not had the aforesaid heads for the last 850 years. Therefore it is plain that the Messiah has come, since authority cannot lie. Further, when the said Moses said that Jesus Christ ought not to be called Messiah, because the Messiah, as he said, should not die, as it is said in the psalm, 'he asked for life from you and you granted it to him' [Psalms, 21: 4], but he ought to live for ever, both he and those whom he will liberate, he was asked whether the chapter of Isaiah, 53, 'Lord, who would have believed . . .' (which according to the Hebrews, begins at the end of chapter 52, where it says, 'Behold my servant will understand . . .') speaks about the Messiah. He firmly asserted that it does not speak of the Messiah at all, but it was proved to him by many authorities from the Talmud, which speak of the passion of Christ and his death, which they prove from the said chapter, that the said chapter of Isaiah is understood of the Christ, and in it the death of Christ and his passion and burial and resurrection are plainly contained. He however, compelled at length by the authorities, admitted that it is understood and explained in reference to Christ. From this it is plain that the Messiah had to suffer and die. Further, since he was unwilling to admit the truth unless compelled by the authorities, when he could not explain the authorities, he said publicly that he did not believe in the authorities which were cited against him, though they were in ancient, authoritative books of the Jews, because, as he said, they were sermons, in which their teachers, for the sake of exhorting the people, often lied. For this reason, he dismissed both the teachers and the scriptures of the Jews. Further, he first denied all, or nearly all, the things which he had previously admitted and which had been proved to him, and then, having been refuted again through authorities and defeated, he was compelled to admit them again. Further, since he could not reply and had been defeated many times in public, and both Jews and Christians were treating him with scorn, he said obstinately in front of everyone that he would not reply at all, because the Jews had told him not to, and some Christians, namely Brother P. de Janua and some respectable citizens had sent to him to advise him not to reply at all. This lie was publicly refuted by the said Brother P. and the respectable citizens. From this it is plain that he was trying to escape from the Disputation by lies. Further, though he had promised in the presence of the lord King and many others that he would answer questions on his faith and law to a small gathering, when the lord King was away from the state he secretly fled away and departed. From this it is plain that he does not dare and is not able to defend his erroneous creed. We, James, by the grace of God king of Aragon, Majorica and Valencia, count of Barcelona and Urgello, and Don of Montispessulanum, truly confess and recognise that each and every one of the words and deeds in our presence and of many others were as is contained above in this present writing. In testimony of this we have caused our seal to be appended in perpetual commemoration.

PART III

THE PARIS AND TORTOSA DISPUTATIONS: TEXTS

9

The *Vikuaḥ* of R. Yeḥiel of Paris: A Paraphrase

From *Vikuaḥ Rabbenu Yeḥiel mi-Paris*, Grünbaum, 1873

(The 'stage-directions' are also paraphrases of incidental matter in the Hebrew account.)

YEḤIEL: What is your complaint?

DONIN: About Jesus our Messiah, who has been blasphemed in the Talmud for many hundreds of years.

YEḤIEL: The Talmud is more than 1,500 years old. *(Turning to the Queen)* Your Majesty, do not compel me to answer him. The Talmud is very ancient and no one has complained about it before. Your learned Jerome knew all Jewish knowledge, including the Talmud, and he would have said something if there had been anything wrong with it.[1] Why should we have to stand for our life against this sinner, who denied the authority of the Talmud and refused to believe in anything except the Torah of Moses without interpretation? But you all know that everything requires interpretation. It was for that reason that we excommunicated him, and from that time he has plotted against us. But we will die rather than give up the Talmud, which is the apple of our eye. Even if you should decide to burn the Talmud in France, it will continue to be studied in the rest of the world, for we Jews are dispersed throughout the world. Our bodies, but not our souls, are in your hands.

A COURTIER: No one is going to touch you.

YEḤIEL: But can you protect us from the mob?

QUEEN BLANCHE: *(angrily)* Do not talk like that! We fully intend to protect you and yours, and our anger will fall on anyone who harms you, for so the Pope has directed. Answer Donin and do not withhold.

YEḤIEL: I appeal to the Pope.

THE JUDGES: It is the Pope who has directed us to hold this inquiry.

YEḤIEL: In that case, I will answer, but if I make a mistake, I represent only myself.

DONIN: Do you believe in the four Orders of the Talmud?

YEḤIEL: I believe in all the laws contained in it, which were deduced by the Rabbis from Scripture. It is called Talmud ('teaching') because of the text 'you shall teach them to your sons' [Deut., 11: 9]. But the Talmud also contains Aggadah, that is, figurative, poetic passages to appeal to men's hearts. Among these are extraordinary things which are hard to believe for a sceptic or heretic or schismatic. But there is no need to answer you about these—you may believe or disbelieve them as you wish, for no practical decision depends on them. Yet I know the Sages wrote only truth. If these passages seem extraordinary, there are many similar passages in Scripture itself: such as the turning of Lot's wife into a pillar of salt, the speaking of Balaam's ass, and Elisha's reviving of the dead. Further, without the Talmud, we would not be able to understand passages in the Bible which appear to contradict each other: for example, one text says that God 'visits the sins of the fathers on the children' [Num., 14: 18], and another text says, 'Children shall not be put to death because of their fathers' [Deut., 24: 16].[2] One text says, 'The Lord descended on Mount Sinai' [Exod., 19: 20], and another text says, 'For from the heavens did I speak with you [Exod., 20: 22], implying that He did not descend.[3] One text says, 'No Ammonite or Moabite may enter the Lord's congregation' [Deut., 23: 4], and yet King David was descended from a Moabitess, Ruth.[4] There is no end to such difficulties, which the Talmud resolves. And if there is difference of opinion about the solution of a legal difficulty, the Talmud decides according to the opinion of the majority of Rabbis, for the Torah instructs us to follow the majority [Exod., 23: 2]. Moreover, where the Biblical law is brief and scattered as in the laws of the Sabbath, the Talmud gives full explanations, gathered into one tractate; otherwise, it would be impossible to understand the law. The Talmud has the authority to decide disputed matters, for the Torah says, 'According to the teaching which they shall teach you and the judgement which they shall pronounce, shall you act' [Deut., 17: 8]; showing that God has handed this authority to the Sages and tradition is a necessity as well as Scripture. The Sages also made enactments of their own, with the intention of guarding the precepts of the Torah and 'making a fence'[5] for them; and the Torah gives them the right to make such enactments too, in the text, 'You shall guard my charge' [Lev., 8: 35]. So anyone who does not study the Talmud cannot understand Scripture, like a man who has been given the inner keys of a house but not the outer keys, and so cannot enter.

DONIN: Swear that you will answer truthfully, and not put us off with falsehood or subtlety.

THE JUDGES: Swear.

YEḤIEL: The Torah requires an oath only in financial matters, not in spiritual matters. Anyway, who are you to demand an oath from me? This is an inquiry, not a trial. You are not my judges, or if you are, I am equally the judge of you.

QUEEN BLANCHE: I request you to swear.

YEḤIEL: I have never sworn an oath in my life, and will not begin to swear now. Moreover, if I swear an oath, it will be open to Donin to say that I have broken my oath whenever I say anything that he does not like, or which is contrary to the Christian faith. Further, the Torah says, 'Thou shalt not take the name of the Lord thy God in vain', that is, where there is no necessity. But I assure you that I will tell the truth, and if anything is too difficult for me to answer, there are others far wiser than I to answer it. For I am the least of them all, and it was not by my desire that I have come before these assembled ecclesiastics to take part in this affair.

QUEEN BLANCHE: Since the matter is so difficult for him, and he has never sworn an oath, let him alone.

DONIN: As an example of the stupidity of the Talmud I cite the following. The Talmud deduces from the text forbidding a man to 'give of his seed to Moloch' that someone who gives *all* his seed to Moloch is not liable, only someone who gives part of his seed to Moloch. Who can possibly believe this, that someone who sacrificed one of his children to Moloch is liable to punishment of death, but someone who piled on wickedness and sacrificed all his children to Moloch goes free?

(The Christian prelates laugh loudly, and the Queen expresses surprise.)

YEḤIEL: There will come a day when you will not laugh and you will repent that you laughed, if you can. Would it not have been better to have listened to my reply before laughing at holy teaching? *(Turning to the Queen)* Your Majesty, who is the greater sinner, he who murders one man, or he who murders two?

QUEEN BLANCHE: He who murders two. And the more people a man murders, the greater sinner he is.

YEḤIEL: You have spoken truth. The Torah prescribes four kinds of capital punishment, and anyone who is executed by one of these methods confesses his sins before his execution, and once he is executed, his sins are forgiven by God, as the Talmud explains, deriving its explanation from the case of Achan [Josh., 7: 25]. So if a man 'passes through' some of his seed to Moloch, he is tried and sentenced to execution, confesses his sins and receives absolution. But if someone 'passes through' all his seed to Moloch, his sin is too great for absolution, and God has not provided execution for him as a means of absolution. For God Himself, in Whose hands are all souls, will judge him as he deserves.

(This explanation pleases the Court.)

DONIN: The Talmud contains blasphemies against Jesus. For example, the Talmud says that Jesus is in hell, and his punishment is to be immersed in boiling excrement [b Gitt., 56b]. *(Turning to the Queen and speaking in French.)* This is in order to make us Christians stink.

YEḤIEL: For the last fifteen years, since you were separated from us, you have sought to ensnare us, but you will not succeed. This Jesus, mentioned here by the Talmud, is another Jesus, not the one whom Christians worship. This was a certain Jesus who mocked the words of the Sages, and believed only in the written Scripture, like you. You can tell this, because he is not called 'Jesus of Nazareth', but simply 'Jesus'.

DONIN: Very well, I will now read out a passage [b Sanh., 43a] which does say 'Jesus of Nazareth'. Churchmen, give your attention to this, and see how this people, which lives amongst you, despises your deity. The Talmud says, 'When Jesus went forth to be stoned, a herald went out before him for forty days, crying, "Jesus the Nazarene goes forth to be stoned because he practised sorcery and enticed to idolatry, and perverted others of Israel. Anyone who knows anything in his favour, let him come and speak in his favour." '

YEḤIEL: *(Answer unknown.)*[6]

DONIN: Here is another passage in which both Jesus and Mary are blasphemed [b Sanh., 67a]. The passage says that someone called

Ben Stada, otherwise known as Ben Pandira, was hanged in Lydda on the eve of Passover. His mother's name was Miriam, 'the hairdresser'; her husband's name was Pappos ben Judah, and her lover's name was Pandira. So Mary is called an adulteress by the Talmud.

(The judges cry out in anger at this.)

YEḤIEL: Do not be angry until you have heard my reply. Mary was our flesh and bone, and we have nothing to say against her, for the Talmud does not even mention her. The 'Miriam' mentioned in the passage quoted by Donin cannot be the same person as Mary, for the locality mentioned is Lydda, not Jerusalem, where Jesus' death took place, and where his Sepulchre is still to be seen. Moreover, Jesus is not even mentioned by name in this passage, but 'Ben Stada' or 'Ben Pandira'. Also, Mary's husband was called Joseph, and this Miriam's husband was called Pappos ben Judah. Also, Mary the Hairdresser is mentioned elsewhere in the Talmud as living in the days of Rav Pappa and Abaye, who lived 700 years after Jesus.

DONIN: There is another blasphemous passage in the Talmud about Jesus. This tells [b Sanh., 107] that Jesus was a pupil of Rabbi Joshua ben Perachia, who fled to Alexandria, accompanied by Jesus, to escape the persecution of King Jannai. Later, on his return from Alexandria, he stayed with Jesus at an inn. Here Jesus offended his teacher by paying too much attention to the inn-keeper's wife. Jesus wished to be forgiven, but Rabbi Joshua was too slow to forgive him, and Jesus in despair went away and put up a brick and worshipped it. The moral given is that a teacher should not be too hard on his pupils.

YEḤIEL: It is easy to see that this Jesus cannot be the same Jesus that Christians worship. For Joshua ben Perachia lived more than 200 years before the Jesus of Christianity, who in my opinion is not mentioned anywhere in the Talmud. Wherever Jesus is mentioned in the Talmud, it is the Jesus who was the pupil of Joshua ben Perachia who is meant. It is quite possible that the Christian deity was also called Jesus, and there were thus two Jesuses, and possibly even two Jesuses from the same town, Nazareth.

(The priests cry out in disbelief)

YEḤIEL: Not every Louis born in France is the King of France. Is it so uncommon that two men should be born in one city, both with the same name, and they should both die the same death?

QUEEN BLANCHE: Tell me the truth on your faith, was there really another Jesus?

YEḤIEL: May I live and return to my house, the Talmud was not referring to the Christian Jesus when it spoke of one who is punished in hell in boiling excrement.

DONIN: I will now cite another example of the blasphemies of the Talmud, this time against God Himself. The Talmud tells the story [b BB, 73b] that Rabbah bar bar Ḥanah once heard a divine voice saying, 'Woe is me that I have made an oath, and who will release me from my oath?' When Rabbah bar bar Ḥanah told this to the Rabbis, they reproved him severely, saying, 'Why did you not say to God, "You are released from your vow"?' Does God mourn over his vows, and can a human being release Him from a vow? Is it not stupid to think that even a human being can be released from a vow by another human being? But the Jews release themselves of their vows every Day of Atonement by their Kol Nidrei prayer. Moreover, three Jews can release another Jew from vows which he may have made to non-Jews; so you can never trust the word of a Jew.

YEḤIEL: Why should there be any difficulty about the Lord repenting of his vow? Is there not full Scriptural authority for the fact that God sometimes repents? Scripture says, 'The Lord repented of the evil He had intended to do to his people' [Exod., 32: 14]. It is clear too that God sometimes makes an oath, for he swore not to repeat the Flood [see Isa., 54: 9]. As for the story that the Sages told Rabbah bar bar Ḥanah that he should have absolved God of his vow, this is not intended literally, but only means that God's vows may be reversed by human beings who devote themselves to repentance and good deeds. As for your remarks about the absolution of vows obtained by the Kol Nidrei prayer, if you only look at the continuation of the prayer you will see that this absolution applies only to unwitting breaches of vows or oaths, not to deliberate breaches. As for your criticism of the law by which three people can absolve a man from his vow, this applies to a vow which affects himself only, not to a vow which affects his neighbour; for the revocation of such a vow requires the consent of the person concerned, as we see in the case of the Gibeonites [Josh., 9], where the vow could not be revoked without the consent of the Gibeonites, even though they had brought about the vow through deception. For Scripture tells us to keep our vows: 'What goes forth from your lips you must keep, and you must perform any vow you have made' [Deut., 23: 24].

DONIN: The Talmud wickedly permits Jews to spill the blood of Gentiles, saying, 'The best Gentile may be killed' [b Sof., 15].

YEḤIEL: You have missed out a very important phrase. The full saying is found in the Tractate Soferim and it reads: 'The best Gentile may be killed in time of war.' The proof is taken from the case of Egyptian attack on the Israelites just before the crossing of the Red Sea. Pharaoh's troops were supplied with horses for this attack by those Egyptians who had previously shown sympathy with the Israelites; which shows that in wartime all members of a hostile nation must be treated as enemies. This is a matter of mere self-defence, for in self-defence it is permitted to kill even a fellow-Jew. Even in wartime, Scripture requires us to seek peace, saying, 'When thou comest nigh to a city to fight against it, you must proclaim peace unto it' [Deut., 20: 10], and this applied even in the case of the Canaanites, whom we were ordered by God to destroy. But when it is not wartime but peacetime, and the nation among whom we live protect us and preserve us, we regard it as wicked to harm either their persons or their property, even as much as a hair of their heads. Has not God warned us and all other nations not to shed blood, by saying in His Ten Commandments, 'Thou shalt not kill'? It is a general principle that whenever the Talmud uses the word 'Gentile', it is referring to the Canaanites; but we are forbidden to deal dishonestly even with them. Moreover, we must treat them kindly, when we have the upper hand over them, for the Talmud instructs us to feed the poor of the Gentiles, along with our own poor, to visit their sick and bury their dead, and not to prevent them from collecting the Forgotten Sheaf and the produce of the Corner of the Field. Moreover, the Talmud instructs us to greet Gentiles politely, and even says that Rabbi Johanan used to rise up in honour of their aged.

THE JUDGES: Tell us, on your faith, can we Christians be saved, according to your religion?

YEḤIEL: You may be saved if you keep the Seven Laws of the Sons of Noah, which were given to all mankind.[7]

THE JUDGES: We have the Ten Commandments.

YEḤIEL: They are excellent and sufficient for you. But this man, Donin, has entered our Covenant and is obliged to keep the 613

Commandments. There is one hell for sinners, whether Jews or Gentiles,[8] as Scripture says [Mal., 3: 19], 'And there will be release for the righteous, who will tread on the ashes of the wicked,' as the same passage says. And the Talmud says that there is both Hell and Purgatory [b RH, 16b].

As for your complaint about our prayer in the Eighteen Blessings which calls for punishment on the 'kingdom of wickedness', saying that this refers to you, this is not the case. The 'kingdom of wickedness' refers to those kingdoms who have persecuted us, such as Egypt, Assyria and Babylon, who massacred, butchered and exiled Israel, and burnt our homes and our Temple. These deserve the name of 'wicked kingdoms'. But as for this kingdom, and the Pope who has given strict orders for our protection and preservation, it is incredible that we should return evil for good. And even if some individuals have harmed us, that does not mean that we are angry at the whole nation. It would not occur to us to do this; on the contrary, it was about such a nation as this that the Talmud has instructed us, 'Pray for the peace of the kingdom.'

DONIN: The Talmud says that God can sin, since He ordered a sin-offering to be given on His behalf for His sin in diminishing the status of the moon in relation to the sun. In this same story, too, a conversation takes place between God and the moon. How can the moon talk without a mouth?

YEḤIEL: The Bible often attributes speech to the heavenly bodies. Also scientists agree that the heavenly bodies are living creatures. God punished the moon for speaking maliciously against the sun, but having punished her, He sought to placate her in order to give her encouragement to repent, and that is why He ordered an offering of appeasement (not a sin-offering) to be made.

DONIN: The Talmud contains many passages directed against Gentiles, saying (a) a Gentile may be left to die, though not actually killed; (b) a Jew who kills a Gentile is not liable to the death penalty, whereas a Gentile who kills a Jew is liable; (c) it is permitted to steal the money of a Gentile;[9] (d) a Jew must not drink wine touched by a Gentile; (e) one may mock Gentile religion; (f) Gentiles are presumed to be habituated to adultery, bestiality and homosexuality; (g) it is forbidden to help a Gentile woman to give birth or to suckle her child; (h) it is forbidden to praise the beauty of a Gentile.

YEḤIEL: These Gentiles mentioned in the Talmud are not Christians. For proof, you may see that we Jews do much business with

Christians, and the Talmud forbids this with Gentiles. Jews have undergone martyrdom countless times for their religion and would not disobey the Talmud if they really thought the people called 'Gentiles' in the Talmud included Christians. Jews have much social intercourse with Christians, and this is forbidden by the Talmud with 'Gentiles', by whom is meant the ancient Egyptians and Canaanites, who were steeped in immorality of every kind. Jews teach Hebrew to Christians, which is forbidden to 'Gentiles'.

DONIN: Why have so many Jews been massacred in Brittany, Anjou and Poitou, if they are God's chosen people? Why doesn't God protect them with miracles?

YEḤIEL: God will perform miracles in Messianic times, just as he performed miracles to save us from Egypt.

DONIN: The Talmud says [b Shabb., 146a] that Gentiles suffer from the impurity which was injected into Eve by the serpent when he cohabited with her; but this impurity was removed from Israel when they stood before Mount Sinai and accepted the Law.

YEḤIEL: This applies to nations like the Egyptians and Canaanites who did not accept the Bible, not to Christians who do.

DONIN: Jews include in their prayer called the Eighteen Benedictions a prayer for the destruction of heretics and slanderers, and this refers to the Christians, as explained by the Jewish exegete Rashi.

YEḤIEL: The prayer refers to apostates from Judaism and to Karaites, not to Christians. As for Rashi's explanation, this is not authoritative, as Rashi is often wrong.

DONIN: The Talmud says that God, after the destruction of the Temple, has only four square cubits of the Law in the world belonging to him. Also, that God weeps for the Temple three times every night. Also, the Talmud contains ridiculous stories about the gigantic stature of Og, king of Bashan, and gigantic animals and birds; and about the Messianic feast, and about people who cheated death, and about Adam having intercourse with all the animals, and about Abraham giving three tongues with mustard to the angels, and about God wearing phylacteries. Also, the Talmud says that the Rabbis have the power to annul laws of the Torah.

YEḤIEL: The Bible testifies that God made His presence dwell 'between the cherubim' in the Temple and in the Temple itself. Now that the Temple has been destroyed, the presence of God can dwell on earth only in the four cubits that surround a man when he studies God's Law. As for God's weeping three times in the night, this too has Scriptural authority [Jer., 25: 30]. The power of the Sages to annul a Scriptural law is only in a case of emergency and temporarily, and this too has Scriptural sanction, as is seen in the case of Elijah, who built an altar outside Jerusalem, in contravention of Biblical law, at a time of emergency. The stories about Og are mere hyperboles and we find similar hyperboles in Scripture: for example, 'The cities are great and fortified up to Heaven' [Deut., 1: 28]. As for the Messianic feast, when Leviathan will be eaten, there are several Scriptural evidences for this. There is Scriptural evidence too that some people evade death: for example, Elijah. As for the Talmudic saying that Adam had intercourse with all the animals, this is deduced from the text which says that God brought all the animals before Adam, but he (Adam) found none suitable to be his mate [Gen., 2: 20]; and at this time there was no prohibition against intercourse with animals. As for other remarks about Adam (that he begat demons by Lilith, and that his height was from earth to Heaven) these too can be defended from the evidence of Scripture. A text says that after living 130 years, he begat 'in his form and image', from which it may be deduced that previously he begat creatures who differed from him in form and image, namely, demons, and as this could not have been from Eve, it must have been from Lilith. And what other explanation is there for the existence of bodily demons, such as are commonly found in this area, and are called by the name 'lutin' or 'fiache'? Another text says that Adam was created 'only a little lower than the angels', so his stature may well have been from earth to Heaven. That angels should eat food is not surprising, since they even once had intercourse with mortal women [Gen., 6: 2].

10

The Christian Account of the Paris Disputation

Prefatory Note

The Latin Original of this account may be found in 'La con troverse de 1240 sur le Talmud' by Isadore Loeb, *Revue des études juives,* vols. I, II, III. The original manuscript (Bibliothèque Nationale, no. 16, 558, fo. 231) is entitled *Extractiones de Talmut* ('Extracts from the Talmud'). It was composed shortly after the burning of the Talmud in 1242, in order to explain to theologians the dangerous contents of the Talmud which had made the burning necessary. The main body of the work was compiled by the convert Thibaut de Sezanne, with the help of two other converts, and consists of a large collection of excerpts from the Talmud. The appendix is the part, however, that mainly concerns us. It consists of thirty-five charges against the Talmud, followed by the 'confessions' of Rabbi Yeḥiel and Rabbi Judah at the trial. This appendix was the work of Nicholas Donin and his associates. The thirty-five charges formed the basis of the accusations made by the Pope in his letters to prominent leaders in 1239, and they also formed the basis of the trial itself.

The 'confessions' are very brief, but give valuable confirmation of the Hebrew account of the trial in several particulars, and throw light on some doubtful matters. The word 'confession' is, of course, misleading, since even the admission that the citations from the Talmud were accurate verbally was labelled a 'confession', irrespective of whether the Jewish disputant disagreed with the Christian view of the scope and meaning of the extract. Judah Rosenthal in his summing-up of his articles 'The Talmud on Trial' (*Jewish Quarterly Review,* vol. 47) says wrongly, 'In general, the

Rabbis admitted the following three main charges: errors, blasphemies in Deum and the *stultitiae*. They denied the charges of: *blasphemiae in Christum* and *blasphemiae contra Christianos.*' In fact, the rabbis did not admit any of the charges, except in the trivial sense that they agreed that the quotations put before them were verbally correct. They disputed the interpretations put upon the extracts. In some cases they said that the passage in question required a symbolic interpretation or was hyperbolic; but this was not any kind of admission, merely a request to read the passages in accordance with their context and genre, not in a literalist way inappropriate to poetical or rhetorical matter.

The Christian account does not allow any sincerity to the replies of the rabbis, frequently adding such comments as 'in saying this, he lied'. Nevertheless, it is a valuable corrective to some of the shortcomings of the Hebrew account, for example, the highly confused version given there of Rabbi Yeḥiel's views on the identity of the Jesus mentioned in the Talmud.

The Text

. . . these are the articles for which Pope Gregory ordered the books which had this content to be burned.

Finally, as a warning for the future and information about the past, I wish you to know the following. For some time the burning of the books of the Talmud containing the extraordinary things outlined above, and others similar to them, was urged upon our most Christian king Louis. Finally, he granted us our request by appointing a group to hear the matter; namely, the Archbishop of Sens, the Bishop of Senlis, and the Chancellor of Paris, now Bishop of Tuscany and papal legate in the Holy Land. So on the day appointed by us, they summoned the teachers of the Jews who were regarded among themselves as experts, and undertook to inquire about the truth of the matters put before them. The first to be brought in was Vino [Vivo] Meldensis,[1] the most expert in their eyes, and a very famous person throughout Jewry. I do not think it superfluous to insert here the depositions of these men.

The Confession of Master Vivo

(1) The said Master Vivo refused entirely to swear an oath.
(2) He said that the book Talmud never lied.

(3) He said that Jesus Noẓri was Jesus the Nazarene, son of Miriam. He was hanged on the eve of Passover. He admitted [that it is said] about him that he was born of adultery and that he is punished in hell in boiling excrement and that he lived in the time of Titus. He says however that this was a different man from our Jesus (but he could not say who else he was, whence it is sufficiently clear that he was lying).

(4) He said further that in the schools they study the Talmud more earnestly than the Bible, and that no one can be called Master unless he knows the Talmud, even if he knows the Bible by heart.

(5) He said further that the Masters had the authority to revoke the command of God about blowing the horn on the first day of the seventh month, and (6) about carrying palms on the fifteenth day;[2] and they might revoke this if it happened to be a Sabbath, lest the horn or palm-branch should be carried on that day through the streets.[3]

(7) He said further that it is written in the Talmud that Gentiles who did not stand on Mount Sinai and did not receive the Law are polluted by the impurity which the serpent injected into Eve when it had coitus with her, and (8) that the Talmud says about Gentiles that animals should not be put into their charge because they are more sexually attracted by the animals of Israel than by their own wives; (9) but Master Vivo says that this is not meant of Christians (believe him who will, he lied).

(10) He also admitted that [it is said that] Adam had coitus with all the animals, and in Paradise too.

(11) He said further that it is in the Talmud that Adam, after he had sinned, 130 years before he begat Seth, begat demons in bodily shape through his semen, which was seized and carried by the wind.

(12) He said further that the whole Talmud, so far as it concerns commandments and judgements and arguments and explanations, was given to Moses on Mount Sinai, not in writing but orally to be learnt by heart.

(13) He also admitted that it is in the Talmud that God said, 'Woe is me that I have sworn, and now that I have sworn, who will absolve me?' And the Masters said that Raba was an ass because he did not reply to the voice of God that spoke thus, 'You are absolved, you are absolved.'

(14) He said further that it is in the Talmud that God curses himself three times every night because he allowed the Temple to be destroyed and gave up the Jews to servitude.

(15) He said further that it is in the Talmud that Elijah the prophet frequented the schools of the Rabbis.

(16) He said further that no Jew would ever feel the pain of the fire of hell and none of them would be punished in any other way in the other world longer than twelve months.

(17) He said further that it is in the Talmud that both the bodies and the souls of the wicked will be reduced to dust, and they will have no other punishment after this, except those who have so rebelled against God that they wished to be gods, and they will be punished eternally; hell will cease, but their hell will never cease.

(18) He said further that three ordinary individuals or one Master who has been in the Promised Land can absolve someone from a vow or oath rashly made, if he regrets it and the matter does not affect anyone else, and even if it was made deliberately; and (19) even if it does affect someone else, provided that person is present, and (20) as an example of this, the case of Zedekiah and Nebuchadnezzar is cited, and (21) also the case of Moses who was told by God Himself to go to Jethro and became absolved of his vow to live with him.[4]

(22) He said further that it is written in the Talmud that anyone who states at the beginning of the year that his oaths and vows in that year are invalid is not bound by them, if he remembers the said statement at the time he makes the vow or oath or promise. But he said that this means vows or oaths or promises made to himself, not to another.

(23) He said further that it is in the Talmud that God exerts himself to teach children every day, and that he sits and plays with Leviathan.[5]

(24) He said further that God asks himself, 'May it be My will that My mercy may overcome My wrath.'[6]

The Confession of Master Judas[7]

(1) Master Judas confessed that it is written in the Talmud that the son called Chatada was the son of Mary and was hanged on the eve of Passover on the eve of Sabbath, because he incited the people and practised sorcery, and the commentary of Salomon Trecensis[8] [Rashi] teaches that he was Jesus Noẓri [the Nazarene], and the commentator Jacob[9] says the same.

(2) He said further that it is in the Talmud that Jesus is punished in boiling excrement in hell, because he mocked the words of the wise, but this does not refer to our Jesus (he lied), but nevertheless

the Jesus referred to was a Jew who lived about the time of Titus or before.[10]

(3) He said further that it is in the Talmud that Rabbi Nathan found Elijah the prophet after the dispute between Rabbi Eliezer and the others, and Elijah told him that God laughed at the time of that dispute, because they refused to believe the voice from Heaven, and God said, 'My children have defeated me, my children have defeated me.'[11]

(4) He said further that there are two Laws and one of them cannot exist without the words of the sages, and that is the Talmud, which contains in it the assertion that the words of the sages deserve to be heeded more than the Written Law, and the penalty for transgressing their words is greater. For it is written in the Law 'to do and not to do' [positive and negative commandments] and there is no death penalty attached to these; but anyone who transgresses the words of the sages merits death.[12]

(6) He further confessed that it is written in the Talmud that they should not send their children to study the Bible, and Salomon Trecensis comments, 'Because to study the Bible draws them to another faith'.[13] And he says that the reason is that there are many difficulties and obscurities which cannot be understood except through the Talmud.

11

A Hebrew Account of the Tortosa Disputation

Translated from Solomon ibn Verga's *Shevet Yehuda*

A copy of the report sent by the great scholar Bonastruk Demaistre to the holy congregation of Gerona in the year 5173, when the leaders of Israel stood in trouble and distress before the Pope at the request of Joshua Halorki, who, after his apostasy, was called among the Gentiles Maestre Geronimo de Santa Fe (the mnemonic for which is 'blasphemer'[1]); for he asked the Pope that the scholars of Israel should come before him, and he would prove to them that the Messiah has come, and is Jesus, and he would prove this from their own Talmud.

And this is the content of the report.

Chiefs of the children of Israel, nobles of Judah, men of 'place and name' [Isa., 56: 5] in your dwelling-places, where you 'rehearse the righteous acts of the Lord' [Judg., 5: 11]; 'there are set thrones' [Ps., 122: 5] for 'Torah and testimony' [Isa., 8: 20], the throne of the Talmud; there you have dwelt from the days of old, may your heart live for ever! What you have known of old may you know now also, that our Saviour 'does not slumber or sleep' [Isa., 5: 27], to save us from those who seek our harm. A shoot that went forth from us and thought to destroy us, and bring low down to the earth our religion of truth—is it not Joshua Halorki? He made plans to pervert us, to show that he was a true Christian and faithful to his new religion, and he asked the Pope to command the leading Jewish scholars to come before him for he wished to prove from their own Talmud that the Messiah had come; and he said to the Pope that when he proved this, it would be fitting to force them to adopt the Christian religion, when he showed true proofs before his high Holiness.

I come now to let you know all that happened, and from it you may know in detail how to reply to a sceptic, and you may know with certainty that we have passed through a measureless danger, for we were before many bishops and lords, and those who sought our condemnation were many.

The representatives of the congregations reached here on the first of January, and in particular, the representatives of the congregations of Aragon, whose attendance was particularly requested by Halorki. From the city of Saragossa came R. Zeraḥia Halevi, and the nobleman Don Vidal ben Benvenista and R. Matithiah Ha-yitshari. From Calatayud—the prince Don Samuel Halevi, and Rabbi Moses ibn Musa. From the city of Huesca—Don Todros Al-constantin. From Alcaniz—Don Joseph ibn Ardot and Don Meir Haligoa. From Doroca—Don Astruk Halevi. From Monreal—Rabbi Joseph Albo. From Monson—Don Joseph Halevi and R. Yom Tov Karkosa. From Montalban—Abu Janda. From Vilesit—Don Joseph Albalag and the scholar Bonjoa and R. Todros ibn Jehia from Gerona, who was a very formidable man.[2]

All the delegates were assembled, and agreed between them who would be the principal speaker before the Pope, and who would be the opening speaker, or 'Arenga', in their language, and they all agreed that the opener should be Don Vidal ben Benvenista, since he was wise in the sciences, and well acquainted with the Latin language; and they agreed that their procedure would not be in the style of the Jews taught in their academies, to interrupt each other and to abuse each other in disagreements, so that they would not be humiliated before the Pope, but that they would behave towards Joshua Halorki, and also towards the bishops, with calmness and moderation, and none of them would lose his temper, even if they should abuse him, and each of them would gently encourage his fellow not to lapse.

Then all we delegates went before the Pope, with the help of God, who 'saves the poor man from one stronger than himself' [Ps., 35: 10]; and the lord Pope received us with a welcoming countenance, and sought to know from us the cities where we dwelt; and he asked the name of each one of us, and commanded that they should be written down. But from this a great fear fell upon us, and we asked the scribe the reason for this procedure, and he told us that there was no harm in it, for it is the usual custom of popes and kings to record their chronicles in their books in every detail.

After that, the Pope said to us, 'Worthies of the people of the

Jews, who were chosen by Him who chose them in days of old, even though they were rejected for their sins! Do not be afraid of the Disputation, for you will not receive any oppression or maltreatment in my presence. Let your thoughts be at rest, and speak with a firm heart. Do not fear and do not tremble. Maestre Geronimo said that he wished to prove that the Messiah had come, and this from your own Talmud. It will be seen in our presence whether the truth is in his mouth, or he has dreamed a dream; but as for you, do not be afraid of him, for in matters of disputation there is equality. And now go and rest in your lodgings, and tomorrow morning come to me.'

And immediately he gave orders that they should give us suitable lodgings, and that they should give us food from his stores or from what we could eat in accordance with our religion. And some of us were happy at the words of the Pope, and some of us were unhappy, as is the character of the Jew.

On Monday, we came before the Pope and found all the great court draped with embroidered cloths, and that was the place for the Disputation. And there were seventy thrones there for the prelates who are called 'cardinals', and 'bishops' and 'archbishops', all of them dressed in golden garments; and all the dignitaries of Rome were there, and some of the burghers and noblemen, nearly 1,000 men, and so it was all the days of the Disputation. And our heart melted and became water; nevertheless, we made the blessing, 'Blessed is he who has apportioned some of his glory to flesh and blood.'

After this, the Pope began, saying, 'You, scholars of the Jews, should know that I have not come here, and I have not sent for you, in order to prove which of our two religions is true; for it is a known thing with me that my religion and faith is true, and that your Torah was once true but was abolished. You have come only because Geronimo has said that he will prove from the Talmud of your Rabbis, who knew more than you do, that the Messiah has come; therefore, you must speak before me on this topic alone.'

After this, the Pope turned his face towards Maestre Geronimo, and said, 'You must begin your proof, and they will answer.'

Maestre Geronimo began: ' "Come now and let us reason together, saith the Lord . . . but if you refuse and rebel, ye shall be devoured with the sword" ' [Isa., 1: 18, 20].

After this, Don Vidal ben Benvenista, the Arenga, opened in the Latin tongue, and the Pope was much pleased by his wisdom and command of language. And in the course of his speech, he complained about Geronimo that someone who comes to argue ought not to enter the debate in a spirit of enmity; for he had quoted, '. . . and if you refuse and rebel, ye shall be devoured with the sword'; before he had proved anything, he had adopted the role of judge and avenger.

The Pope replied, 'You are right; but do not be surprised at this bad behaviour, for he is one of you!'

The opening of Don Vidal was: ' "Behold, we have come unto thee" [Jer., 3: 22], for you are our lord.' And after him Don Samuel Halevi said, ' "Show us thy mercy, our lord, and grant us thy salvation" ' [Ps., 85: 7]. And finally, they implored the Pope to free them from this Disputation, because the Jews were not experienced in the methods of syllogism and logic, with which Geronimo, who was expert in them, had already begun; the Jewish topics of thought being all derived from tradition.

The Pope replied, 'If you have made this request from fear, I have already assured you, and "it has gone forth from my mouth and I shall not go back from it" [Isa., 45: 23]. But if it is because you are not acquainted with the methods of logic, whenever Geronimo enters into logic and syllogism, do not answer him a word, but when he speaks of proofs from tradition, answer him with tradition.'

After this, since considerable time had elapsed, the king [?] said that they should go to eat, and return the following morning. And so it was done. And the Pope gave orders that lords and other important people should escort us. And we said in our hearts, 'Would that our end may be like our beginning!' And on that day we went to the synagogue, where there was a great gathering, and with a voice of weeping and entreaty we prayed to the Rock of our salvation that he should turn our darkness into light, and that there should not go forth from our mouths a stumbling-block, before all those lions who stood against us. And then, before a numerous congregation, with a humble soul and a low spirit, and with 'a broken and contrite heart' [Ps., 51: 17], Rabbi Zeraḥiah Halevi began to preach, and the beginning of his sermon was, 'Like is cured by like, and opposite by opposite.'[3] And he gave a wonderful explanation of this, which cannot be understood except face to face,[4] and he concluded his sermon with prayer and entreaty.

On Tuesday, was the commencement of the Disputation, and Maestre Geronimo opened thus: 'In your Talmud it is written, "The world will be six thousand, two thousand of chaos, two thousand of Torah, and two thousand, the days of the Messiah"

[Sanh., 97a]. It is clear from this saying that the Messiah comes in the last 2,000; who is he but our Saviour?' And Halorki preached on this at length, according to his desire, until the Pope said to him, 'Geronimo, I have known for some time that you are a great preacher, but we have come here only for the proof which you promised, so be careful not to digress into sermons.' And he turned his face to the delegates and said, 'Give your answer about this saying.'

Don Vidal ben Benvenista said, 'Our lord the Pope, let us know the characteristics of the Messiah, and then it may become clear whether he has come; for if there should be found in someone who has come the characteristics of the Messiah, we too will acknowledge him.'

Said the Pope, 'This is not an answer to what you have been asked, for the inquiry was not about the characteristics of the Messiah, but whether the Talmudic saying asserts that he has come. You are already acting as Jews do in arguments, for when they are asked about one thing, they shift to another.'

Don Vidal replied, 'In this beginning of ours we were acting in the manner of the wise, for it is fitting to speak first about the essence of a matter, and afterwards about its accidental properties. And so the Physicist[5] has written. But if this method does not appeal to our lord, we shall not proceed in it. I reply about the Talmudic saying itself, and I say that Geronimo the scholar has taken from the saying what is of use to him and what gives him some help, and he has left out the part that is against him. The end of the saying goes as follows: "And because of the increase of our sins, all these years have been lost." This shows clearly that he has not come.'

Geronimo replied, 'It seems that you have not understood the saying, or perhaps you pretend that you do not understand. The words "and two thousand, the days of the Messiah" is a saying of the prophet Elijah, who said it to his pupils, who said it in his name, as is shown by the expression, "The Tanna of the House of Elijah teaches". This is well known to Talmudists. But it was the Talmudists, or the men of the Talmud who fixed the saying in their books, who added, "And because of the increase of our sins", this being in accordance with their opinion that Jesus was not the Messiah. Elijah, however, in accordance with his status as a prophet and one who knew the truth, said, "two thousand, the days of the Messiah", according to what was known to him by the gift of prophecy.'[6]

Rabbi Zeraḥiah Halevi now replied, 'Our lord Pope! If someone comes to prove a thesis, how can he prove it in a matter which can bear various interpretations? And how can he call it a confirmed proof? Geronimo says that the end of the passage was composed by the Talmudists, and he has made this explanation in order to support his opinion, but an opponent could say that both the end of the passage and its beginning were said by Elijah, urging this in order to support his side of the argument; and if neither side has a proof or confirmation for his explanation, at the least the matter should remain dubious; so how can Geronimo prove thence what he seeks to prove? For he who differs from him will say, "If you have come to prove your case thence with your explanation, I will form another explanation to prevent you from proving it." And when you say to me, "But whence is your proof?" I will reply, "And whence is *your* proof?" Moreover, since he comes against us with our Talmud—he must know that it is the way of our Talmud that when an explanation is not compelling because of a difficulty made against it, and the expression "perhaps" is used, and no reply is made, the matter remains refuted until the offerer of the explanation goes and seeks another supporting argument. Moreover, it is more fitting that we should say that a single passage was said by one man than that it was said by two; for in such a case, the Talmud usually says, "Said Rav Ashi . . ." or "Said so-and-so". Because of the increase of our sins, all these years have been lost." Moreover, we said, for this very reason, in our opening speech before our lord, that we should examine anyone who has come, to see whether he possesses the characteristics of the Messiah or not, and if we found in that man the characteristics of the Messiah—then we would change the Talmudic saying to the explanation of Geronimo; and if we did not find in him the characteristics of the Messiah—then *our* explanation will be proved true.'

Said the Pope, 'There can be no doubt that you are right in saying that anyone who comes to prove a matter ought to cite a passage that commands agreement and compels assent and cannot bear another interpretation.'

Geronimo replied, 'Our lord Pope, my argument does not depend on this passage alone, for I have many other passages.'

Returned the Pope, 'This man has already lost the character of a Christian disputant and returned to being a Jewish disputant, running away to another side, when the first side has proved weak. It is fitting that you should answer the words of the Jews about this passage.'

Geronimo replied, 'Did not Elijah come many ages before the Jews were exiled? We are compelled to say, therefore, that some other man said the words, "And because of the increase of our sins"—someone who existed in the Exile. And even if we say that it was the pupils of Elijah who said it—were not his pupils close to him in time? But it must be that the Talmudists made this comment, in accordance with their opinion, as I said.'

Don Vidal then replied, 'Our lord Pope, even allowing that the Talmudists made the comment—let us come to what Elijah said. His words are, "and two thousand, the days of the Messiah". If the Messiah has come, he should have said, "and at the end of the four thousand, the Messiah will come," or "and at its beginning the Messiah will come", that is, at the beginning of the fifth thousand, or "at such-and-such a time, the Messiah will come". As it is, the possibility is left open that he will come at the end of the "two thousand".'

Geronimo replied, 'It is because he wanted to say that the whole period of two thousand would be the Messianic Age, and after that, at the seventh thousand, the world would be destroyed.'

Said Rabbi Joseph Albo, 'This too has been answered by what has already been said, and our lord Pope agreed to it; and that is, that another explanation has been made, and there is no compelling force in *your* explanation. Moreover, the Talmudists, through whom you have brought your proof to us, themselves fixed that passage in the Talmud, and they were not in the habit of fixing something that was against their opinion; and they said that there were two limits for the Messiah: either the time sworn by God, or the time when Israel were in a state of readiness and repentance; and therefore, the passage does not set a definite time for the days of the Messiah, but it says, "and two thousand, the days of the Messiah", that is to say, these years are set aside for the coming of the Messiah; and if the Jews are fit, he will come at the beginning of the period, and if they are not fit at the beginning but are fit in the middle, the Messiah will come in the middle of the period; and if they are not fit in the middle but are fit at the end, the Messiah will come at the end; but his coming will not be delayed longer than those 2,000 years.'

Said the Pope, 'And why will you not say that if the *Christians* are fit, he will come immediately, and if not—he will delay until the end of the 2,000 years?'

Said the delegates, 'One does not say that a Redeemer will come except for those who dwell in exile. For those who dwell in security—what need have they of a Redeemer? But the Messiah is needed for a people who dwell in exile and subjection.'

Said Geronimo, 'And why will you not agree with my explanation?'

The delegates replied, 'And why will you not agree with our explanation? We have already said that there is no proof from something that does not compel agreement; and the lord Pope has agreed in this, and will not retract his view; and you know the status and importance of our teacher Solomon Yitsḥaki—and his explanation is like ours.'

Said Geronimo, 'I stand by my position and my religion, that the Messiah has come. You who say that he has not come—the onus of proof is on you.'

Said the delegates, 'Let the prelates, who understand the truth, say on whom is the onus of proof. For, on the contrary, I came first, by many ages, when I accepted the Torah of Moses, and he who comes to detach me from my prior right, must accept the burden of proof.'

The prelates then replied, 'It is so, beyond doubt, as you say. We are surprised at Geronimo, for he has spoken incorrectly, and not as he undertook originally to bring proof; and we have come here, at the command of the Pope, to uphold the truth.'

Said the delegates, 'Our lord has already shown us what we asked of him, "Show us thy mercy, Lord," and the rest of the verse, "and grant us thy salvation", applies to you prelates; not as Geronimo began, saying, "you will be devoured by the sword". Does he think that it is out of obstinacy that we have preserved our religion up to this day in the face of the victorious powers and kingdoms? Let the rule and the power and the glory be yours, as we have seen today, and from the day that we came, we have seen the completeness of your greatness and importance. We have upheld this Torah only because it was given to us in the presence of 600,000, and with strong signs, and with the revelation of the glory of God; and we considered that we had no right to detach ourselves from it unless He who gave it should come Himself and say, "Believe in such-and-such." But not just because Geronimo comes and says to us "Abandon it!" And perhaps his intention in this is to reach high rank like yourselves; and "He who trieth hearts" [Ps., 7: 9] knows what is in his heart.'

Geronimo replied, 'What is in my heart is what I have said, that the Messiah has come; and this passage is not the chief basis of my argument, but "they will help every one his neighbour" [Isa., 41: 6].

Said the Pope, 'I have already told you that this is not valid. As for what you have said—"they will help every one his neighbour"—woe to him who needs supports to keep him up, and has not the strength to stand up himself. For the vine, because of its weight, needs supports to keep it up, which is not necessary for the cedars of Lebanon, which, on the contrary, act as supports for others.'

After this, the Pope gave us leave to go, and we went joyfully to eat our food; for on that day Geronimo 'found no help' [Gen., 2: 20].

On Thursday, Geronimo began with a passage near to the first one. It goes: 'Elijah said to Rav Judah, "The world will be not less than eighty-five jubilees, and in the last jubilee, he will come." He said to him, "At the beginning or the end?" He said to him, "I do not know." '[8]

The scholar R. Matitihiah replied, 'This passage does not confirm at all that Jesus is the Messiah, for he did not come at that time, since it does not add up to the number of jubilees.'

Geronimo replied, 'I did not say in my opening speech that Jesus was the Messiah, but that the Messiah has come; and it does not matter whether this was ten years or ten days ago.'

Said the delegates, 'Let our lord see and judge! If it was not Jesus—in whom some sign of greatness and wisdom appeared—who can it be? Matteo the madman, or Marvaste the fool?'

Said the Pope, 'Why do you not understand Geronimo? He is one of you, and comes at you with cunning. If you say that the Messiah has come, as appears from the Talmudic passage, the Disputation is over. And if you say that it is possible that he has come, but it is not Jesus, then he will tell you the answer to your question: whether it is Matt or Pico.'

Said the delegates, 'Our lord, you have seen well; and we could not know what hatred and malice sought to do.'

After this, R. Matitihiah said to Geronimo, 'Sir scholar, before trying to prove from the Talmud that the Messiah has come, why do you not bring a proof for the opposite from the Talmud itself, which says, "Blasted be the breath of those who calculate the end!"' [b Sanh., 97b].

The Pope spoke up, 'I have heard this saying before, and was curious to know its meaning.'

Said R. Matitihiah, 'We have no interpretation but the plain meaning, that a curse is pronounced on him who makes reckonings and says when the Messiah will come. For this will result in great harm to the people, for when the predicted time arrives, and the

Messiah does not come, they will despair, and the hearts of those hoping for salvation, bound in the fetters and bonds of hope, will be weakened. Moreover, there is a transgression in this matter, for God has hidden it from all the peoples and from all the prophets, and yet this man attempts to reveal it by calculation.'

But at this, the Pope was strongly enraged, and said, 'O people of madmen! O the rejected ones! O foolish Talmudists! And was Daniel, who calculated the end, a fit person to have said about him, "Blasted be his breath"? It seems truly that you and they are sinners and rebels.'

Don Todros spoke, 'O our lord Pope, if the Talmudists are such fools in his eyes, why does he bring proofs from them to confirm that the Messiah has come? One does not bring proofs from madmen.'

At this the Pope was angrier still. Then Don Vidal spoke again, 'Our lord Pope! It is not in accordance with the custom of his Holiness that he should be angry in matters of disputation; and permission was given to this extent; unless we have transgressed in some other way and have stumbled in our words—and for such an occasion we said, "Show us, our lord, your mercy!" '

The Pope replied, 'Do not try to hoodwink me with words! What do you reply about that saying, "Blasted be the breath of those who calculate the end"?'

Said Don Vidal, 'The expression *meḥashev* in Hebrew means one who calculates and comes to a conclusion by reckoning; but a prophet, or one who speaks by the Holy Spirit, is not called *meḥashev* but *ro'eh*, for so the prophet has said: "Where is the house of the seer [*ro'eh*]" [I Sam., 9: 18], for he "saw" truth by the gift of prophecy.'

And on this, the Pope was appeased, and he said, 'If we come to speak the truth, this seems right to me, and this is the solution for an understanding mind.'

And we went out of there that day, and in the morning we returned; but in our lodgings a strong quarrel had taken place between us and R. Matithiah and R. Todros, for they had not kept or put a muzzle on their mouths. And when we came, we said to Geronimo, 'Our lord scholar, before you bring a proof from the Amoraim that the Messiah has come, why do you not bring a proof from the latest of them, and the chief of them, Rav Ashi,[9] who said, "Before that, do not expect him. Afterwards, you may await him." For it may be seen that at that time, the Messiah had not come.'

Geronimo replied, 'I have already said to you that one should not bring a proof from someone who did not believe that the Messiah had come. For he [Rav Ashi] spoke according to his opinion and faith; but the first saying was said by Elijah the prophet, and he, as a prophet, knew the truth.'

Then the delegates rose up and said to him, 'Our lord, tell us, was Rav Ashi a clever man or a fool? Was he a wicked man or a righteous man?'

Geronimo answered, 'There is no question that he was a great sage and saint, as appears from his sayings.'

Said they, 'How then did he contradict the words of the prophet Elijah? Therefore, we are constrained to say one of two things: either that Elijah was not Elijah the prophet and made a mistake in his opinion;[10] or that he was Elijah, and Rav Ashi understood the meaning of his saying when he explained it in the way he did; for if he had been in doubt in the matter he would have taken the narrower interpretation in the case of a prophetic utterance; and why should we seek to be wiser than Rav Ashi?'

Geronimo replied, 'Even if I should agree with you that this is the meaning of that saying, what will you say about the second saying about the number of the jubilees? For it has no explanation except the one which I gave.'

R. Joseph Albo jumped up and said, 'The meaning of this saying is that the world will not be *less* than this, but it could be more; for if one should say, "I will not give up this for less than twenty," there is nothing to prevent him from giving it for forty or fifty. So it is possible that the world will last very much longer; and in the last jubilee, the Messiah will come.'

Said the prelates, 'According to this, there is no definite time for the Messiah.'

R. Matithiah replied, 'This is not surprising to us; for even on your view, there is no definite time, for the passage says, "and two thousand, the Messiah".'[11]

And while these things were going on, we noticed that they were writing down all our words, and a strong fear fell into our hearts, for we thought that the intention was that the scribes would falsify our remarks, and later, the Pope would say, "You spoke thus!" And the result would be that we would be convicted by our words, and we would not be able to call the scribe a falsifier, since he was a scribe well known to the Pope. So we agreed to be guarded in our speech, and to keep silent as much as possible; but this proved impossible, for the Pope ordered us to reply in every matter to that man Geronimo; and if we did not reply, 'there was one law for us, to be put to death' [see Esther, 4: 11]. So we adopted the plan that only one of us would speak, and if his words pleased the Pope, well and good, but if not, we would say that his reply was not agreed by all of us, and that it was a mistake, and our opinion differed from his.

And for that day, the Disputation was at an end.

When we returned in the morning in fear and terror, Geronimo began by quoting a certain passage [Ekhah R., 1: 51] which goes, 'It happened with a certain man, etc.' until '. . . the Messiah has been born'. Said R. Judan, 'It is written in Scripture: "and Lebanon shall fall by a mighty one. And there shall come forth a rod out of the stem of Jesse" [Isa., 10: 34 and 11: 1].' Said Geronimo, 'See, it is clear from this passage something that you cannot contradict, that on the day of the Destruction of the Temple, the Messiah was born.'

The scholar ibn Astruk replied, 'This passage has already been discussed by the great ones of the world in the Disputation between the Master of Gerona [Naḥmanides] and Fray Paul. The beginning of that Disputation was that Fray Paul wanted to prove that the Jews ought to be called Canaanites, since they adopted the Canaanite way of life and lived in their land, while the Christians ought to be called "Israel", since they have entered the place of the Jews.'[12]

Said the Pope, 'And what did the Master reply to this?'

Said he, 'His answer was that he who enters the place of his brother ought to inherit his goods; and if the Christians have entered our place, why have they not inherited our true goods? They are: prophecy, and fire from Heaven, and the Urim and Thummim, and so on. Yet behold! we Jews, when we lost these things, have never found them in the hand of another; from which it can be seen that it is the intention of Him who gave them to keep them until He sees whether we will repent, and then He will return them to us as at first.'

Said the Pope, 'And before whom was that Disputation held?'

They said, 'Before the saintly King Don Pedro the elder.'[13]

He asked further, 'And what did Fray Paul reply to Maestre Moses?'

Said he, 'He was silent and did not answer.'

The Pope returned, 'That king was a saint, but not a sage. And Fray Paul's failure to reply was untypical of his wisdom; for he could have said that we Christians have no need of these things, after the coming of our Saviour, who promised the salvation of our souls, and entered the status of a man in order to rescue the souls of the fathers. But however these things may be, there is no answer in this to what is said in the quoted passage: that the Messiah has already been born.'

Said Don Vidal,[14] 'The Master explained that it does not mean that he was born literally; and even if it does mean that he was born literally, there is no contradiction in this, for he may have been born on that day and lives in the Garden of Eden. Rambam [Maimonides] has written that the Messiah was not born on the day of the Destruction, but the meaning is that from that day onwards a man is born in every generation who is fit to be the Messiah, if only Israel prove fit; and the intention of the speaker of this saying was to awake people's hearts to repentance, and to explain to them that the Messiah is not dependent on a fixed time, as was the Babylonian exile. And Don Hasdai gave the same explanation.'[15]

The Pope answered in anger, 'When you came to my court, it was not to tell us what your commentators say, but what you yourselves say. What have I to do with the explanations of outdated authors? It is vain and ridiculous to say that the Messiah has been born but has not come. For if the matter depends on the merit of the Jews, why was he born? Let the matter be delayed, and let him be born on the day when they are ready and fit.'

Said the delegates, 'And if they should be fit today, and the Messiah is born today, could a new-born babe lead them? Even Moses at the age of eighty had to have divine help, and the help of his brother and the seventy elders!'

Said the Pope, 'There were 600,000 of them and more.'[16]

The delegates replied, 'In a place where understanding is great, there is no need of a judge, for the intellect of a human being is fit to be his judge; and that generation, according to the tradition of the Talmud was "a generation of knowledge", and we are gnats, compared with them; each man of us needs ten judges, because of the smallness of our understanding.'

Said the Pope, 'In this I agree with you; for each one of you needs a king and a judge. But let us return to our subject.'

Then rose up one of the inhabitants of Rome[17] and said, 'Our lord Pope, there are ambiguous expressions, as is agreed by Jews and Christians, and the word "born" is such an ambiguous expression. For example, "Before the mountains were born [brought forth]" [Ps., 90: 2], or "what the day may bring forth [give birth to]" [Prov., 27: 1] or "they conceive mischief and bring forth [give birth to] vanity" [Prov., 15: 35]; and all these are expressions of conception in the mind. Moreover, when Scripture says, "and Lebanon shall fall by a mighty one", and after that, "And a rod shall come forth," this does not necessarily mean that it will be immediately, and it could be a long time afterwards; and the verse comes to comfort them for the destruction of the Temple, and to say to them that they will yet return to their original state. And if it is possible that this is the meaning of the verse, why should we assume that the author of that saying meant to say that he came immediately? But it seems that it means that the Messiah, because of his importance, came into the mind of God. Similarly, the Talmudists said, "Seven things came before the creation of the world," and one of them was the "name of the Messiah". They used the expression "creation" for something that did not really exist, meaning that it arose in the thought of God because it was essential for the completion of the Creation that the whole world should come to believe in One God. And so it means that on the day of the Destruction of the Temple, the creation of the Messiah arose in the thought of God, but the people were not fit for his immediate coming, and the exile was still needed for the dissolving of the sins of earlier days and to make whole every transgression and sin [see Dan., 9: 24].'

And the Disputation was suspended for that day.

In the morning, when we returned, we said to Geronimo, 'The Targum uses the expression *ityalad* as a translation for the Scriptural Hebrew *nolad,* which means "will be born" in the future; the Scriptural phrase being "a child shall be born unto the house of David, Josiah by name"; and this did not happen [i.e., the reign of Josiah] for another 500 years.'

Geronimo replied, 'The word *nolad* gives no indication of tense, but can mean either "will be born" or "was born".'

We all said, 'But this is a confirmation and help for what we have said. For we say that it [the Midrash] means "will be born". On your own admission, there is no necessity to accept your interpretation, and the building you have built has been destroyed.'

Geronimo tried to put right his first words, but could not, and he was very much put to shame, and expatiated at length on other proofs; but all of them understood that his aim was to 'make straight what he had made crooked' [see Eccles., 7: 13]. And when we saw that we had the upper hand, we said, 'It would be good for us now if we could depart with honour,' and we set on certain lords, by bribes, to speak to the Pope, and also many prelates to speak to Joshua Halorki, to put an end to the Disputation. But we were not successful, for the Pope said, 'Willy-nilly, Geronimo must prove what he promised!'

And on the morning of the reading of the lection 'Remember . . .', the Pope said, 'You Jews are speaking in a confusing manner. What sensible person would say that the Messiah has been born and has been alive in the Garden of Eden so many years. How could he live 1,400 years?'

We said to him, 'This difficulty was raised by Fray Paul, and the Master answered that Adam lived 1,000 years, and just as it is possible to live for 1,000 years, it is possible to live for more; for we should not deny something just because we have not seen it. Moreover, according to tradition, Enoch and Methuselah are still alive in the Garden of Eden.'

Said the Pope, 'This is like someone who answers one difficulty with another. For this too goes beyond reason.'

Then Rabbi Astruk jumped up and said, 'Our lord Pope! While you believe so many far-fetched things about your Messiah, allow us to believe one about our Messiah.'

On this, the Pope was much moved, and we were afraid that his wrath would go forth like fire, and we said to the Pope, 'Our lord! Our colleague has not spoken well, and entirely without our agreement. And he spoke by way of jest—not that he had the right to do so, for the Pope is not like one of us, engaging in familiar discourse.' And we returned to what we had said in the beginning: 'Show us, our lord, your mercy!'

We went to our lodging, and we all cried out against Rabbi Astruk, saying, 'Fie on you, and on your words, for you have put a sword in the hand of our enemies; and it is not according to our agreement that we should speak in the way you spoke. Our affairs were going well with the Pope, and he was more on our side than on Geronimo's; but now that the Pope has become angry, who will shield us, except the mercy of Heaven? But one ought not to rely on a miracle, where one's merits are in doubt.'

And on that day, we fled from there in shame and confusion, and we returned in the morning with great trembling and fear; but God granted us grace, and we found the Pope in a good mood.

And Geronimo returned to the subject, saying, 'If you believe that the Messiah has literally been born, I will show you that he has been revealed.'

Said the delegates, 'We do not believe that he was literally born, but we have said that the author of that saying may have understood the matter so.'

The Pope spoke: 'You, Geronimo, whence will you prove that he has been both born and revealed?'

Said he, 'Our lord Pope, because it is said in the Talmud, "Said Samuel: whence can one derive that the Messiah was born on the day that the Temple was destroyed? From the verse, 'before she travailed, she brought forth' " [Isa., 66: 7]. And Jonathan translates [in Aramaic]: "Before the disaster comes, you will be released, and before the quaking of the Destruction comes, the Messiah will be revealed."' [See Bereshit Rabbati, p. 131.]

We delegates replied, 'The Targum of Jonathan is not part of the saying; but the saying of Samuel is quite separate from the Targum, which meant that when the Messiah would come, he would come suddenly, like a woman who gives birth suddenly, as it is said, "Before she travailed, she brought forth." And the Targum did not mean to say the same thing as R. Samuel, but came to disclose that when the Messiah comes, he will come suddenly, which the Sages have already disclosed, saying, "Three things come unexpectedly" [b Sanh., 97a].'

Said the Pope, 'It is enough for me that you say that the Messiah has been born.'

We said to him, 'But we say that Samuel, the author of that saying, held that opinion mistakenly; but the Targum, which is an inspired work, did not say the same thing as Samuel, but explained the verse by saying that when the Messiah came, he would come suddenly. But it is our belief, and the belief of every Jew, that if a person comes who gathers the dispersed of Israel, and builds the Temple, and all the peoples assemble to him, and are all called by the name of God, then we will say that he is our Messiah.[18] And any saying that says the reverse of this has some other interpretation. Further, that saying which Geronimo cited says, "At his heels will the Temple be built"; and where is the Temple which was built in the time of Jesus?'

On this, Geronimo was not able to reply; but he embarked on other topics on which he spoke at length. Then the Disputation was adjourned two days until the fifteenth of February, when the Pope sent for us. And when we came before the Pope, he returned to that saying of Samuel to the effect that the Messiah had been born.

Then the Pope said, 'Last night I was thinking how you misled us with your words when you said that *nolad* is an ambiguous word, and could mean either "will be born" or "was born". However that may be, the truth of the matter is that Jesus was born long before the Destruction, for he was born in the year 3,671 after the Creation, and the Destruction of the Temple was in 3,828; so he was born 150 years before the Destruction!'

Said Don Vidal, 'Our lord Pope, we have an agreed principle in the Talmud that even if many interpretations are given of a verse, none of them ever abolishes the plain meaning; as is said plainly: "A Biblical verse never loses its literal meaning." When an Amora comes and removes a verse from its literal meaning, we say, "This is by way of metaphor, and it has some secret meaning or intention." And we do not believe that figurative interpretation as against the literal meaning. And Geronimo cannot deny that this is an understood principle in the Talmud. Therefore, let our lord take the Bible before him and see that those verses do not speak at all about the matter of your saviour, for when it is said, "Before she travailed, she gave birth," the reference is to Jerusalem, as it is said immediately afterwards, "Rejoice ye with Jerusalem" [v. 10]; and if it were said about your saviour, why is such surprise expressed—"who hath seen such things" [v. 8]? Is it said that it is a wonder that one man should be born in one day? Especially one of whom it is said that he is partly divine, or God's son! Especially, too, as it says next, "Shall a nation be born at once, for as soon as Zion travailed, she brought forth her children." And what has the birth of a nation to do with the saviour? But it speaks about the future, the time of the gathering of our exiles, for when they will be gathered by Divine power with great suddenness, then it is appropriately said, "Who hath heard such a thing?" Further, how does it say, "and ye shall be comforted in Jerusalem" [v. 13], when after the birth of Jesus, Jerusalem was destroyed?'

On this, Geronimo said, 'Since you contradict the sayings of the Talmud, I will show proof from Biblical verses which you will not be able to contradict. It is written in your Torah, "The sceptre will not depart from Judah, or a ruler from between his feet, until Shiloh shall come." And the Targum translates, "until the Messiah comes". And see, you have neither sceptre nor ruler—so how does it say that it "will not depart"?'

Rabbi Astruk answered, 'We have already said in our opening speech that any Scriptural verse or Talmudic saying that has various interpretations has no compelling force to confirm an opinion or article of faith; and you, lord Geronimo, know the interpretations of ibn Ezra and the comments of the great ones of earlier and later times. We too, if you wish to hear, will say about it one of two interpretations. The first is that it means that the sceptre will not depart eternally from Judah, but sometimes they will have a sceptre of Judah, and sometimes there will be an interruption and it will depart temporarily; and this course of events will continue until the coming of the Messiah; for when the Messiah whom we await comes, there will be no more interruption. The second interpretation is that we find in the word *'ad* a *yethiv,* which is a punctuation mark signifying a pause; so that the meaning is: "The sceptre of Judah will not depart for ever; for there will be Shiloh, that is, the Messiah, who will return the sceptre to Judah" '.

Geronimo replied, 'We are not obliged to believe in punctuation marks, for the Torah was not given with them.'

Said Don Vidal, 'O sage Geronimo! You believe in what helps your intentions, but in what is unpleasing to you, you do not believe! Let us offer yet another interpretation: that this word *'ad* may be as in "for I will not leave thee, until [*'ad*] I have done that which I have spoken to thee of" [Gen., 28: 15]. Is the meaning of this verse that God would desert him after He had done what He had spoken of? No, the meaning is like a man or a king who says to one of his servants, "I will not forsake you until I make you into a great lord." He does not mean that he will forsake him then. And so Scripture says, "There will not be lacking some kind of appointment or officialdom among the Jews until Shiloh comes, until the time arrives for the coming of Shiloh, to whom shall be the gathering of peoples" [Gen., 49: 10].'

Said Geronimo, 'Why should I accept your interpretation, and not accept what was said by Moses ha-Darshan, as quoted by Rashi in his Commentary; Rashi, the greatest of the commentators learnt from him and said that "the sceptre shall not depart from Judah" refers to the Chamber of Hewn Stone, which was put in the portion of Judah, and this expression "sceptre" refers to the Sanhedrin. And since the Sanhedrin has departed, the sceptre of Judah has departed, that is, the Sanhedrin which was in Judah.'

Said the delegates, 'We do not understand what is supposed to be proved by this interpretation. Moreover, Moses ha-Darshan was a preacher, not a Talmudist; further, the saying does not mean this, for it is Jacob's saying to his sons.'

Up to here, I found written, but I did not find written the end of the affair. But people have told me, by second-hand report, that the delegates went forth with great honour despite the great distresses that befell them and the congregations that hoped for their salvation.

12

The Christian Account of the Tortosa Disputation

Translated from the Latin protocols,
edited by A. Pacios Lopez, in volume 2 of
La Disputa de Tortosa, 1957

Preface

In the following pages some samples are given of the Christian account of the Tortosa Disputation, contained in the voluminous minutes ('protocols') kept by the papal notary at the sixty-nine sessions of the disputation. The protocols are preceded by two tables of contents: (1) a summary of topics discussed in the disputation as a whole; and (2) a summary of the topics discussed at each individual session. Translations of these two summaries are included here, as they give a convenient conspectus of the aims and achievements of the disputation from the Christian point of view.

From the protocols themselves, translations are given of: (1) Session 4 (10 February 1413). This session corresponds to part of the Hebrew account translated above, and also has interesting connections with the Barcelona Disputation. (2) Session 54 (15 February 1414). There is no Hebrew account of this session. Rabbi Astruk ha-Levi here replies to one of Geronimo's arguments. He contends that the Talmudic passages cited by Geronimo are both tentative and ambiguous, and that the Aggadah is in general a matter of 'opinion'. Geronimo, in his reply, asserts that the Jews are bound to treat the whole of the Talmud as holy writ, and he develops his theory that the Talmud was in the main composed as a counterblast to the growing success of Christianity, though it also contained ancient traditions derived from prophetic sources (such as the circle of Elijah) supporting the claims of Christianity. He carries his argument to such lengths that he asks the Pope to 'condemn' the rabbis as 'heretics and transgressors of their own religion' (because they refuse to accept the authority of the Aggadah) and demands that they should be subjected to 'grave penalties' (see Part I, p. 89). Geronimo's speech is typical of his style of argument, with its mixture of rabbinical learning, audacious inventions, and Aristotelian logic. He continues his speech by replying to the Jewish contention that no one has yet appeared who has fulfilled the Old Testament prophecies about the Messianic era. Geronimo's answer is twofold: (a) some of the Messianic prophecies mentioned were fulfilled at the time of the return from the Babylonian captivity; (b) others were intended figuratively, not literally, and, in their figurative sense, were fulfilled by Jesus. Geronimo ends the session by alleging that the Jewish argument about the Messiah contains a basic contradiction.

Contents: Subjects

In this present book or proceedings, sixteen subjects are dealt with; they are numbered and indicated as follows.

First is the subject of the things in which Christians and Jews agree in faith, and the things in which they disagree. This is contained in the first and fifty-eighth sessions, where the sign *A* is put in the margin.

Second is the subject of the twenty-four attributes of the Messiah; this is treated in the first and fifty-eighth sessions, and the letter *B* is put in the margin as an indication.

Third is the subject of the times assigned for the coming of the Messiah, which have long ago passed. This is contained in sessions 2, 3, 6, 8, 9, 10, 11, 12, 13, 14, 15, 46, 47, 49, 51, 52, 57, and 61, with the sign in the margin of the letter *C*.

Fourth, that in the time of the destruction of the Temple of Jerusalem, the Messiah had been born. This is to be found in the fourth and fifth sessions, marked in the margin of the book by the letter *D*.

Fifth, that at the time of the said destruction of the Temple, not only had the Messiah been born, but he had also come and had been revealed. This is treated in the fifth, seventh, and fifteenth sessions, and is designated in the margin of the book by the letter *E*.

Sixth, that the Messiah was to come in the year in which the

Passion of our Lord Saviour Jesus Christ took place. This is in the eighteenth and twenty-first sessions, under the sign of the letter *F*.

Seventh, that the prophecies which speak of the deeds of the Messiah, such as the rebuilding of the Temple and the gathering-in of Israel and the comforting of Jerusalem, should be understood in a spiritual, not a material, sense. This is in sessions 1, 7, 23, 24, 26, 31, and 36, and are marked by the letter *G*.

Eighth is the subject of the twelve questions of the Jews about the acts performed by the Messiah. This is treated in sessions 23, 24, 27, 28, 29, 30, 31, 32, 33, 34, 35, 36, 39, 40, 41, 42, 43, 44, 45, and 62, under the letter *H*.

Ninth, that the Mosaic Law is neither perfect nor eternal. This is contained in the thirty-second session, under the sign of the letter *L*.

Tenth is the subject of the holy Sacrament of the Eucharist. This is in session 33, under *M*.

Eleventh, the manner of the composition of the tractates called the books of the Talmud. This is in session 44, under *N*.

Twelfth, that a Jew must necessarily believe the entire contents of the Talmud, whether they are explanations of the Law, or legal decisions, or ceremonies, or homiletic material, or edicts, commentaries, additions or novelle made about the said Talmud; nor may a Jew deny anything of it. This is in session 54, marked with the letter *P* in the margin.

Thirteenth, what is the definition of an article of religion; and it is shown that it is not an article of the Jewish faith that the Messiah has not come. This is treated in session 59, under the sign *Q*.

Fourteenth, it is made clear how 'faith', 'scripture' and 'article of faith' are defined, and this is in session 61, under the letter *R*.

Fifteenth is the subject of the abominations, heresies, obscenities and nonsensicalities which are contained in the Talmud. These are in sessions 63, 65, 66, and 67, with the letter *T*.

Sixteenth, that the Jews are in their present captivity only because of the sinful and groundless hate which they had for the true Messiah, the Lord Jesus Christ. This is in sessions 13 and 35, under the letter *S*.

Contents: The Sessions

The following are the daily sessions in the present proceedings, numbered at the top of the pages, 1st, 2nd, 3rd, 4th, etc.

In the first session is placed the opening address which Master Ieronimus directed to the Jews, in order to show them the intention of the Most Sacred lord, our lord Pope Benedict XIII, in the present mode of instruction.

In the second: to prove that the dates and times decided by ancient teachers for the advent of the Messiah have passed, Master Ieronimus cited the authority of the passage concerning 'six thousand years'. The rabbis of the Jews replied to this citation, and the said Master Ieronimus answered them.

In the third: to prove the aforementioned proposition, a passage was cited concerning 'eighty-five jubilees'. The Jews replied to this citation, and the said Master Ieronimus answered them.

In the fourth: a passage about 'the Arab' was put forward, to prove that when the Destruction of the Temple took place, the Messiah had been born. The rabbis replied to this citation, and our lord the Pope answered them so conclusively that one of the most important rabbis admitted in that session that the Messiah had been born; but said that he had nevertheless not revealed himself nor 'come'.

In the fifth: Master Ieronimus repeated the conclusions of the preceding sessions, and then the rabbis confirmed what had been said, namely, that the Messiah was born around the time of the Destruction of the Temple, but that he had never been revealed. And Master Ieronimus, in order to prove that the Messiah had revealed himself, cited the prophecy of Isaiah, where it is said, 'Before she travailed, she brought forth' [Isa., 66: 7]. The Jews replied concerning this prophecy, and Master Ieronimus answered them.

In the sixth: to confirm that the Messiah had come, Master Ieronimus cited the prophecy of Jacob, 'The sceptre shall not depart from Judah . . .' [Gen., 49: 10]. The Jews replied, and Master Ieronimus answered them.

In the seventh: the Jews argued again about the things they had said on the previous day. They were questioned again whether they wished to say anything about what had been proved to them, namely, that the Messiah had been born and revealed. And one of the rabbis began to make new interpretations of the passages cited; and a full reply was made to these interpretations.

In the eighth: Master Ieronimus repeated all that had been transacted on the preceding days; but some of the rabbis repeated the above-mentioned interpretations. Finally, by order of our lord

Pope, the master of the Holy Palace summed up, with the conclusion that the Messiah had been born.

In the ninth: the said Master Ieronimus stated formally that both from the citation of 'The sceptre will not depart from Judah . . .' and from other citations, it had been proved that the Messiah had come, and it did not seem that adequate reply had been made to these citations; and he asked the Jews whether they had anything to say, as they would be heard willingly. And then one of the said rabbis proposed another new interpretation of the said prophecy; and a comprehensive reply was made to him by the said Master Ieronimus. Then also, by order of our lord the Pope, the Head of the Dominican Order summed up against the said Jews, and at this point, the Jews, complaining, denied everything that they had previously conceded. Therefore, our Most Holy lord Pope ordered that the said Disputation should be begun anew, and that everything to be propounded from both sides should be put into public writing, notaries being assigned for this purpose.

In the tenth session, the said Master Ieronimus put forward in writing the authoritative passage of the 'six thousand years', showing from it that the Messiah had already come, refuting or replying to the arguments that they were able to make against what Master Ieronimus had offered; in which written argument they cited prophecies which, in their opinion, proved that the Messiah had not yet come.

In the eleventh session, Master Ieronimus divided the reply of the Jews into seven parts, and replied to each one in turn.

In the twelfth session, there was a rejoinder of the Jews to the reply of Master Ieronimus. Then there was the sur-rejoinder of the said Master Ieronimus. And in that session, ten Jewish notables were baptised, together with their wives and families.

In the thirteenth session: this concerns the opposition by the Jews to the answers of Master Ieronimus, and the reply of that Master which he made to the Jews, giving them to understand, by six points, that their statements were erroneous.

In the fourteenth: a scroll was offered, on the part of the Jews, of which the contents were that the Jews were convinced that they had answered sufficiently; it referred too to their lack of knowledge and ability, saying that they did not know anything else to reply; but they wished to remain in their opinion and belief. And on the said day, eleven Jews were converted to the faith, together with their wives and families.

In the fifteenth: concerning a new proof made by Master Ieronimus from six authentic rabbinical citations from the Talmud, that the Messiah has already come. And concerning the reply of the Jews that the aforementioned citations should be understood figuratively; and concerning the command of our lord Pope that they should clarify the aforementioned figures, and name which teacher posited them.

In the sixteenth: concerning the replies of a Jew to the proofs of Master Ieronimus, saying that he was not bound to give credence to the aforementioned citations; and even if he should give faith to them, he tried to prove that it did not follow from them that the Messiah had come.

In the seventeenth: of the division of the reply of the Jews into twelve parts, and the proof by Master Ieronimus that the replies of the Jews were ineffectual. And concerning the scroll of the Jews, maintaining that they wished to reply something different from what they had said before: that they did not know any more.

In the eighteenth: the proof by Master Ieronimus that the Messiah had to come at the very time when the Passion of Christ occurred. And he cited three passages for this proof: first, 'a child is born . . .' [Isa., 9: 6]; second, 'The sceptre shall not depart from Judah'; third, a passage in the Talmud saying, 'They read: ten miracles were performed . . .'

In the nineteenth: the feeble reply of the Jews to the aforementioned citations; and finally they said that they did not know any more.

In the twentieth: the rejoinder of Master Ieronimus to the aforementioned replies of the Jews, dividing it into twelve parts, saying that those replies could not pass.

In the twenty-first: concerning the scroll of the Jews containing their perseverance in the previous replies, and that they did not know any more. And concerning the explanation made by Master Ieronimus to the Jews about the 'weeks' of Daniel, to confirm the foregoing conclusion.

In the twenty-second: the reply of the Jews about the aforementioned 'weeks', and the rejoinder of Master Ieronimus to the said reply, refuting it by five arguments; and finally, the reply of the Jews, that they did not know any more. And while this was going on, many of the Jews were converted to the faith.

In the twenty-third: the address made by Master Ieronimus, on the text, 'Return, ye backsliding children' [Jer., 3: 22]. In this he showed the obduracy of the Jews, and by sure arguments proved that events which the Jews derived from Scripture, such as the rebuilding of the Temple, the gathering of the people, and the prosperity of Jerusalem, should be understood in a spiritual sense; and concerning the twelve questions about the acts of the Messiah.

In the twenty-fourth: a long-winded reply by the Jews, trying to excuse themselves for their obduracy, and trying to prove that all the prophecies speaking of the Messiah should be understood in a material and temporal sense. And concerning the reply to the twelve questions.

In the twenty-fifth: the analysis by Ieronimus of the reply of the Jews, though long-winded, into four sections. And on that day, he recalled what was said in the first section.

In the twenty-sixth: a summing-up of the second and third sections, teaching clearly that a great part of the prophets who speak of the Messiah must necessarily be understood in a spiritual sense.

In the twenty-seventh: to show that the replies of the Jews to the twelve questions were false. And he proved, concerning the first question, by five citations, that the place of the nativity of the Messiah was the area called Bethlehem Ephrata.

In the twenty-eighth: the proof by many notable citations and arguments that the Messiah was to be born without the carnal seed of a father and without human corruption on the part of his mother, which was contrary to their contention in their reply.

In the twenty-ninth: the proof that the Messiah must be truly God and man, contrary to their reply.

In the thirtieth: concerning the advent of the Messiah, which must be for the salvation of souls for the spiritual life, etc., and that in his coming, the sin of our first parent was remitted, and that, before him, all souls went to Hell. That he had to suffer death and his Passion in order to wipe out the said sin, despite what the Jews had said in their 3rd, 4th, 5th, and 6th questions.

In the thirty-first: it was proved that the Messiah had to save in general the whole human race, contrary to what the Jews replied in their seventh question. Further, it was proved that the word 'Israel' signifies the whole people which came to the doctrine of the Messiah.

In the thirty-second: it was proved that the Messiah had to give a new law and teaching, contrary to what the Jews replied in the eighth question. Further, that the Mosaic Law was neither perfect nor eternal.

In the thirty-third: it was proved that in the time of the Messiah all animal sacrifices which were made in antiquity in the Temple of Jerusalem had to cease, which was contrary to what the Jews replied in their ninth question. Further, it was proved that there had to be made only sacrifices of bread and wine, in the manner which is done today in the Holy Church of God.

In the thirty-fourth: it was proved that the ceremonies of the Mosaic Law, such as the prohibition of kinds of food and the confining of the priesthood to the tribe of Levi, and so on, had to cease in the time of the Messiah, contrary to what the Jews replied in their tenth question.

In the thirty-fifth: it was clearly proved how it is that the captivity, in which the Hebrew people is today, has no other cause than their ingratitude and causeless hatred[1] which the Jews had towards the true Messiah, namely, Christ; which was contrary to what they replied in the eleventh question.

In the thirty-sixth: it was proved how the Jews moreover must not acquire or conquer or possess the Holy Land, contrary to what they replied in the twelfth question. Further, it was proved that the Land and Jerusalem, promised in the prophecies in the time of the Messiah, signify spiritual glory.

In the thirty-seventh: concerning what the Jews tried to urge against the proofs made in the 25th and 26th sessions. Further, the manner in which Master Ieronimus summed it up, dividing their objections into seven parts.

In the thirty-eighth: how Master Ieronimus summed up the remaining objections in the said sections.

In the thirty-ninth: how the Jews replied, saying that, after deliberation concerning the sur-rejoinder made by Master Ieronimus, they did not care to say anything more, as being people who did not know anything more in these matters, yet trying to disprove the proofs made concerning the first question, and making various interpretations of the texts adduced by Master Ieronimus, who destroyed the aforesaid interpretations by manifold arguments.

In the fortieth: how the Jews tried to disprove the citations made by Master Ieronimus in the second question, making false interpretations of the prophecies; and how Master Ieronimus by adequate reasons showed the emptiness of these interpretations.

In the forty-first: how the Jews strove to disprove the citations made by Master Ieronimus in the 3rd, 4th, 5th, and 6th questions, and how he disposed of their arguments and difficulties.

In the forty-second: how the Jews tried to disprove the citations made by Master Ieronimus in the 4th, 5th, and 6th questions, which objections Master Ieronimus destroyed with adequate reasons.

In the forty-third: how the Jews strove to object to the citations made by Master Ieronimus in the 7th and 8th questions, and how he demolished their arguments.

In the forty-fourth: how the Jews tried to object also to the citations made by Master Ieronimus in the 9th, 10th, 11th, and 12th questions, and how Master Ieronimus nullified them by irrefutable arguments.

In the forty-fifth: the reply which the Jews handed over, saying that, after consideration of the sur-rejoinders made by Master Ieronimus in the twelfth question, they did not intend to add anything, as they believed themselves to have answered well, and that they did not know anything more in the matter.

In the forty-sixth: how Master Ieronimus, by order of our lord Pope, recited the arguments and citations already made, by which it had been proved that the Messiah had already come, rounding them off finally in detail.

In the forty-seventh: how Master Ieronimus completed the details of the said citations, requesting the Jews to give some other argument, if they had one, or confess that they had been defeated. Further, he requested that a public record should be made of the confession.

In the forty-eighth: how our lord commanded his whole Curia and all the rabbis to be assembled, and remarked to them that in the last two sessions an account had been given of the whole previous proceedings, and when his Holiness had requested of the Jews whether they wished to give further replies, all had said 'No' except Rabbi Ferrer and Rabbi Mathtias and Rabbi Astruck, to whom he had ordered to be given a copy of the proceedings so far. In order to listen to them, he appointed certain cardinals and prelates in particular. Further, he assigned certain professors in Sacred Writ to instruct the Jews who had said that they did not wish to dispute further, since they did not know any more.

In the forty-ninth: concerning a certain memorandum which Rabbi Ferrer and Rabbi Mathatias had newly handed over against the citations made by Master Ieronimus, on the question of whether the Messiah had already come, and in particular against the citations of 'six thousand years' and 'eighty-five jubilees', making certain arguments and objections against Master Ieronimus, and interpreting the said citations in a false and quibbling manner.

In the fiftieth: how Master Ieronimus, in order to nullify the quibbles and arguments and objections made by the said two rabbis, laid down a certain principle, and then divided all their words into three sections, and in that session disproved the first section by very sufficient proofs.

In the fifty-first: the arguments which Master Ieronimus gave against the second section mentioned above, disproving three objections made by them.

In the fifty-second: how Master Ieronimus showed by argument the quibbling and illogicality contained in the third section, namely, in the interpretations given by the two rabbis of the above-mentioned two texts.

In the fifty-third: how Rabbi Astruch presented a memorandum containing eight points; but he undertook to speak and expound before our Lord and his Curia the third point, since the two first did not properly touch on the matter in dispute; and how Master Ieronimus replied to the said point.

In the fifty-fourth: how the said Rabbi Astruch read out the fourth point of his memorandum, and how Master Ieronimus replied.

In the fifty-fifth: how Master Ieronimus replied to some remaining arguments of the fourth point.

In the fifty-sixth: how the aforesaid rabbi read out the 5th, 6th, 7th, and 8th points of the said memorandum.

In the fifty-seventh: how Master Ieronimus replied against the said last four points of the said rabbi, refuting all his words, and showing the quibbles in them, and attacking a certain false figure which the said rabbi gave in the said seventh point.

In the fifty-eighth: how the said rabbi read out the first two points which he had omitted, and Master Ieronimus annihilated all his arguments, and showed by reason how the main conclusion had been well drawn, namely, that the Messiah had already come.

In the fifty-ninth: how Rabbi Ferrer gave a memorandum against the arguments made by Master Ieronimus in the previous sessions. In this, he proposed ten propositions and six arguments. And he based himself mainly on saying that the Messiah had not yet come, and that this was an article of Jewish faith, and therefore, granted that the texts cited by Master Ieronimus showed literally that the Messiah had come, nevertheless they should not be understood so, but an interpretation should be made that would not be contrary to the above-mentioned article of faith.

In the sixtieth: how Master Ieronimus, replying to the said Rabbi Ferrer, had two aims: first, to show the great inconsistency of that rabbi and of the others in all their disputes; and second, to clarify two kinds of fallacies or evasions which the said rabbi employed in his memorandum. In particular, he dealt with one proposition, on which the said rabbi based his whole memorandum, namely, that the Messiah must be awaited as long as the Jews remain in captivity, and that this an article of the Mosaic Law. Master Ieronimus constructed eight arguments, all very weighty, to prove that the said proposition, in the way it was understood or proposed by Rabbi Ferrer, was false; nevertheless, understood in accordance with the Catholic faith, it could be true, and in that case, its oppositon could be shown to the meaning given to it by the rabbi.

In the sixty-first: how Master Ieronimus made certain distinctions in relation to the terms 'faith', 'scripture' and 'article'; and replied in detail to each of the ten propositions and six arguments of the said Rabbi Ferrer. In particular, he showed the disingenuous quibble which the said Rabbi Ferrer proposed on the texts concerning the six thousand years and the eighty-five jubilees.

In the sixty-second: how Master Ieronimus, by order of our Lord the Pope, before him and his holy Curia and in the presence of the Jews, read out a summary of all the proceedings, from the day when the Disputation commenced up to that day, from session to session, including twelve interrogations which he made of the Jews, as recorded; and how then a great multitude of Jews became converted to the holy catholic faith.

In the sixty-third: how Master Ieronimus cited certain texts containing the vanities, obscenities and heresies of the Talmud, requesting the rabbis that if they could excuse such things they should do so, but if not, the said Talmud should be condemned. And they denied that it was literally so, as he alleged. And then our lord ordered that the books of the Talmud should be brought before him, and Master Ieronimus showed the Jews all the things just as he had alleged in the texts themselves.

In the sixty-fourth: how a certain statement was offered by all except Rabbi Ferrer and Rabbi Joseph Albo, to the effect that they, because of lack of ability, did not know how to reply or to excuse in any way such abominations of the said Talmud.

In the sixty-fifth: how our lord made a very holy and merciful exhortation. Then Master Ieronimus made an address, of which the theme was 'Seek the Lord while he can be found' [Zeph., 2: 3]; and he made a summary of the whole previous proceedings, both the proofs of the Messiah and the abominations of the Talmud. On the same day, Rabbi Joseph Albo and Rabbi Astruch presented a written statement in defence of the said abominations. A sufficient reply to this statement was made by the reverend master Andreas Bertrandi, the Almoner of our lord the Pope. Then master Salomon, a Jew, rabbi of the congregation of Tortosa, made certain arguments, trying to defend the said Talmud.

In the sixty-sixth: how Master Ieronimus replied to a certain statement issued by the Jewish community in which it was said that the compilers of the Talmud were learned men of good life. He replied that the contrary was the truth, proving how they were lacking in knowledge, and how they sinned in all the seven deadly sins; and the same Master Ieronimus made seven notable arguments against the contentions of master Salomon, drawing effective conclusions from them.

In the sixty-seventh: concerning an address which Master Ieronimus made, by order of our lord the Pope, in the form of a narration and an admonition. Then Rabbi Astruch, in the name of all the Jews, offered a statement the content of which was that they did not know how to defend the said abominations nor did they give any credence to them; and all the Jews asserted that they were in accord in the said reply, except two Jews, namely, Ferrer and Joseph Albo.

In the sixty-eighth: how on the part of all the Jews, and on behalf of them, and in the name of their community, the said statement was presented in the villa of San Mateo to the aforesaid our lord the Pope, in the presence of the lords Cardinals and other members of the Curia, as is the custom. And how at that moment, our lord the Pope ordered that the sentence ordained by himself against the Talmud should be published in the presence of all the Jews, and with it the other edicts ordained by his Holiness, about the way of life of the Jews and their relations with Christians.

In the sixty-ninth session, the titles and contents of the aforesaid edicts and sentence [were read out].

Session IV

On the next day, Friday the 10th of February of the abovementioned year, the said Master Ieronimus opened by saying that

Rabbi Ferrer, in the previous sessions, had said that the text concerning 'six thousand years' was followed by the words, 'Because of our sins so many years have passed beyond the predicted date, and the Messiah has not yet come.' Master Ieronimus had denied that the words 'the Messiah has not yet come' were in the text of the Talmud, while Rabbi Ferrer continued to assert that they were. Consequently, in the presence of the said Pope, our lord, and of his whole Curia, the said Master Ieronimus showed certain books of the Talmud in which the content was just as Master Ieronimus had frequently alleged.[2]

Then, in order to prove more clearly and efficaciously that the Messiah had come, he cited a certain text of the Talmud in the book called Berahot [Berakhot] of the Jerusalem Talmud, in the chapter 'Haya core' [Haya qore']:

'It happened that while a certain Jew was ploughing, one of his oxen lowed, and an Arab who was passing by, hearing the sound, said to the Jew, "Hebrew, son of a Hebrew, loose the oxen, stop your work, for your Temple is destroyed." And then the ox lowed a second time, and the Arab said, "Hebrew, son of a Hebrew, fasten up your oxen and return to your work, for your Messiah has been born." Then the Jew asked the Arab, "Where is he?" The Arab replied, "In Bethlehem, in the land of Judaea." '

To this text, Rabbi Astruch replied that it was correct, and was so written in his book. To prove this he drew out an ancient folio and held it in his hands, and from it read out that the Jew who was ploughing became a seller of children's shoes in order to find out who was the mother of the Messiah. Nevertheless, he added that the story was contained in the commentary on Jeremiah's Book of Lamentations, and therefore referred to the destruction of the First Temple, not the Second Temple.

Then Master Ieronimus put forward very many arguments to prove that the story referred to the destruction of the Second Temple.

Then the said rabbi argued that the Messiah had indeed been born, but had not yet come.

The said Jew was then interrogated by our lord the Pope, who asked, 'Where has he been since he was born?' The Jew replied, 'At Rome, according to the opinion of some, and in the opinion of others, in the terrestrial paradise. And even if the words seem to mean literally that the Messiah has come, they mean something different.' But he was not willing to add what this meaning was. Strongly urged, however, by the Pope to express his view more clearly, he came out with assertion that Jews do not await the Messiah for the salvation of their souls, but for good times and the prosperity of the body; since their souls, even if the Messiah should never come, were saved. When he was deservedly reproved by the Pope for saying 'even if the Messiah should never come', he said that he was assuming the impossible for the sake of argument. And then he changed the words, saying that he had meant 'even if he should not come until the end of the world'.

When the other Jews were asked whether Rabbi Astruch's responses seemed good and legitimate, Rabbi Matathias and Rabbi Joseph Albo, and some others, said that he had replied well. Then our lord Pope drew out conclusions from this. Then Master Todros, a Jew, said that the story made up about the Arab and the Jewish ploughman, since it was fictitious, should not be regarded as authoritative, since in such stories it was permissible to accept the good and reject the bad. And Rabbi Astruch supported this, adding, 'The words of the Bible, of approved teachers, and of the comments of Rabbi Hyna [Huna] and Rabbi Asse [Ashi] are regarded as authoritative; but homiletical passages are open to criticism.'

Master Ieronimus, however, urged with many arguments that the said quotation was in the proper text of the Talmud, within matter regarded as fully authoritative by the Jews, transmitted by Rabbi Hyna and Rabbi Hasse, whose sayings all Jews were obliged to believe.

Then our lord the Pope summed up by concluding the truth of the said propositions, that the Messiah had both come and been born. Master Salomon Ysach [Solomon Isaac],[3] however, said that Rabbi Astruch had replied badly and insufficiently, since the above story was true and authentic, but it did not prove that the Messiah had been born. For the word *nolad,* though its principal significance was 'to be born', can mean many other things, of which one was 'to be conceived in the imagination', and this was a case of such a meaning.

To this Master Ieronimus replied that a word should never be understood in an inappropriate way if in the context it can be understood appropriately. Therefore the word *nolad,* though it might have a different meaning elsewhere, when it is applied to a person whose nature is to be born, should mean nothing other than to be born.

At this, the said Master Salomon ceased to speak.

SESSION LIV

On Saturday, the seventeenth of the said month of February, the said Rabbi Astruch continued his remarks as follows:

'Against the fourth point I reply: that Master Ieronimus in his epilogue failed to mention all the arguments which had been offered on the part of our speakers, paying attention to the sayings of our side only to a very small degree.

'First we said that the whole treatment of the said Master Ieronimus and many of his proofs are based on homiletical material and stories about the lowing of cattle, and such things, which we are not bound to regard as authoritative. Indeed Rabbi Moses said, "I altogether disbelieve this story." Our wise men say that they are not in such a category that anything should be proved from them, nor should one argue against them, since they speak figuratively and metaphorically.

'Further we said, and firmly hold by way of our tradition, that the Messiah has not yet come, and this because there has not been a man in the whole world in whom all the acts of the Messiah and his operations as expressed in the prophecies have come together. And if any words in this homiletical material should be found relevant, if they are in agreement with the prophecies or their declarations, we accept them; and if they deviate from them, they ought to be explained figuratively, in such a way that they are in no way an obstacle to faith or our belief. And if we do not know how to explain them, this is because of lack of knowledge on our part, not because of any defect in our faith.

'Further we said that all the statements which the aforesaid Master Ieronimus quoted are by men who firmly held and asserted that the Messiah had not yet come, and for that reason endured many sufferings and martyrdoms. If therefore a man of good authority should say: "The Messiah has come; but I believe that he has not come yet, and because of this I intend to endure or suffer martyrdom or sufferings or tortures," there is no doubt that every person believes in what he puts into action; by saying verbally "he has come", he means that he will come shortly, if we are worthy, or some other such explanation. So also we ought to follow what they followed and believed, and to explain their writings in a way which is in harmony with their actions; especially as none of them said clearly that the Messiah had come, unless to say "the years of the Messiah are so many" and such expressions. And if they had understood him to have come already, they would have said plainly, "The years since the Messiah has come are so many."

'Further, from the same people from whom we derive, by the way of tradition, the law of Moses and the interpretation of its commands and ceremonies, we derive also, by the way of tradition, what are the conditions of the Messiah and his operations. Whence it follows necessarily that the Messiah has not yet come. Just as, therefore, we ascribe no doubtfulness to the interpretation made by them of the commandments of the ceremonies, so we must not ascribe any doubtfulness to the acts of the Messiah, and anything which is incompatible with that tradition we must interpret in such a way that it becomes compatible. If however we do not know how, we ought not to separate ourselves in any way or deviate from our faith or belief.

'These arguments we have expressed, for the most part, so that the whole disputation may be resolved, and so that we may be defended from all the proofs of Master Ieronimus, or from this kind of disputation, and to say that from all this no conclusion can be drawn against our faith and belief, nor ought to be drawn.

'Now therefore, lords, let anyone who wishes consider carefully whether in view of all these arguments there is any sense in this kind of disputation, or whether any conclusion contrary to our faith or belief ought to be drawn. Certainly it seems to me that by every judgement of the natural intellect it should not.

'Further, particular responses which we made about the authority of "six thousand years" were two interpretations, of which the aforesaid Master Ieronimus in his epilogue mentioned only one, and of that he quoted only one argument, though we put forward many arguments to prove that this said authority is opiniative and presumptive, whether one considers the tenor of its authority, or its compiler, or its opponent.

'First as to its tenor, this text is a simple expression, not a prophecy, nor said by the prophet Elijah; and it speaks of the future and the redemption of the Messiah that it is something hidden and secret both from the wise men by the way of tradition, from the prophets by the way of prophecy, and even from the angels by the way of glory. Rabbi Moses of Egypt says in his book called Soffrim [Shofetim]: "About the fact of the Messiah, no one knows how all these things will be until they happen. And the wise do not have it from tradition," etc.

'From the tenor therefore it follows that the text speaks in the manner of opinion or conjecture, not with certitude.

'Secondly, it is plain by the teacher's saying (as he himself states), "And because of our sins", etc. that it was not bound of necessity to happen in that way and not in another. Therefore it is plain that he spoke by way of opinion, and therefore he said, "And because of our sins which are many, there resulted all the things that then resulted, and the son of David has not yet come." If however he had said this by determining with certitude, he ought to have said, "And because of our sins, which are many, the Messiah has already come at such-and-such a date, and we did not recognise him."

'Thirdly, the compiler Rabasse [Rav Ashi], who was a pronouncer or compiler of authority, comments on that saying about jubilees as follows: "From then, expect him." It seems that he did not hold that first saying as certain; for if he held it as certain how could he say, "Expect him"?—if he had already come over two hundred years before?

'Further, he believed and supported the view that the Messiah had not yet come.

'Fourthly, as to opposition: for first the authority who speaks about jubilees is opposed to him, and also many others. In the same book called Sanhedrin, Abimi interprets: "The days of the Messiah will be to Israel as the days from the creation of the world until now." Rabbi Naḥman says, "as from the days of Noah until now." And there are very many other sayings which contradict this one.

'Therefore from these arguments it follows that this text is merely an opinion.

'Besides, I am moved by strong wonder how anyone can prove from this text that the Messiah has come. And I speak thus, for the sake of example: If one were to say, "Twelve months make a year, three of spring, three of summer, three of autumn and three the days of winter," there is no doubt that, by common sense, winter would not be as certain as the other times, since he did not say "three of winter" as he said "three of spring"; but it seems that those days are days which by good and right judgement ought to make winter unless doubt arose through some planet or constellation which might occur to make the time warm. Similarly, this man too when he said, "Two thousand years of the *days* of the Messiah", and did not say, "Two thousand years of the Messiah", as he said, "Two thousand years of chaos", seems to be saying that those days, by right and good judgement, ought to be the days of the Messiah, unless doubt arises because sins prevent it, as he said, "And because of our sins", etc.

'From this therefore it is obvious that it is not certain that the Messiah has come, as it was certain that the Law was given at the beginning of the second 2,000 years; so it should not be said that from this it can be proved that the Messiah has already come.'

To these things, read out as above by the same Rabbi Astruch, the said Master Ieronimus replied in the following form:

'About the fourth point, in which the said Rabbi sweats mainly to oppose the argument made by me above, I say that if good and thorough scrutiny is made of what is contained diffusely in the writing offered by him on this point, his attack can be divided into two parts: In the first, namely, he wishes to assert that to four general and universal arguments put or read out by the Jew in the proceedings above I did not reply.

'In the second, that interpretations have been made by Jews on the authority of the "two thousand years", and he wishes to show that I have not adequately opposed these.

'About the first part of the aforesaid four arguments, to which the aforesaid Rabbi says I have not replied, he says that it was stated on the part of the Jews that they were not bound to give credence to the Talmudic authorities quoted by me, since they are stories and homiletical expressions, called in Hebrew, "hagadoth". In support of this he quotes the words of Rabbi Moses of Egypt and Rabbi Moses of Gerona.[5]

'Replying immediately to this argument, I say that, according to the order of correct disputation (though the said Jews and especially the aforesaid Rabbi have striven to prove that from the said authorities my conclusion cannot be drawn), first this issue ought to be decided, and by them admitted or accepted, before we come to the demonstration that they are bound to show faith in the aforesaid authorities, as I have said very often in the proceedings.

'Nevertheless, so that I may bow to their proceeding, I will not expatiate further, and before proceeding to further matters, with the help of divine grace, I shall show how what the said Rabbi said fails to illuminate this matter; but the Jews are bound and obliged to show faith in the aforesaid authorities, just as much or more than in the words of the prophets.

'And so that it may be given to all to understand plainly what I intend to state in this matter, it behoves you to know how this teaching, called the Talmud among the Jews, took root when that tribe or society of rabbis named the Pharisees, who were in the time of the Second Temple, as can be plainly shown, through their adverse fortune, or rather obstinacy, did not acknowledge the true Messiah who then came, but had groundless hate for him, despite the fact that they witnessed great miracles, which were done every day in his name. This hatred indeed was the cause of the Destruction of the Temple, and their captivity, as is plain in very many places in the Hebrew books, where it is asked what was the cause of the captivity; to which it is answered that it was nothing other than "groundless hatred". Clinging to your error, however, you declare that this was said because of the hatred which you bear among yourselves for each other, which was sufficient to bring you into so cruel a captivity, and to keep you or chain you in it for such a long time. But a truer and more certain cause was the hatred stated above.

'Then the aforesaid rabbis, after they saw the Messiah crucified and dead, thought that from then on no mention would be made of him, nor of his teaching. Then when they saw that his teaching was prospering greatly through all parts of the world because of the preaching of his disciples, and in what way they interpreted the law of Moses and commanded observance such as the Church now observes, whence it followed that the ceremonies which they themselves observed were annulled, they took thought to arrange and renew those ceremonies in their writings. This scripture they called the Mishna, which is the same as the "second Law", setting up the rumour that God had given all this to Moses by word of mouth.

'Seeing also that the Catholic faith grew much more and increased, to such an extent that a great part of the Jews of the whole world, and the whole Roman Empire, and Helena the mother of the Emperor, and all the heathens from the various parts of Italy had been converted to the said Catholic faith, to such an extent that they occupied the greatest part of the world, and a little before, the Blessed Jerome who with great diligence and the co-operating help of God, assembled the various codices of the Holy Scripture from various parts of the world, had translated them from the Chaldaic and Hebrew tongues into the Latin tongue: when the aforesaid rabbis considered carefully all these things, thinking themselves lost, and fearing lest their teaching might be lost, they took thought that the teaching previously made was not sufficient, and they arranged in addition, or added, another teaching with an arrangement concocted by themselves and very diffuse, known among the Jews as the Talmud. In this they explained all the other ceremonies, with their manner of observance, one by one or in the minutest detail; placing in it many things which they knew their ancestors had received from revelation, they included also many vile things, wicked and unspeakable, against the true holy faith, and against the Saviour our Lord Jesus Christ, and very many blasphemies and follies, and many other things which were against the law of Moses and the law of nature, vile and filthy things, to name which would cause abomination in the ears; the ultimate reason for all these things being that they saw that the Evangelical teaching was prospering and increasing.

'On this you have the authority of Rabbi Moses of Egypt in the prologue Maddag [Madd'a],[6] where he says that the reason why the oral law was put into writing was that they saw that an evil kingdom was spreading or widening and being prosperous through the world.

'And so that great authority might be reserved for the said tractate, they adopted the ruse of saying that God had given not only the five books of Moses, but also another oral law, like the Talmud, to them. And so they give such great authority to the said Talmud that they say that what is written in it is of greater strength and validity that what is written in the law of Moses.

'And therefore they say about the book the Talmud that the words of the teachers who composed and compiled it have more validity that the words of the written law.[7] And according to the assumption which they make, forsooth, that that law derives from God's own mouth, they act rightly to ascribe to it greater faith and authority than to the law of Moses. For if our lord the Pope gives me an instruction in writing, and on the other hand gives me an instruction with his own mouth or orally, it is not turned into doubt, and I may acknowledge that I ought to obey each of them, yet I shall ascribe without error or reproach a validity of greater strength or efficacy to the instruction given by his own mouth than to that given to me in writing.

'It follows then that he who believes that the Talmud is the oral law ought to give it greater faith than the law of Moses.

'Yet the rabbis will say, "This applies only in that part of the book or code named the Talmud which is the exposition of the commandments of the law, and what kind of ceremonies ought to be observed. That is what came through the tradition of Moses, and alone is to be called the oral law, and which alone a Jew is bound to believe even more than the law of Moses. Sermons, however, and stories called 'haggadot', in which are included all the texts which I quoted above, are not included in the oral law nor do they come through the divine tradition of Moses, nor to us from Moses. And therefore we are not obliged to believe them."

'I reply that it is not so. I prove this by various texts: and first through the book Sanhedrin, where it is said that whoever says that the whole law is or was given to Moses on Mount Sinai, except one of the thirteen exegetical principles which are in the book called the Talmud, with which the law is expounded, that it is said about him in the law that he has disparaged the law of God and his soul ought to be damned.[8]

'Further, Rabbi Moses of Egypt says in the book called Soffrim in the laws of rebels, chapter three, similar words: "Whoever does not believe in the oral law is not only a rebel, but also a heretic, and whoever kills him is rewarded."[9]

'And certainly in such a matter, where so great a punishment is appointed, if by chance any texts ought to be excepted from it, truly those teachers ought to declare it in their compositions. But since they except nothing from it, it seems that all of it is meant. And we can say further that the words of Rabbi Moses and the imposition of so great a punishment are spoken rather about the "haggadot" than about the rest, when he said, "He who does not believe in the oral law, or believe the oral law". "Belief" is mainly relevant to talking about the haggadot, for they are sermons about divine matters and the facts of the Messiah and the resurrection and the creation of the world and about hell and Paradise, because as for the other things which are in the Talmud, which you suggest are more authoritative, I think, such as law-suits, civil and criminal judgements, and the observance of ceremonies, it is not appropriate to talk of "believing" these, but rather of observing or practising. Belief, however, is more appropriate in matters which concern faith and revelation, and not practice.

'From this therefore it is plain that all the words of the Talmud are the oral law.

'But, so that this may be made more clearly plain, and so that I may remove from you the false covering or veil with which you have veiled or striven to veil yourselves, not because a Jew really professes this, nay, you have faith in all the particularities of the said Talmud, but when you are not able to find any other evasion, you try to excuse yourselves with this—I will show therefore a certain authoritative statement which is in Medras Cohellet [Midrash Qohelet], that is, the moral commentary on Ecclesiastes, which was stated by Rabbi Joshua the son of Levi, who is one of the most ancient and authoritative people whom you have ever had. This authority is about the text of Solomon, where it is said, Ecclesiastes, 1: "Nor can anyone say, Behold this is new; for it has already preceded in the generations which were before you."

'It is written in Deuteronomy [9: 10], "God gave to me the tablets of stone written by the finger of God. And on them was according to all these words." Said Rabbi Joshua, son of Levi: "Instead of 'on them', there is 'And on them'; instead of 'all', there is 'according to all', instead of 'words', there is 'the words', instead of 'commandment', there is 'all the commandment': to show that the Bible and the Mishna, and the decisions of the Talmud, and additions and stories and homilies, and whatever any teacher would teach for his time, and whatever any disciple of authority would rehearse before his teacher, all was said and given to Moses on Mount Sinai."[10]

'Behold it is plain that that teacher of yours gives a clear opinion that what you deny came through the tradition of God to Moses himself, and to you from Moses.

'Whence I form the following argument:

'Whatever the rabbis said is the oral law.

'As for the haggadot quoted by me, they were spoken by the rabbis.

'Therefore, the haggadot are the oral law.

'The major premise is proved through Rabbi Joshua. The minor is obvious in the books. Therefore the conclusion follows.

'Having proved that the haggadot are oral law, I form another syllogism as follows:

'A Jew is obliged to observe and believe all the oral law, with all its parts.

'But the haggadot are oral law.

'Therefore a Jew is obliged to believe and observe the haggadot.

'The major is proved by the Talmudic passages quoted above, and by Rabbi Moses. The minor has been sufficiently proved by me. Therefore the conclusion follows by necessity, namely, that the haggadot quoted by me you are bound to believe and observe.

'This belief in the Talmud they took to such lengths that not only do they wish to make it equal to the Scripture of the law of

Moses, but they even wish to uphold stubbornly that it is of greater sanctity and greater validity. And whoever transgresses it is involved in greater punishment.

'It is said in the Talmud, in the book Baba Meciha [Bava Metsi'a] in the chapter which begins "Hellu Meciho" [*'elu metsi'oth*], that there is a greater obligation to honour a teacher than a father. And Rabbi Solomon [Rashi] declares that this is meant of a teacher who has taught him the Talmud or talmudic knowledge, not of him who has taught him the Bible.

'Further it is said in Sanhedrin, in the chapter which begins Bencorer [*Ben sorer*], that one who denies anything of the law is not deserving of death, but one who denies something of the Talmud is deserving of death.[11]

'Whence it follows that you have committed or perpetrated a great crime when you denied the authoritative passages of your Talmud, and you are deserving of great punishment.

'And not only is it proved that you are obliged to believe homilies and haggadot of the Talmud by the aforesaid authorities and arguments, but also by the practice of many prayers which you make in your Synagogues, and many ceremonies which you Jews observe, which are based on haggadot of the Talmud, it can be plainly proved. For it is certain that the authority on which prayers are based must be especially righteous and holy. It is not to be presumed that any prayer would be composed unless it were valid and authentic.

'First, then, there is one haggada, where it is said that Elijah himself was Finees [Phinehas], the nephew of Aaron the high priest. And this assertion is based on a similarity in their titles, one with the other. For Phinehas was in the time of Moses, and Elijah in the time of King Ahab. Nevertheless from that haggada follows a certain prayer at the end of the Sabbath, and it begins at the kindling of a light; this prayer is commonly called Havdala among the Jews, and in it they pray to God that Elijah, who is Phinehas, may come soon, together with the Messiah the son of David.[12]

'Further, on the day of atonements, that is, of pardons, which they regard as the most sacred of the whole year, in the first prayer which the Jews make, they say a certain passage, where mention is made of a certain haggada which is in Sanhedrin, in the chapter which begins Cohen Gadol, which says thus: "Forty days before a creature is formed in the womb, a revelation or heavenly voice goes out saying, 'Such a daughter will be for such a one.' "

'Further, on the same day in passages which they say mention is made of a certain haggada which in the book of Nedarim in the chapter which begins Arbaha Nedarim, where it is said that Abraham had acquaintance with God when he was three years old.

'And these passages and prayers which are said in the Synagogues, which are based on haggadot of the Talmud itself, a man could adduce many more; and not only prayers, but also many ceremonies based on haggadot.

'It says, for example, in the Talmud, in the book called Meguilla, that when the ten sons of Haman were hanged, their souls were separated from their bodies in one instant. In virtue of that haggada there is a ceremony in the Synagogues that on the day of the feast of Purim, when the rabbi reads the story of Esther, and reaches the place where the names of the ten sons of Haman are mentioned, in which naming there are twenty-one vowels, all those twenty-one vowels the rabbi who is reading is bound to recite and say in one single inhalation or inspiration or drawing of breath, not recalling or withdrawing or diminishing his inhalation or breath in the middle, nor making any pause for breath. If however he does not do this, they make the said reader start again from the beginning. And certainly there is no Jew who would then dare to say, "It is not the law, and I do not believe that haggada." For if he did say that, he would be regarded by them as a heretic, and for that he would be punished by death. But these rabbis here, who continually deny before us Talmudic authorities, since these do not make for supporting their error, have not yet been punished by any penalty.

'There is too another haggada in the Talmud, where it is said that God has ordered Elijah that at whatever hour a circumcision is performed of any Jew, the said Elijah should attend there.

'By virtue of this haggada, the ceremony, forsooth, is performed in such a way that two chairs are prepared, forsooth, one at the right hand where Elijah is supposed to sit, and this chair is covered splendidly with white cloths and silks. At the left hand sits an elder holding the boy on his knees for the circumcision.

'And similarly, very many ceremonies could be quoted for you.

'People, therefore, who ascribe such great force and validity to the Talmudic haggadot, both in prayers and in ceremonies, how do they not fear or be afraid in such a notable and excellent assembly or place, to repudiate them brazenly and deny them?[13]

'Indeed it would be worthy and just that Our Most Holy Lord the Pope, who is required to make everyone observe his religion or belief, to condemn seriously without mercy the said rabbis as heretics and transgressors of their own religion and belief and as those who have taught and teach false doctrine, and to exact grave penalties from them, as serious delinquents. So far against the first argument.

'The second argument, which they say was put by them and not answered by me, is this: that the Jews by way of tradition hold firmly that the Messiah has not come. And this inasmuch as there has not been anyone in the world in whom all the operations of the Messiah and all his deeds, as expressed in the prophecies, have come together. Whence they mean to conclude that, even if the Messiah should be shown by Talmudic quotations to have been born, they should be explained figuratively, so that they may not contradict the prophecies.

'To this I reply that it is plain that the said rabbi has not studied well the content of these proceedings, for if he had examined it carefully, he would not have said that I did not reply sufficiently to this argument. Indeed, I say that, according to what is plain in the said proceedings, a certain paper was offered to me by them, in which all the prophecies which they could put forward to show all the acts which they say the Messiah will do were contained in full, meaning to assert that until now those acts have not been fulfilled. To this I replied at length in the said proceedings. For in the arguments which they offered in the said paper, on Tuesday the seventeenth of May, they laid down six kinds of conditions which in Scripture the Messiah ought to have: first, namely, that after their captivity he would gather them in the promised land and live in it.

'Secondly: that in the bringing-back of the said captivity, miracles were to be performed.

'Thirdly: that the Temple and Jerusalem were to be physically restored.

'Fourthly: that in the time of the Messiah, the ceremonies of the Mosaic law of sacrifices and other similar things which were performed in antiquity would have to be observed.

'Fifthly: that the Messiah would govern the whole world.

'Sixthly: that in the time of the Messiah the wars of Gog and Magog would be waged and completed.

'To prove these six conditions, you took care to quote from the Bible as many texts as you could find with all your best efforts. Of these some were relevant, and some were not.

'After this, on the twenty-ninth day of the aforesaid month, I began to reply to you on this, explaining clearly by my words, how some of the texts which you had quoted above spoke of the time of the Messiah, and some did not; and that those that did speak of the time of the Messiah were fulfilled in the coming of our Saviour Jesus Christ, in all the acts which you ascribe or attribute to the Messiah.

'First, about the assembling of the lost people to the promised land, and about the building of the Temple. If these words "land" and "Jerusalem" are understood and taken according to their proper and true meaning, in the prophecies touching this aspect, I have proved copiously through sayings of the ancient talmudic rabbis, that they ought to be understood in the prophecies in the same sense as they receive in the holy orthodox faith.

'Further, I have proved equally to you that at his coming the ceremonies which used to be observed at that time in the ancient law were to be changed, and the animal sacrifices were to cease. And also I have no less fully made plain through true texts how the true sacrifice in the time of the Messiah, acceptable to God, had to be only that of the bread and wine.

'Further, I have proved that all the miracles predicted by Isaiah and the others for the time of the Messiah were fulfilled by the coming of our Saviour Jesus Christ. All these things are contained in the broadest extent in the above proceedings, so that it is superfluous to repeat anything more about them.

'In addition you cited many other prophecies which, as you assert, were to be fulfilled in the time of the Messiah, of which many are in the 30th chapter of Deuteronomy, some in the 28th chapter of Ezekiel, and in the 37th and 39th; and Jeremiah, ch. 16, and Micah, ch. 7, and Isaiah, ch. 11 and 49 and 52, showing that all the aforesaid prophecies show that the expected return of the captivity from various parts of the world must happen, and a return to the land, and its rebuilding and consolation as much and better than before.

'To these texts I replied that all the aforesaid texts are not to be understood of the time of the Messiah, but they were all really and in fact fulfilled in the exodus of the Babylonian captivity and its return to the land; and that at that time they assembled not only from Babylonia but from various parts and regions of the Persians and Media and Asia and Egypt; and then all the good things in all these prophecies previously announced were fulfilled. And this I proved amply through very many prophecies, and in one of them, namely Jeremiah, ch. 29, where it is said: "Thus saith the Lord:

when seventy years have been accomplished in Babylon, I shall visit you, and rouse for you my good spirit, and lead you back to that place. For I know the thoughts which I think of you, saith the Lord, thoughts of peace and not of affliction."

'In particular, the said prophet says, chapter 42, speaking in the same style: "I will build you and not destroy you: I will plant you, and not pluck you up; for I have been appeased by the evil I have done to you."

'Further, Isaiah, chapter 11, says, "It shall be on that day, that the Lord will set His hand again the second time to recover the remainder of His people."

'And so that I may confirm this truth more to you, and show you clearly that you ought not to expect the Messiah any more, and that all the aforesaid prophecies have passed their time, I showed you plainly through the authority of the Talmud that the Hebrew people was never to possess the land more than twice; and this is proved by a text in the book called Yebamot, and in addition in the Ceder Holam [Seder Olam], of which the tenor is thus: "A rabbi asks: is it possible that Israel may have a third possession in the land, in time to come? He replies: No: for Scripture says in Deuteronomy, chapter 30: 'And the Lord will lead thee into the land which thy fathers possessed, and thou shalt possess it' [v. 5]. Since Scripture names possession twice, it shows that they would have a first possession and a second, but never a third possession" [b Yev., 82; Seder Olam, 30].

'Then replying to this, you said that this sentence was linked with another sentence about the first-fruits of the land of Israel, and that it was not a sentence by itself. I replied to this that it was indeed a sentence by itself, for even though in the book Yebamot there is the said sentence about first-fruits, nevertheless in the book called Ceder Holam the sentence is by itself, not mixed with any other matter. And thus it is clear that in the time of the Messiah, you were not to return to the aforesaid land to possess it.[14]

'From this it followed necessarily that those prophecies which you cited in this Disputation were to be fulfilled completely in the time of the Second Temple, when they were brought back from the Babylonian captivity.

'Then you went back and reshaped the argument, saying that my argument had no place, since the predictions of the prophets applied to the whole of Israel, and in the prosperity of the Second Temple only those were involved who were brought back from the

Babylonian captivity, who were of the tribe of Judah, but not all Israel.

'I, however, satisfying this point, said that in the book of Nehemiah, chapter 7, it is said: "The priests and the Levites and all Israel lived in their states." And since it is said "all Israel", which means the whole, nothing is excluded. Whence it follows that all the benefits and prosperity promised to all Israel were fulfilled.

'After all this had passed by, you replied that you did not know anything more to say, as can be seen plainly in detail and in general in the proceedings; and on this it is superfluous to dwell or speak further. Yet so that you may be informed more deeply in this matter, and may see more clearly, I will show you that even if it were as you say, and the benefits of the Second Temple applied only to the tribe of Judah, the prophecies nevertheless were directed at all Israel. For this I adduce for you a text which says this same thing to the letter, in the book called Midras Thehillim [Midrash Tehillim], that is, homilies on the Psalms, on Psalm 76, where it is said: "God is known in Judah, and his name is great in Israel" [v. 2]. The rabbis comment thus: "In the hour when our Lord acts mercifully to Judah, it is just as if he acts mercifully to all Israel, for all Israel are called by the name Judah, since Israel is called by a fourfold name: Jacob, Israel, Ephraim and Judah."

'It is therefore quite plain that when the benefits mentioned in the said prophecy occurred in Judah, the prophecies were adequately fulfilled.

'Behold therefore how plain is the rabbi's error, which I have omitted to repeat and pillory again,[15] since it has been very sufficiently pointed out and proved in the foregoing sessions. It seems needless to repeat it, all the more, in view of the remarks of the said rabbi in his fourth argument and his assertion in the second main part of this point, and also his citation of the rabbi Moses of Egypt.

'Manifestly plain is the blindness of the aforesaid rabbi and how he contradicts himself. For in the first two places, he asserts that there are certain acts and operations of the Messiah expressed in the prophecies, and indeed other acts which they know of through tradition from those from whom they received the law of Moses and its interpretation. In the second section, however, he adduces the said Rabbi Moses, alleging that it is not known how the acts of the Messiah will be, or are to be, until they happen, since they are very hidden.[16] Hear, then, I ask, and see how plain is this contradiction: to say that the Messiah has not yet come because the acts which he was to perform by the declaration of the prophets have not been fulfilled or done: and then to assert that the acts are so hidden that no one can know them until they have been done or fulfilled, as you will hear further more fully.

END OF FIFTY-FOURTH SESSION.

Notes

Introduction

1. An interesting discussion between an unnamed Jewish scholar and Gilbert Crispin took place about 1090. This was a dialogue before some friends, rather than a public disputation (see *Gisleberti Crispini Disputatio Judei et Christiani,* ed. B. Blumenkranz, 1956, Utrecht). Brief details exist of public disputations which took place at Burgos (1375), Ávila (1375), Pamplona (1373) and Granada (*c.* 1430).

1. The Paris Disputation, 1240

1. See Grayzel, 1966, p. 339.
2. Grayzel, 1966, p. 241 n. 96.
3. See Rosenthal, 1956–57, p. 146 n. 4.
4. 'Censorship' is really a misnomer as applied to the Talmud at any period, for censorship implied that the book, once censored, was authorised and permitted to the faithful. The Talmud always remained a proscribed book, even when expurgated. The first such expurgation took place in 1263, ordered by James I of Aragon, after the Barcelona Disputation. Frequent expurgations took place in the fifteenth century, but the Talmud was also condemned to be burnt. The 'battle of the books' in the early sixteenth century was on this issue, Johann Pfeffercorn advocating the complete suppression of the Talmud, while Johann Reuchlin defended the Talmud even from expurgation. Expurgation of the Talmud and other Jewish books continued even into the twentieth century in some areas, notably Tsarist Russia.
5. See Rabbinowitz, 1867–76.
6. See Loeb, 1888, pp. 86 f., where the history of this argument is given.
7. Katz, 1961, Chapter 3.
8. Ibid., Chapter 10.
9. Only recently, in 1236, a massacre of Jews by crusaders had taken place in Poitiers and Anjou. This massacre was condemned by Pope Gregory IX.
10. Aquinas, *Summa Contra Gentiles,* ii: 25. Among modern theologians who have tried to modify his doctrine are A. M. Fairbairn, C. H. Weisse, H. Lotze and A. Ritschl.
11. This story is not included in the Hebrew account, but is included in the thirty-five charges on which the proceedings were based, and is explicitly mentioned in the Christian account ('Confession of Master Judas', item 3, see p. 167).
12. Loeb, 1881, p. 255.

2. *The Barcelona Disputation, 1263*

1. Yet one outcome was the expurgation of the Talmud ordered by James I in 1263. Also Pope Clement IV demanded the destruction of the Talmud in 1267.
2. Defenders of the authenticity of the Midrashim quoted in *Pugio Fidei* are J. J. Brierre-Narbonne (1939), and Saul Liebermann (1939). The opposite view is taken by Y. Baer (1942).
3. The Palestinian Talmud (j Pe'ah, 2: 6, 17a) says, 'No *halakhah* may be derived from the *'aggadot.'* Hai Gaon (*Otzar ha-Geonim,* Ḥagigah, 59–60) states, 'Everyone may interpret them as he thinks fit.' Some strong anti-Aggadic statements in the Talmud are: R. Zeira (j Ma'as., 3: 9, 51a), 'turning over and over and conveying nothing'; R. Joshua b. Levi (j Shabb., 16: 1, 15c), 'He who writes it down has no share in the world to come, he who preaches it is excommunicated, and he who listens to it receives no rewards.'
4. Talmage, 1975.
5. Loeb, 1887.
6. Bonastrug, or Astrug (Astruch, etc.) was a common name among Jews of S. France and E. Spain, and Astruc is still a common surname of Jews in France. It is equivalent to the Hebrew *mazal,* or *mazal tov,* meaning 'good luck'. It is clear from one document (Denifle, 1887, document 8) that this was Naḥmanides' alternative name. There is the complication, however, that three other documents (Regné, 1910–19, nos. 262, 315, 316) refer to an Astrug de Porta 'who in controversy [*disputando*] had said something insulting about Jesus Christ'. This Astrug de Porta appears to have been a rich, landed man, brother of Benveniste de Porta, a high official (baillif, or *bayle*) of King James. Cohen (1964, p. 190) takes the view that this man was the same as Naḥmanides, but all others think him a different man (see Roth, 1950, p. 142). This man was punished by a large fine and also by exile, which later, however, was revoked.
7. Naḥmanides' finely poised position between rationalism and anti-rationalism can be seen in his letter to the rabbis of France (Letter 2 in Chavel, 1963, vol. 1), on the occasion of the anti-Maimunist controversy of 1232. Here Naḥmanides showed his sympathy with both rationalists and traditionalists. Graetz oversimplified Naḥmanides' attitude as one of mere compromise or peacemaking (see Chavel's valuable remarks in his introduction to the letter). Baer too (1961, I, pp. 103 f.) has oversimplified Naḥmanides' attitude as basically sympathetic to the anti-Maimunists. Baer also (I, p. 245) quotes Naḥmanides on Exod., 13: 6, to show his allegedly anti-rationalist philosophy: 'One cannot be said to profess the faith of Moses unless he believes that all phenomena to which we are subject are miracles every one, not caused by any natural law.' This view (shared by Judah Halevi) cannot be called anti-rationalist except in the narrowly philosophical sense of the term. It does not make Naḥmanides anti-scientific; for Berkeley, Hume and modern logical empiricists hold a similar view (i.e., that there is no logical link between recurrences of physical phenomena) while remaining keenly interested in scientific research. In his letter, Naḥmanides quotes approvingly the statement of Maimonides (*Guide,* Part 1, ch. 70) that the Jews previously possessed many books of science which were lost at the time of the exile, thus necessitating study of non-Jewish science.
8. John Scotus Erigena, in fact, chose as his triad of attributes corresponding to the Trinity, 'being', 'wisdom' and 'life'. See pp. 144 ff.
9. Roth rightly points out that the name 'Pablo Christiani' is an 'impossible hybrid'. However, since this name has become familiar to all readers of Jewish history, it is retained in this book.
10. See Campanton, 1891, and Abramson, 1971.
11. Cohen (1964, p. 175) puts forward the theory that Pablo Christiani had a cunning

strategy of alternately putting forward arguments to prove the Messiah to be divine, and to prove that he was human, thus presenting a rounded picture of the Messiah as God-man. However, Christiani had no need to prove to Naḥmanides that the Messiah would be human, as this is just what Naḥmanides was arguing himself. Christiani had no such alternating strategy; he was trying to prove that the Messiah would be *mortal,* in the sense that he would die in the course of his mission. He confused mortality, however, with crucifixion. Naḥmanides was quite willing to admit that the Messiah would be mortal in the sense that he would eventually die of old age.

9. *The* Vikuaḥ *of R. Yeḥiel of Paris: A Paraphrase*

1. Actually, Jerome did attack the Talmud, or at least the Mishnah *(Contemnentes legem Dei, et sequentes traditiones hominum, quas illi deuteroses vocant;* in Isaiam, 59, 12 [PL, 24, 603]). See Simon, 1964, pp. 116 f.
2. See b Ber., 7a. The contradiction is resolved by the Talmud as follows: 'One verse deals with children who continue in the same course as their fathers and the other verse with children who do not continue in the course of their fathers.'
3. See Mekhilta, Bahodesh, IX, near end. Rabbi Akiva's solution is that the upper heavens were lowered on this occasion to the top of the mountain. Rabbi's solution, however, is that the expression 'came down' is figurative.
4. See b Yevamot, 76b. The solution is that the prohibition applies to Moabite men but not to Moabite women.
5. See Mishnah, Avot, 1: 1. 'They [the men of the Great Synagogue] said three things: Be deliberate in judgement; raise up many disciples; and make a fence round the Torah.'
6. Yeḥiel's reply to this as given in the text is too stupid to be credible: 'If they stoned him, we are guiltless, as we weren't there. Also, you can't blame us for what is written in the Talmud, as we didn't write it, it was written long ago. It is surprising that this is the only mention in the Talmud of the execution of Jesus. The Rabbis must have foreseen that you would question us about it, and therefore did not mention him further.' This contradicts Yeḥiel's statement that the Christian Jesus is not mentioned in the Talmud at all. The question at issue, of course, was not whether the Jews of the time of Yeḥiel were to be blamed, but whether the Talmud did in fact contain offensive remarks about Jesus. The whole reply is probably the work of Joseph ben Nathan Official, who did not have information about the reply of Yeḥiel at this point. Yeḥiel's actual reply must have been that the 'Jesus of Nazareth' mentioned here was not the Christian Jesus, but some other Jesus, also from Nazareth. We find Yeḥiel arguing precisely this at a later point.
7. See b Sanh., 56a: 'Seven commandments were given to the sons of Noah: to establish a system of laws; to refrain from blasphemy; from idolatry; from adultery and incest; from murder; from robbery; and from eating flesh cut from a living animal.' These Noahide laws are regarded by the Talmud as a basic code of decency obligatory for all mankind. The Noahide laws of the Talmud were frequently cited by John Selden and Hugo Grotius in their attempts to work out the principles of international law. The Talmud regards the Jewish law, or Torah, as binding only for Jews (except where it coincides with the Noahide laws). It is not a universal law, or means of universal salvation, but a special rule for the 'nation of priests' (i.e., those born Jews and those who elect to join them by conversion). This applies particularly to ceremonial laws, such as the dietary laws, which were never intended to have universal application. Gentiles achieve salvation by adhering

to the Noahide laws, without needing to become Jews: 'The righteous men of the nations of the world have a share in the World to Come' (t Sanh., 13; also b Sanh., 105a). See Steven S. Schwarzschild (1961–62). See also Shabtai Rosenne, 'The Influence of Judaism on the Development of International Law', 1958, *Netherlands International Law Review*, 5, pp. 128–30.

8. Relevant to this is charge 15 in the thirty-five charges drawn up by Donin before the disputation (see Rosenthal, 1956–57, p. 154): 'It is written in their Talmud that Jews cannot suffer in hell longer than 12 months, and that the punishment in the gehenna cannot exceed 12 months, but that Christians stay in hell forever.'

9. This charge is based on an ambiguous expression *(hitir mamonan le-yisra'el)* in b BQ, 38a. The normative Jewish view is clearly explained in b BQ, 113a–b: all deception or cheating of gentiles is forbidden. For the other charges listed here, see Part I, pp. 30–34.

10. The Christian Account of the Paris Disputation

1. i.e., of Meaux. Vivo is a kind of translation of the first element in the name Yeḥiel.
2. See b Rosh Hashanah, 29b.
3. See b Sukkah, 13b–14a (revoking m Sukkah, 3: 13–14). See also *Shulhan Arukh*, Oraḥ Hayyim, 658: 2.
4. See b Nedarim, 65a, for both these cases.
5. See b Avodah Zarah, 3b.
6. See b Berakhot, 7a.
7. i.e., Rabbi Judah ben David of Melun.
8. *Trecensis:* i.e., of Troyes. Solomon ben Yitzḥak (Rashi, or Yitzḥaki) was the greatest of the Biblical and Talmudic commentators.
9. This is probably Jacob Tam, the grandson of Rashi, and the most distinguished of the Tosafists.
10. See Part I, pp. 26–30.
11. See Part I, pp. 35–36.
12. See b Eruvin, 21b (also b Berakhot, 4b). See p. 222, n. 7.
13. This refers to the teaching of Rabbi Eliezer in b Berakhot, 28b: 'keep your children from *higgayon.*' The meaning of this word is disputed, but Rashi ('Salomon Trecensis') does explain it as Bible-study, saying, 'Do not accustom them to too much Bible-study, as it draws . . .' (The sentence seems defective in our text of Rashi, and probably ought to be supplemented, in the light of Donin's citation, by the words ' . . . to heresy'. Rashi also gives an alternative interpretation of the word *higgayon* as 'childish chatter'.) Rashi evidently derived his explanation of *higgayon* as 'Bible-study' from the Geonic literature, where a similar explanation is found, together with an explicit mention of the danger of heresy (see *Otzar ha-Geonim*, I, 2, p. 39,). The meaning is not that Biblical study should be discouraged (it was the first essential step in all Jewish education; see m Avot, 5: 21), but that it should not be studied in isolation from Talmudic interpretations. However, it is very doubtful whether *higgayon* in the Talmudic passage does mean Bible-study. S. Liebermann (1950, p. 103) thinks it means 'logic'. M. Jastrow (1926, p. 331), thinks it means 'recitation' or 'verbal memorising'.

11. A Hebrew Account of the Tortosa Disputation

1. Hebrew *megadef,* an acronym based on the initial letters of *M*aistre *G*eronimo *d*e Santa *Fe*.

2. The ascriptions of locations are in fact incorrect in some particulars. Astruk Halevi came from Alcaniz, not from Doroca. Joseph Albo came from Doroca, not Monreal.

3. Shochat suggests that the expression 'like is cured by like' *(ha-domeh ba-domeh mavriy')* is derived from Aristotle, *De Generatione et Corruptione,* II, 8: '*omnia enim eisdem aluntur quibus constant*' ('all things are nourished by things of the same substance as themselves'). This Aristotelian passage, however, deals with nourishment, not cure; the whole passage is biological, not medical. Moreover, the Aristotelian passage provides no parallel to the second part of Rabbi Zeraḥiah's theme, 'and opposite by opposite' *(ve-ha-hefekh ba-hefekh).*

Much more closely parallel are the two medical tags, *similia similibus curantur* and *contraria contrariis curantur.* These are the formulae, respectively, of two therapeutic systems, homoeopathy and allopathy. The Latin translation of *Shevet Yehudah* (1651, Gentio) confirms this interpretation by its rendering, '*similia similibus, contraria contrariis, curantur*'.

The starting point of Rabbi Zeraḥia's sermon, therefore, seems to have been a discussion of homoeopathy and allopathy, two methods of therapy which would have been familiar (though not by those names) to his rabbinical hearers, several of whom were practising physicians. But what was the relevance of such a discussion to the circumstances of the disputation? This is a matter of conjecture. A plausible reconstruction of Rabbi Zeraḥiah's sermon, in outline, might be as follows (the terms 'homoeopathy' and 'allopathy' are here put anachronistically into Rabbi Zeraḥiah's mouth, for the sake of brevity):

> Brothers, we meet this Sabbath in difficult circumstances. We and our fellow-Jews are facing a determined attempt to convert us to Christianity. Is there any comfort to be found in our situation? Let me remind you of two methods of therapy well known to physicians: homoeopathy ('like is cured by like') and allopathy ('opposite is cured by opposite'). Both are valid methods, depending on the condition of the patient. Homoeopathy is the method by which a patient is treated by the application of a substance which, when used on a healthy person, would produce symptoms similar to those from which the patient is suffering. Allopathy is the method by which a patient is treated by the application of a substance which, in a healthy patient, should produce symptoms opposite to those from which the patient is suffering. An inflammation of the skin, for example, might be treated homoeopathically by the application of nettles or bee-stings, or allopathically by the application of ice.
>
> What is the disease from which our Jewish people in Spain is now suffering? It is loss of faith in Judaism. This disease takes two forms: a leaning towards Christianity, and a leaning towards Averroist atheism. These are two opposite extremes: Christianity being an excess of irrationalism, and Averroism an excess of rationalism. One is faith without reason, and the other is reason without faith. Between these two extremes lies the health of Judaism, a balance between faith and reason.
>
> The present Christian missionary campaign may act as a twofold therapy. First, there could be a homoeopathic reaction. Many Jews, we observe, lean towards Christianity until they encounter intense Christian propaganda, which has a counter-effect.
>
> Second, many Jews who lean towards atheism are also influenced towards a return to Judaism by listening to Christian propaganda. Their reaction is, 'I am an atheist, but if there *were* a true religion, it would be Judaism, not Christianity.' This reaction is often the beginning of a favourable reassessment of Judaism. This is an allopathic reaction—a

cure of over-rationalism by an application of over-irrationalism, resulting in the restoration of a healthy balance.

Thus we may take some comfort from the present Christian onslaught: both homoeopathically and allopathically, it may cure many of our brethren from their twofold spiritual disease.

Note: The convenient terms 'homoeopathy' and 'allopathy' were coined by S. C. F. Hahnemann (1755–1843), the founder of the modern system of homoeopathy. The mottoes *similia similibus curantur* (sometimes *curentur*) and *contraria contrariis curantur* were often used by Hahnemann, but were of medieval provenance. Hahnemann is thought to have derived his system partly from Paracelsus (1495–1541), but the idea of using minute doses was Hahnemann's own, and was not part of the original definition of homoeopathy. The words *similia similibus curantur* occur in the Geneva edition (1658) of the works of Paracelsus, as a marginal heading of one of the paragraphs, and this has been held to be the earliest authenticated occurrence of the formula. As we have seen, however, it was preceded by the use of both the homoeopathic and the allopathic Latin formulae in Gentio's translation of ibn Verga (1651). It may be that our letter of Bonastruc Demaistre on the Tortosa Disputation, deriving from the first half of the fifteenth century (with additions by the editor Solomon ibn Verga in the early sixteenth century), contains the earliest known use of the homoeopathic and allopathic formulae, though in a Hebrew, not a Latin, form.

4. *cannot be understood except face to face* Braude (1952) translates 'can be understood only when heard'. The Hebrew suggests, however, that the content of Rabbi Zeraḥiah's sermon was such that it would be unwise to repeat it except in the company of Jews. The previous note indicates the reason: the sermon was a counterblast against Christian missionary activity, suggesting that Christianity was a disease to be cured, as far as Jews were concerned.
5. i.e., Aristotle.
6. Geronimo here gives an illustration of his two-tier method of interpreting the Talmud, ascribing the part of the passage which does suit his thesis to a later, post-Christian, stratum.
7. Pope Benedict is objecting to the view that the coming of the Messiah depends entirely on the spiritual state of Jews and not of Christians; his coming should arise from the progress of the whole world. Benedict is here entering into the Jewish standpoint and suggesting an amendment in it—for from his own point of view as a Christian, the Messiah has already come. The Jewish answer, however, envisages the Messiah as a national saviour, not as a world-saviour. This is rather to underplay the universalism of Jewish messianism. This interesting exchange reflects a moment of real Jewish-Christian dialogue.
8. On this reckoning, the coming of the Messiah would be about 440 CE, while on the previous reckoning, the 'days of the Messiah' would commence at about 240 CE.
9. The Amoraim are the rabbis of the later period, from the time of the redaction of the Mishnah to the time of the closing of the Talmud. Rav Ashi, who died 427 CE, is credited with being one of the chief redactors of the Talmud.
10. The reference here is to the first saying, about the two thousand years which are 'the days of the Messiah'. This saying is in the name of 'Tanna debe Eliyyahu' (lit. 'a teacher of the house of Elijah'), and there is some doubt about what this expression means. In the other Hebrew fragment (Halberstam, 1868), much more is made of the Jewish side of this doubt. In the present account, this matter is somewhat garbled, as can be seen from Geronimo's next speech, which makes sense only if the passage involving Rav Ashi has not yet been discussed in this session.

11. This argument of Rabbi Matithiah is not clear.
12. This argument does not appear in Naḥmanides' account of the Barcelona Disputation, nor in the Christian account. See p. 144. The topic is also missing from the other Hebrew fragment of the Tortosa Disputation.
13. The reference is to Pedro III, the successor of James I of Aragon. This is simply a mistake.
14. Don Vidal is given many learned speeches in this account, but not in the other fragment. In historical fact, he was not a learned man, but a courtier and diplomat. Later he became converted to Christianity. See Marx (1944, pp. 86, 93) for the conjecture that he was given a prominent role in this account as a compliment to his descendant of the same name.
15. These arguments are not found in any extant writings of Maimonides or Ḥasdai Crescas.
16. The argument at this point is obscure, and Shoḥat seems right in maintaining that it is an addition of Ibn Verga.
17. 'Rome' should be 'Tortosa'. Ibn Verga was evidently vague about the location of this disputation, and thought it must be Rome, since it took place before the Pope. The original reading was probably, as Shoḥat suggests, 'one of the inhabitants of the city'. The other Hebrew fragment has, 'Then rose the sage Maistre Solomon Maimon of the congregation of Tortosa.'
18. See Maimonides, *Mishneh Torah*, Melakhim, ch. 11.

12. The Christian Account of the Tortosa Disputation

1. The Talmud says (b Yoma, 9b) that the reason for the destruction of the Temple was 'causeless hatred' *(sin'at hinam)*, i.e., between rival factions of Jews. Geronimo's argument, however, stemming from *Pugio Fidei*, is that 'causeless hatred' means hatred of Jesus, and that therefore this Talmudic passage is a confirmation of the Jews' sin in rejecting Jesus.
2. The actual text reads 'but through our many iniquities all these years have been lost' (b Sanh., 97a). Rabbi Ferrer (Zeraḥiah) must have argued that this text *implied* that the Messiah had not come, as in the Hebrew account (p. 172): 'this shows clearly that he has not come'.
3. See Hebrew account, p. 180. The Christian account here confirms the second Hebrew account (Halberstam, 1868), which attributes this argument to 'Maistre Solomon Maimon' (see p. 90). This scholar, as the Christian account shows elsewhere, played a prominent part on the Jewish side, and is usually called 'Salomon Ysach' in the protocols. Nothing more is known about him. See p. 198, where he is called 'Master Salomon, a Jew, rabbi of the congregation of Tortosa' *(magister Salomon, iudeus, rabi aliame dertusensis)*. The designation 'magister' or 'maestre' was given to rabbis who had achieved status for their scholarship in non-Jewish circles as well as in the Jewish community (e.g., Naḥmanides and Gersonides).
4. The papal notary (according to Pacios Lopez's edition) transcribes incorrectly throughout the protocols 'Soffrim' for 'Softim' (Shofetim), perhaps by confusion with the Talmudic tractate Soferim.
5. i.e., Maimonides and Naḥmanides.
6. *Sefer Madd'a*, 'The Book of Knowledge', is the first volume of Maimonides' *Mishneh Torah*. In this introductory volume, Maimonides explains the general principles of Judaism.
7. See b Eruvin, 21b: 'Rava said [expounding Eccles., 12: 12], "Be more careful in the observance of the words of the Scribes than in the words of the Torah. . . . whoever

transgresses any of the enactments of the Scribes is worthy of death." ' (See also b Berakhot, 4b.) At the Paris Disputation, Nicholas Donin also cited this passage, but as an example of Talmudic heresy, since Judaism ought to be based, he argues, solely on the Old Testament (see Part I, pp. 24–25, and Paris Disputation, p. 161). Geronimo quotes the same passage with the very different intention of insisting on the necessity of belief in the Talmud for Jews, thus hoping to counter the Jewish contention that Aggadic passages of the Talmud were not authoritative. Actually the above passage in Eruvin is merely a hyperbolic exegesis, intended to emphasise that the right of the scribes to enact new laws (as a 'fence' to the Torah) is itself derived from Biblical authority (Deut., 17: 10). The expression *hayav mittah* ('is worthy of death') is often used hyperbolically, without literal legal force, e.g., b Shabb. 114a, 'A scholar upon whose garment a grease-stain is found is worthy of death.'

8. 'Even if he admits that the whole Torah is from Heaven excepting a single point, a particular *qal va-homer* [*a fortiori*] deduction or a certain *gezerah shavah* [argument from likeness of expressions]—he is regarded as one who "hath despised the word of the Lord" [Num., 15: 31]' (b Sanh., 99a). Geronimo is here being disingenuous. The Masorah (the traditional text of the Bible) and the conclusions arrived at by the two methods of deduction mentioned were regarded as having the status of *halakhah le-Mosheh mi-Sinai* (Sinaitical law) and therefore as *de-'uraita* (of Biblical authority). The Talmud, however, does not regard all its own provisions as being in this category. Very many of its laws are regarded as *de-rabbanan* (of rabbinical status), i.e., as having less than Biblical authority. This meant that such laws carried lower penalties, could be repealed by a rabbinical council, and could even be disregarded in a time of emergency *(sha'at ha-deḥaq).* See Z. H. Chajes, *Mevo ha-Talmud,* ch. VI–IX.

9. *Mishneh Torah*, Shofetim, Mamrim, 3: 'He who does not acknowledge the Oral Law is not a "rebellious elder" but he is in the category of the heretics [*'apiqorsin*].' Our text gets this slightly wrong by saying 'not only a rebel', but whether the error is that of Geronimo or of the papal notary cannot be decided. Maimonides goes on to explain that the penalty of death for a 'heretic' applies only to heresiarchs, not to their followers or descendants.

10. This quotation from Midrash Qohelet is wrongly and meaninglessly punctuated in Pacios Lopez's edition. The Latin should be punctuated as follows:

> *Scriptum est Deuteronomio 'dedit michi Deus tabulas lapideas cum digito dei vel eius scriptas, et super eas sicut omnia verba.' Inquit rabi Osua, filius Levi: 'Super eas: "et super eas"; omnia: "sicut omnia"; verba: "illa verba"; preceptum: "totum preceptum". Ad ostendum quod. . . .'*

Rabbi Joshua's point is that the superfluous expressions in the Biblical verse are intended to hint that in addition to the Written Law (with which the verse is ostensibly concerned) there is also an Oral Law of equal authority. (Note that the last phrase commented on by Rabbi Joshua does not appear in our Biblical text.)

11. This saying does not appear in the chapter cited, or anywhere else in the Talmud.

12. There is actually no mention of Elijah in the Havdalah ceremony, but it is customary to sing songs mentioning Elijah before or after the Havdalah. The singing of such songs does not imply, of course, that Talmudic or Midrashic legends about the future coming of Elijah on a Saturday evening have the force of articles of belief.

13. That certain liturgical customs were derived from Aggadic notions does not, of course, elevate such notions into dogmas of faith. Geronimo must have been well aware of this.

14. In Seder Olam, ch. 30, the saying 'there will be no third possession for you' is cited not 'by itself' but in connection with the laws of tithes, fallow-years *(shemittot)* and jubilees. The saying does not, of course, deny that Israel will occupy the Land of Israel in the time of the Messiah. It asserts that the holiness of the Land did not lapse after the destruction of 70

CE (as it did in the time of the Babylonian exile); therefore no act of resanctification or repossession would be necessary in Messianic times. The practical corollary was that the payment of first-fruits, tithes, etc. was still in force in the Land of Israel, even after the destruction of the Temple. This is a minority view, not the accepted law, which regards the continued payment of first-fruits, etc. after the destruction as having only rabbinical, not Pentateuchal, force. The whole matter is discussed also in b Niddah, 46b. Again, it is hard to believe that Geronimo was putting forward his argument sincerely, since his interpretation has plausibility only when the passages cited are taken completely out of context.

15. The Latin word is *repillogare,* which I have not been able to find in any dictionary of medieval Latin.

16. See Maimonides, *Mishneh Torah,* Shofetim, Melakhim, 12: 2. (See p. 202.) Maimonides is quite definite that the Messiah will redeem Israel from exile and will set up his kingdom in the Land of Israel. Maimonides directs a warning, however, against those who wish to be too dogmatic about the *details* (e.g., the exact date of the Messiah's coming, whether he will be preceded by Elijah, etc.). There is thus no real contradiction in the argument of Rabbi Astruk, who follows Maimonides in distinguishing between the broad outlines of the Messiah's coming (which he regards as known) and the details (which he regards as unknown). The Jewish case is that the Christian disputants, both at Barcelona and Tortosa, wished to insist on a definite and dogmatic interpretation of certain scattered Jewish Aggadot (which in the Jewish tradition were regarded as tentative and obscure), while ignoring the main outlines of Jewish messianic expectations, which were clear enough, and were unfulfilled in Jesus.

Bibliography

Relevant works published since the first edition of this book appeared in 1982 are listed in the Additional Bibliography on page 8.

Abbreviations in Bibliography

Enc. Jud.	*Encyclopaedia Judaica*
ET	*English translation*
HUCA	*Hebrew Union College Annual*
HTR	*Harvard Theological Journal*
JQR	*Jewish Quarterly Review*
MGWJ	*Monatsschrift für Geschichte und Wissenschaft des Judenthums*
REJ	*Revue des Études Juives*

Abraham ibn Daud. 1969. *The Book of Tradition: Sefer ha-Qabbalah,* ed. Gerson D. Cohen. London: Littman Library of Jewish Civilization.

Abraham ben Moses Maimonides. 1959. *Peyrush ha-Torah,* ed. S. D. Sassoon, tr. E. J. Wiesenberg. London.

———. 1821. *Milhamot Adonai.* Vilna.

Abramson, Shraga. 1971. *Kelalei ha-Talmud be-divrei ha-Ramban.* Jerusalem.

Abravanel, Isaac. 1954–60. *Peyrush,* 4 vols. Jerusalem/Tel Aviv.

Albo, Joseph. 1930. *Sefer ha-Ikkarim,* ed. I. Husik, 4 vols. Philadelphia.

Altaner, B. 1933a. Die fremdsprachliche Ausbildung der Dominikanermissionäre während des 13 und 14 Jahrhunderts. *Zeitschrift für Missionswissenschaft und Religionswissenschaft* XXIII.

———. 1933b. Zur Kenntnis des Hebraeischen im Mittelalter. *Biblische Zeitschrift* XXI.

Amador de los Ríos, J. 1875. *Historia de los Judíos de España y Portugal.* Madrid.

Aquinas, Thomas. 1882. *Works.* Rome.

Augustine. 1945. *City of God,* tr. J. Henley, 2 vols. New York.

Bacher, W. 1884, 1890. *Die Agada der Tannaïten,* 2 vols. Strasbourg.

———. 1878. *Die Agada der babylonischen Amoraer.* Strasbourg.

———. 1892–99. *Die Agada der palestinensischen Amoraer,* 3 vols. Strasbourg.

Baer, Yitzhak. 1923. *Untersuchungen über Quellen und Komposition des Schebet Jehuda.* Berlin.

———. 1930–31. On the Disputations of R. Yeḥiel of Paris and R. Moses ben Naḥman (Hebrew). *Tarbiz* II: 172–87.

———. 1931. Die Disputation von Tortosa (1413–1414). *Spanische Forschungen der Görresgesellschaft* III: 330ff.

———. 1939. *Abner Aus Burgos, Korrespondenzblatt des Vereins zur Gründung und Erhaltung einer Akademie für die Wissenschaft des Judentums.* Berlin.

———. 1942. The forged Midrashim of Raymund Martini, and their role in medieval religious polemic (Hebrew). *Memorial Volume to Asher Gulak and S. Klein.* Jerusalem.

———. 1961, 1971. *A History of the Jews in Christian Spain,* 2 vols. Philadelphia.

Baron, Salo W. 1952–75. *A Social and Religious History of the Jews,* 16 vols. Philadelphia.

Benedict, B. Z. 1950–51. On the history of the Torah centre in Provence (Hebrew). *Tarbiz* XXII.

Benjamin of Tudela. 1907. *Itinerary.* tr. M. N. Adler. London.

Ben Sasson, H. H. 1966. Jewish–Christian disputation in the setting of humanism and Reformation in the German Empire. *HTR,* LIX: 369–90.

———. 1969. *Toledot 'Am Yisrael* II. Jerusalem.

Berger, E. 1895. *Histoire de Blanche de Castille.* Paris.

Bloch, Joseph S. 1927. *Israel and the Nations.* Berlin/Vienna.

Blumenkranz, B., ed. 1963. *Gisleberti Crispini Disputatio Judei et Christiani.* Utrecht.

———. 1960. *Juifs et Chrétiens dans le Monde Occidentale.* Paris.

———. 1963. *Les Auteurs Chrétiens Latins du Moyen Age sur les Juifs et la Judaisme.* Paris.

Braude, W. G. 1968. *Pesikta Rabbati,* ET. New Haven, Conn.

Braude, M. 1952. *Conscience on Trial.* New York.

Brettle, S. 1924. *San Vicente Ferrer und sein literarischer Nachlass.* Münster.

Brierre-Narbonne, J. J. 1939. *Commentaire de la Genèse de R. Moïse le Predicateur.* Paris.

Campanton, Isaac. 1891. *Darkhei ha-Talmud,* ed. I. H. Weiss. Wien.

Castro, A. 1954. *The Structure of Spanish History.* Princeton, N.J.

Charles, R. H. 1899. *A Critical History of the Doctrine of a Future Life in Israel, in Judaism and in Christianity,* London.

Chavel, H. D. 1960. *Naḥmanides* (biography). New York.

———. 1963. *Kitvey Rabbenu Mosheh ben Naḥman,* 2 vols. Jerusalem.

Cohen, A. 1927. *The Teachings of Maimonides.* London.

Cohen, Martin A. 1964. Reflections on the text and context of the Disputation of Barcelona. *HUCA* XXXV: 157–92.

Copleston, F. C. 1961. *Medieval Philosophy.* New York.

Coulton, G. G. 1938. *Inquisition and Liberty.* London.

Crescas, Hasdai. 1410. *'Or 'Adonai.* Ferara.

Davies, W. D. 1948. *Paul and Rabbinic Judaism*. London.

de Bofarull y Sans, F. 1911. *Jaime I y los Judios*. Barcelona.

de Gayangos, P., ed. 1883. *The Chronicle of James I, King of Aragon*, tr. J. Foster. London.

de Tourtoulon, Ch. 1867. *Jacme Ier le Conquérant*. Montpellier.

Denifle, H. 1887. Quellen zur Disputation Pablos Christiani mit Mose Nachmani zu Barcelona, 1263. *Historisches Jahrbuch der Görres-Gesellschaft* VIII: 225–44.

Dinur, B. Z. 1961–65. *Yisrael ba-Golah*, 2nd ed., 5 vols. Tel Aviv.

Dubnov, Simon. 1967–73. *History of the Jews*, tr. Moshe Spiegel, 5 vols. New York/London.

Efros, I. 1924. *Philosophical Terms in the 'Moreh Nebukim'*. New York.

———. 1974. *Studies in Medieval Jewish Philosophy*. New York/London.

Eisenstein, J. D. 1928. *Otzar Vikuḥim*. New York.

Epstein, A. 1949–50. Rabbi Mosheh ha-Darshan mi-Narbonah. *Kitvey Rabbi Avraham Epstein*. Jerusalem.

Etheridge, J. W. 1862–69. *The Targums of Onkelos and Jonathan ben Uzziel on the Pentateuch*, 2 vols. London.

Finkelstein, L. 1926. *Commentary of David Kimhi on Isaiah*. New York.

Friedlaender, M. 1877. *Essays on the Writings of Abraham ibn Ezra*, London.

Funk, F. X. 1941. *A History of the Church*, 2 vols. ET. London.

Genovés, V. 1943 *San Vicente Ferrer en la politica de su tiempo*. Madrid.

Gilson, E. 1955. *History of Christian Philosophy in the Middle Ages*. New York.

Ginzberg, L. 1909–38. *The Legends of the Jews*, 7 vols. Philadelphia.

Goldstein, M. 1950. *Jesus in the Jewish Tradition*. New York.

Girbal, C. E. 1870. *Los Judíos de Gerona*. Gerona.

Graetz, H. 1897–1911. *Geschichte der Juden*, 11 vols. Leipzig.

Grayzel, Solomon. 1966. *The Church and the Jews in the XIIIth Century*. New York.

Greenstone, J. H. 1906. *The Messiah Idea in Jewish History*. Philadelphia.

Grünbaum, S., ed. 1873. *Vikuaḥ Rabbenu Yeḥiel mi-Paris*. Thorn.

Guttmann, J. 1964. *Philosophies of Judaism*, tr. D. W. Silverman. Philadelphia.

Hadassi, Judah. 1971. *Eshkol Hakofer* (Karaism), ed. Leon Nemoy. New York.

Halberstam, A. 1868. Anonymous Hebrew account of the Tortosa Disputation (Hebrew). In Kobak's *Jeschurun* VI: 45–55. Bamberg.

Ha-Meiri, Menahem. 1948–67. *Bet ha-beḥirah*. Israel.

Heer, Friedrich. 1967. *God's First Love*. London.

Heinemann, I. 1949. *The Methods of the Aggadah* (Hebrew). Jerusalem.

Herford, T. R. 1903. *Christianity in Talmud and Midrash*. London.

Horodezky, S. A. 1952. *Jewish Mysticism* (Hebrew). Tel Aviv.

Ibn Verga, Solomon. 1947. *Shevet Yehudah,* ed. A. Shochat. Jerusalem.

Jacob ben Elie. 1868. Letter on Pablo Christiani. *Jeschurun* VI: 29–30.

Jacobs, L. 1973. *A Jewish Theology.* London.

James I of Aragon. *Chronicle.* See de Gayangos, P.

Jastrow, M. 1926. *A Dictionary of the Targumim, the Talmud Babli and Yerushalmi, and the Midrashic Literature.* New York.

Jellinek, A. 1938. *Bet ha-Midrash,* 2nd ed., 6 vols. Jerusalem.

Jerome. *Commentary on Isaiah.* Migne PL, vol. 29, 87.

Joseph ben Nathan Official, *Vikuaḥ Rabbenu Yeḥiel mi-Paris.* See Wagenseil, J. C.; Grünbaum, S.; and Eisenstein, J. D.

Judah Ha-levi. 1927. *Kitab al-Khazari,* tr. H. Hirschfeld. New York.

Katz, Jacob. 1961. *Exclusiveness and Tolerance.* Oxford.

Kaufmann, Y. 1929–32. *Golah ve-Nekhar,* 2 vols. Tel Aviv.

Kayserling, M. 1890. *Biblioteca Española-Portugueza-Judaica.* Strasbourg.

———. 1865. Die Disputation des Bonastruc mit Fra Pablo in Barcelona. *MGWJ* XIV: 308–13.

Kimhi, Joseph. 1972. *Book of the Covenant,* ed. F. Talmage. Toronto.

Kisch, A. 1874. *Papst Gregor des Neunten Anklageartikel gegen den Talmud.* Leipzig.

———. 1874. Die Anklageartikel gegen den Talmud und ihre Vertheidigung durch R. Jehiel ben Joseph vor Ludwig dem Heiligen in Paris. *MGWJ* XXIII: 10–18, 62–75, 123–30, 155–63, 204–12.

Kohut, A. 1955. *Aruch Completum,* 9 vols. New York.

Kook, S. C. 1953–54. The Date of the Burning of the Talmud in France (Hebrew). *Kirjath Sepher* XXIX: 281ff.

Kook, S. H. 1935. Yeḥiel of Paris (Hebrew). *Zion* V: 97–102.

Krauss, S. 1902. *Das Leben Jesus nach jüdischen Quellen.* Berlin.

———. 1898. *Griechische und Lateinische Lehnwörter in Talmud, Midrasch und Targum.* Berlin.

Lasker, I. J. 1977. *Jewish Philosophical Polemics against Christianity in the Middle Ages.* New York.

Lea, H. C. 1906. *A History of the Inquisition in the Middle Ages.* London.

Levy, Raphael. 1964. *Trésor de la Langue des juifs Français au Moyen Age.* Austin.

Lewin, A. 1869. Die religionsdisputation des R. Jehiel. *MGWJ* XVIII: 97ff, 145ff, 193ff.

Liebermann, S. 1955–62. *Tosefta ki-feshutah,* 5 vols. New York.

———. 1950. *Hellenism in Jewish Palestine.* New York.

———. 1939. *Shekiin.* Jerusalem.

Little, A. 1936. The Mendicant Orders. *Cambridge Medieval History* VI: 741ff. Cambridge.

Loeb, I. 1881. La controverse de 1240 sur le Talmud. *REJ* II: 253ff, and III: 39ff.

———. 1888. *Joseph Haccohen et les Chroniques Juifs.* Paris.

———. 1887. La controverse de 1263 à Barcelone. *REJ* XV: 1–18.

Luce, S. 1881. Catalogue des documents du trésor de Chartres relatifs aux juifs sous le règne de Philippe le Bel. *REJ* II.

McGiffert, A. C. 1932–33. *A History of Christian Thought,* 2 vols. New York.

Maimonides, Moses. 1957–65. *Mishneh Torah,* 15 vol., ed. S. T. Rubinstein. Jerusalem.

———. 1963. *Guide for the Perplexed,* tr. Shlomo Pines. Chicago.

———. 1963b. *Mishnah im Peyrush R. Mosheh b. Maimon,* ed. and tr. into Hebrew by J. Kafih, Jerusalem.

———. 1972. *Iggerot ha-Rambam,* ed. J. Kafih, Jerusalem.

Mandonnet, P. 1913. Preachers, Order of. *Catholic Encyclopaedia* XII.

———. 1938. *Saint Dominique,* 2 vols. Paris.

Margoliouth, R. 192-. *Vikuaḥ ha-Ramban.* Lemberg.

Martini, Raymund. 1687. *Pugio Fidei adversus Mauros et Judaeos.* Leipzig/ Frankfurt.

Marx, A. 1944. *Studies in Jewish History and Booklore.* Philadelphia.

Mekilta de-Rabbi Ishmael. 1933. ed. and tr. J. Z. Lauterbach, 3 vols. Philadelphia.

Migne, I. P. 1844. *Patrologia Latina.* Paris.

Milḥemet Ḥovah. 1710. Constantinople.

Millas Vallicrosa, J. M. 1960. Extractos del Talmud y alusiones polemicas de la Biblioteca Catedral de Gerona. *Sefarad* XX: 17–49.

———. 1940. Sobre las fuentes documentales de la controversia de Barcelona en el año 1263. *Anales de la Universidad de Barcelona: Memorias y comunicaciones,* pp. 25–44.

Moore, G. F. 1927–30. *Judaism,* 3 vols. Oxford.

Moses ha-Darshan. 1940. *Midrash Bereshit Rabbati,* ed. Ch. Albeck. Jerusalem.

Naḥmanides, Moses. *Vikuaḥ.* See Wagenseil, J.C.; Steinschneider, M.; Margoliouth, R.; Chavel, H. D.; Eisenstein, J. D.; Braude, M., tr.; and Rankin, O. S., tr.

———. 1967. *Peyrush ʿal ha-Torah,* ed. H. D. Chavel, 2 vols. Jerusalem.

Neubauer, A. and Driver, S. R. 1876. *The 53rd Chapter of Isaiah According to the Jewish Interpreters.* Oxford.

———. 1887. *Medieval Jewish Chronicles.* Oxford.

———. 1888. Jewish Controversy and the *Pugio Fidei. The Expositor,* third series, vol. VII, pp. 81–105, 179–97.

Origen. 1869. *The Writings of Origen,* 2 vols., tr. F. Crombie. Edinburgh.

Ozar ha-Geonim. 1928–44, ed. B. M. Lewin, 13 vols. Jerusalem.

———. 1966. ed. H. Z. Taubes, 1 vol. Jerusalem.

Pacios Lopez, A. 1957. *La Disputa de Tortosa,* 2 vols. Madrid/Barcelona,

Parkes, James. 1934. *The Conflict of the Church and the Synagogue.* London.

Paul of Burgos. 1475. *Scrutinium scripturarum.* Mantua.

Perles, J. 1858. Über den Geist des Kommentars des R. Moses ben Nachman zum Pentateuch. *MGWJ* VII: 81ff, 117ff.

Pillemont, G. 1955. *Pedro de Luna. Le dernier pape d'Avignon.* Paris.

Posnanski, A. 1904. *Schiloh.* Leipzig.

———. 1922–23. Le Colloque de Tortose et de San Mateo (7 Février 1413–13 Novembre 1414). *REJ* LXXIV:17–39, 160–68; LXXV:74–88, 187–204; LXXVI:37–46.

Poliakov, Leon. 1974. *The History of Anti-Semitism.* 3 vols. London: Littman Library of Jewish Civilization.

Potthast, Augustus 1875. *Regesta Pontificium Romanorum,* 2 vols. Berlin.

Quétif, J. and Ekhard, J. 1719. *Scriptores Ordinis Predicatorum.* Paris.

Rabbinowitz, R. N. 1867–86. *Diqduqei Soferim,* 15 vols. Munich.

Rankin, O. S. 1956. *Jewish Religious Polemic.* Edinburgh.

Regné, Jean. 1910–19. Catalogue des actes de Jaime I, Pedro III et Alfonso III, rois d'Aragon, concernant les juifs 1213–91. *REJ* LX–LXX.

Renan, E., and Neubauer, A. 1877. Les rabbins français du commencement du quatorzième siècle. *Histoire littéraire de la France* XXVII:562–69. Paris.

Rosenthal, J. M. 1956–57. The Talmud on Trial. *JQR* XLVII:58–76, 145–69.

———1960. Sifrut ha-vikuaḥ ha-anti-notsrit 'ad sof ha-meah ha-shemoneh-'esreh. *Areshet* 2.

Roth, C. 1932. *A History of the Marranos* Philadelphia.

———. 1950. The Disputation of Barcelona (1263). *HTR* XLIII:117–44.

Ruether, Rosemary. 1974. *Faith and Fratricide.* New York.

Sarachek, J. 1932. *The Doctrine of the Messiah in Medieval Jewish Literature.* New York.

———.1935. *Faith and Reason: The Conflict over the Rationalism of Maimonides.* Williamsport, Pa.

Schechter, S. 1896. Nachmanides, in *Studies in Judaism.* London.

———.1909. *Some Aspects of Rabbinic Theology,* London.

Scholem, G. 1941. *Major Trends in Jewish Mysticism.* Jerusalem.

———. 1948. *The Early Kabbalah, 1150–1250* (Hebrew), Tel Aviv.

Schwarzschild, Steven S. 1961–62. Noachites, *JQR* LII:297–308:LIII:30–65.

Seder Olam. 1894, Ed. B. Ratner. Vilna.

Silver, A. H. 1927. *A History of Messianic Speculation in Israel.* New York.

Simon, M. 1964. *Verus Israel,* 2nd ed. Paris.

Stein, S. 1969. *Jewish-Christian Disputations in 13th-century Narbonne.* London.

Steinschneider, M. 1860. *Nahmanidis Disputatio Publica pro fide Judaica.* Stettin/Berlin.

Swift, F. Darwin. 1894. *The Life and Times of James the First the Conqueror.* Oxford.

Talmage, Frank Ephraim. 1975. *David Kimḥi: the Man and the Commentaries.* Cambridge, Mass. / London.

———. 1968. David Kimḥi and the rationalist tradition. *HUCA* XXXIX:177–218.

Twersky, I. 1962. *Rabad of Posquières.* Cambridge, Mass.

Urbach, E. E. 1968. *Ba'aley ha-Tosafot* (especially ch. 9). Jerusalem.

Vacandard. 1922. *Dictionnaire de théologie catholique* VII:2016f, 'Inquisition'.

Valls-Taberner, F. (1953). *San Ramon de Penyafort: Obras Selectas.* Madrid.

Wagenseil, J. C. 1681. *Tela Ignea Satanae.* Altdorf.

Weiss, I. H. See Campanton, Isaac.

Wertheimer, S. A. 1950–53. *Battei Midrashot,* 2 vols. Jerusalem.

Williams, A. L. 1935. *Adversus Judaeos.* Cambridge, England.

Wolfson, H. A. 1929. *Crescas' Critique of Aristotle.* Cambridge, Mass.

———. 1956. *The Philosophy of the Church Fathers.* Cambridge, Mass.

Zacuto, Abraham ben Samuel. 1924. *Sefer ha-Yuḥasin,* ed. M. Filipowski. Frankfurt.

Zurita, G. 1669. *Anales de la Corona de Aragón.* Zaragoza.

General Index

Abaye, 157
Abimi, 203
Abraham, 36, 46, 48, 122, 136, 137, 161, 210
Abraham ibn Daud, 29
Abramson, Shraga, 217
Abravanel, Isaac, 88
Abu Janda, 169
Acre, 80
Adam, 114, 130; curse of, 118; intercourse of, with animals, 36, 161, 162, 165; mortality of, 116; sin of, 51, 117; and spirit of God, 48, 140
Adam de Chambly, 22
Aggadah: allegorical nature of, 46–47, 57, 72, 90, 154; authority of, 36, 44, 48–49, 74, 115; critical remarks on, in Talmud, 217; and dogma, 223; Geronimo on, 207–10; spelling of, 110; and theology, 93
Agrippa II (king), 125
Ahaz (king), 129
Akiva, 156, 218; mistake of, re Bar Kokhba, 120; role of, in formation of Mishnah, 104
'akum, 30–33
Albigensians, 10, 13
Albo, Joseph, 50, 92, 169, 178, 197, 198, 200, 220
Alconstantini family, 79
Alexander the Great, 106
Alexander Jannaeus, 26, 111, 157
Allopathy, 220–21
Amaziah (king), 129
Amoraim, 221
Andreas Bertrandi, 198
Angels: cannot believe in Trinity, 63, 146; intercourse of, with mortal women, 162
Anti-Maimunists, 69, 217
Antiochus Epiphanes, 105
Apocrypha, 43
Aquinas, Thomas, 34, 62, 80, 216
Arab (in Midrash), 110, 199
Arenga, 169, 170
Aristotle, 46, 84, 88, 172, 220, 221
Arnold de Segarra, 98, 128, 132
Arnold of Segura. *See* Arnold de Segarra
Ashi, Rav, 104, 177–78, 200, 203, 221
Astruc (name), 217
Astrug de Porta, 217
Astruk Halevi, 84, 169, 185, 187, 195, 196, 198, 199, 200–204, 220, 224; on longevity of Messiah, 182; on toleration, 86–87
Athronges, 27
Augustine: argument of, about Trinity, 65, 144
Averroism, 94, 220
Azariah (king), 129

Babylon, 141
Babylonian Captivity, 105, 106, 108, 109, 124, 149, 188, 212, 214, 223
Baer, Yitzhak, 13, 23, 57–66, 67, 89, 98, 103, 147, 217
Balaam's ass, 154
Baptism: of Jews, 191, 197
Bar Kokhba, 31, 43, 120, 121
bat qol, 35
Benedict XIII (pope), 82, 85, 91, 168, 183, 190, 197, 198, 221; claim to papacy of, unsuccessful, 94; interventions in disputation of Tortosa, 169, 174, 176–77, 182
Benjamin of Tudela, 21
Ben Pandira, 26, 157. *See also* Jesus
Ben Sasson, H. H., 120
Ben Stada, 26, 157. *See also* Jesus
Benveniste de Porta, 81, 217

Berkeley, George, 217
Bethlehem, 110, 193
Bezalel, 141
Bible: authority of, 115; study of, allegedly discouraged, 167, 219
Bishop of Gerona. *See* Peter of Castellnou
Bithiah, 129, 130
Blanche of Castile (queen), 22, 153, 155, 156, 158
Blumenkranz, B., 123, 216
Bodo, 123
Bonastrug (name), 217
Bonastrug de Porta, 59, 79, 217. *See also* Naḥmanides
Bonjoa, 169
Braude, M., 13, 221
Brierre-Narbonne, J. J., 217

Caleb, 130
Canaanites, 159, 179
Campanton, Isaac, 217
Canon Law, 47
'causeless hatred', 194, 222. *See also* 'groundless hate'
Censorship: of Talmud, 25, 132, 216; of Maimonides, 132
Chajes, Z. H., 223
Chamber of Hewn Stone, 185
Chavel, C. B., 14, 76, 78, 115, 144, 217
Christian Fathers, 47
Christian Hebraists, 46
Christianity: an Aggadic religion, 48–49; contrasted with Judaism, 220–21
Christians: alleged remarks against, in Talmud, 30–34; not *goyim*, 32, 160–61
Church, 53
Church of England, 118
Clement IV (pope), 80, 217
Cohen, Martin A., 13, 57, 68–74, 111, 132, 133, 217
Constantinople edition (of Naḥmanides' *Vikuaḥ*), 131
Conversos, 84
Council of Constance, 94
Council of Elvira, 32
Council of Laodicea, 32
Council of Pisa, 94
Council of Vienne, 41
Covenant, 50
Crescas, Ḥasdai, 50, 88, 92, 180, 222
Crispin, Gilbert, 216
Crusades, 40
Cyrus, 124, 125

Daniel, 41, 111, 149, 177, 192
Dante, 62, 116
Darius, 124
David (king), 43, 55, 111, 129, 133; descent of, from Moabitess, 154; prefiguring Messiah, 137
Davies, W. D., 19, 112
Day of Atonement, 158, 209
Desmaîtres, Bonastruc, 82, 168, 221
Denifle, Heinrich, 57, 61, 63, 64, 65, 66, 76, 132, 217
de-rabbanan, 223
derush, 46, 112
de-'uraita, 223
Disputations: Ávila, 216; Barcelona, 39–81, 97–150; Barcelona, agenda of, 58, 60–61, 103, 147; Barcelona, dates of, 114; Burgos, 216; Granada, 216; Pamplona, 216; Paris, 19–38, 153–67; Tortosa, 82–96, 168–215
Dominicans (Preaching Friars), 12, 22, 39, 40, 56, 59, 60, 69, 70, 73, 75, 79, 80, 98, 100, 114, 133, 142, 147, 191
Donin, Nicholas, 20, 22, 23, 24, 25, 26, 30, 35, 41, 51, 153–67, 219, 223
Duran, Profiat, 28, 143

Earthly Paradise, 46, 116, 199. *See also* Eden, Garden of
Ebionites, 55
Eden, Garden of, 52, 116, 138
Egyptians, 159
Eighteen Benedictions, 25, 160; *birkat ha-minim*, 161
Eisenstein, J. D., 76, 136
Eliezer (servant of Abraham), 129
Eliezer (rabbi), 35, 167, 219
Eliezer of Tarascon, 80
Elijah, 37, 71, 111, 113, 114, 117, 162, 166, 167, 209, 210, 223; in Garden of Eden, 129, 148; longevity of, 114, 162; prophesying Messiah, 172–74, 176, 178
Elisha, 154
Enoch: in Garden of Eden, 129; longevity of, 114
Esther, 210

Eucharist, 189, 194, 212
Eve, 36; cohabited with serpent, 51, 161, 165; curse of, 118
Eved-Melekh the Ethiopian, 129
Evil spirits, 47
Excommunication, 49
Exilarchs: rule of, 106; right to licence judges, 107
Exodus, 50
Ezra (Book of), 109

Faith: should not be disturbed by disputation, 86
Fairbairn, A. M., 216
Ferdinand of Aragon (king), 84, 91
Ferrer (rabbi), 195, 196, 197, 198, 199, 222. *See also* Zeraḥia Halevi
Ferrer, Vincent (saint), 83, 84, 93
'fiache', 162
Fire from heaven, 179
Fourth Lateran Council, 22
Franciscans (Minorites), 20, 22, 114, 133, 147
Freud, Sigmund, 36, 52

Galileo, 88
Gehenna, 117, 118. *See also* Hell
Gentiles: cheating of, forbidden, 219; Christians not reckoned as, 160–61, 165; Talmud on, 159, 160, 165
Gentio, G., 220
Geoffrey of Belville, 22
Geonim, 44
Gerona, 83; Trinity discussed at, 144, 148
Geronimo de Santa Fe, 47, 82–94, 168–215, 221–24: accuses Jews of heresy, 188, 211; on Messiah, alleged Jewish contradiction about, 214, 224; snatches text of Midrash, 90; style of, 188; Talmudic theory of, 187, 205–8. *See also* Halorki, Joshua
Gersonides. *See* Levi ben Gershom
gezerah shavah, 223
Gibeonites, 158
Gilles of Cervello, 133
"gloria", 139
Gnosticism, 43
God: attributes of, 145; blasphemies against, alleged, 34; impassibility of, 34, 145; laughter of, 167; phylacteries of, 161; prayer of, to Himself, 166; sin-offering of, 160; vows of, 158, 165; weeping of, 161, 165
Gog and Magog, 127, 211
Gospel of Nicodemus, 118
goyim. See *'akum*. *See also* Gentiles
Graetz, Heinrich, 57, 217
Grayzel, Solomon, 216
Greece, 141; rule of, over Jews, 106
Greek philosophy, 35
Gregory IX (pope), 21, 80, 216
Grotius, Hugo, 218
'groundless hate', 189, 205. *See also* 'causeless hatred'
Grünbaum, S., 153
Guillaume, Maestro, 111

Haggadah (Passover), 115
Hahnemann, S. C. F., 221
Hai Gaon, 217
Halakhah, 36, 74, 115
halakhah le-Moshe mi-Sinai, 223
Halberstam, A., 221, 222
Halorki, Joshua, 82, 168, 169, 182. *See also* Geronimo de Santa Fe
Ham, 36
Haman, 210
Ha-Meiri, Menahem ben Solomon, 33
Hasmonean dynasty, 105, 106
Havdalah, 209
Hebrew: taught to Christians, 161
Helena, 205
Hell, 52, 160, 165, 219; harrowing of, 118. *See also* Gehenna
Henry VIII (king of England), 81
Heresy, 23, 49; contrast between Jewish and Christian view of, 92–93
Herod I (king), 106
Herodian dynasty, 106
Hezekiah (king), 55, 129
higgayon, 219
Hillel (son of Judah III), 107
Hiram (king of Tyre), 117; in Garden of Eden, 129
Holy Land: not to be possessed by Jews, 194, 213, 223
Homoeopathy, 220–21
Humanism: of Judaism, 36
Hume, David, 217
Huna (Rav), 200
Hyperbolic expressions, 223

Ibn Ezra, Abraham, 46
Ibn Gabirol, Solomon, 23
Ibn Verga, Solomon, 144, 168, 222
Idolatry, 54. *See also 'akum*
Incarnation: doctrine of, 54, 63, 119
Infallibility of the Church, 36
Inquisition, 12, 23, 25, 80, 83
Isaac, 46
Islam, 39
'ispaqlaria, 139
Israel: Land of, 106, 107; Ten Tribes of, 105; as title claimed by Christians, 179

Jacob, 46, 109, 141
Jacob Tam, 219
James I (king of Aragon), 12, 40, 50, 56, 59, 65, 69, 73, 79, 80, 81, 98, 119, 142, 147, 217; and censoring of Maimonides, 132; and censoring of Talmud, 132, 216; complex character of, 143; interventions of, in disputation, 114, 117, 135; on Jesus' messiahship, 142; and Naḥmanides, 146; on Trinity, 145
Jastrow, M., 109, 219
Jehoash (king), 129
Jeremiah: as Suffering Servant, 112
Jerome, 128–29, 153, 205, 218
Jerusalem, 26, 80
Jesus, 24, 52, 104, 105, 106, 107, 111, 121, 122, 124, 143, 157, 176, 183; and Abraham, 138; as Ben Pandira, 26; disciples of, executed, 97–98; Divine status, did not claim, 28, 143; and harrowing of hell, 118; in Hell, 26, 27, 156, 166; Maimonides' view of, 132; Messiahship, one of many claimants to, 14, 120; stoned, 156; Talmud, blasphemed by, 156–57, 206; in Talmud, no mention of, 26–29, 156, 218. *See also* Ben Pandira, Ben Stada
Jethro, 166
Jewish badge, 22
Jews: cultural deterioration of, 88; expulsion of, from Spain, 94; persecution of, 83, 92, 161, 216; right of, to Holy Land, denied, 194, 213, 223
Joab, 130
Job, 35, 79
Johanan (rabbi), 159
John Scotus Erigena, 217
Jonah Gerondi, 79
Jose the Galilean (rabbi), 136
Joseph Albalag, 169
Joseph Halevi, 169
Joseph ibn Ardot, 169
Joseph ben Nathan Official, 20, 218
Josephus, 26
Joshua, 141
Joshua ben Ḥanania (rabbi), 35
Joshua ben Levi (rabbi): on Aggadah, 217; in Eden, 129; and Elijah, 113–14; on Oral Law, 208, 223
Joshua ben Peraḥia, 26, 28, 111, 157
Jubilee, 223
Judah (tribe), 105, 108, 109, 185
Judah ben David, of Melun, 21, 29, 163, 166–67, 219
Judah Halevi, 46, 62, 217
Judah ben Isaac, 21
Judah de la Cavalleria, 81
Judah the Prince (rabbi), 104, 218
Judas of Galilee, 27
Judan (rabbi), 179
Judge: liability of, 107

Kabbalah, 13, 44, 72
Karaism, 19, 41, 161
Katz, Jacob, 32, 216
Khazars, 50
Kimḥi, David, 46, 62
'Kingdom of wickedness', 160
Kol Nidrei, 158
Korah: three sons of, in Eden, 129
Krauss, Samuel, 139
Kronos, 36

Lasker, D. J., 144
Law: in Judaism, 48
Leiden MS (of the *Vikuaḥ* of Naḥmanides), 76, 131
Leo Hebraeus. *See* Levi ben Gershom
Levi (tribe), 135–36
Levi ben Gershom (Ralbag), 80, 88, 222
Leviathan, 162, 166
Lieberman, Saul, 217, 219
Lilith, 162
Loeb, Isidore, 38, 57, 58, 59, 61, 66, 114, 144, 146, 163, 216, 217; alleged mistake of, 130; on Naḥmanides' alleged flight, 142
Logic, 171

Lot's wife, 154
Lotze, H., 216
Louis (name), 157
Louis IX (king of France), 21, 22, 80, 103, 164
'lutin', 162
Lydda, 26, 157

Maestro (title), 106, 107
Maimonides, 13, 46, 50, 62, 69, 73, 74, 79, 88, 104, 206, 214, 222; called a liar, 132; Epistle to the Yemen of, 121; on heretics, 223; on Messiah, 119, 180, 202, 224; on mortality of Messiah, 130–31; Sefer ha-Mitzvot of, 115; thirteen principles of faith of, 93
Margoliouth, R., 76
Marius Victorinus, 144
Martini, Raymund, 41, 43, 44, 58, 80, 90, 98
Marx, A., 222
Mary, 30, 157
Masorah, 223
Matathias. *See* Matithiah ha-Yitzhari
Matithiah ha-Yitzhari, 169, 176, 177, 178, 195, 200, 222
matzah, 60
Media, 141
Meir Haligoa, 169
Menasseh (king), 129
Mered, 130
Messiah, 14, 41, 42, 43, 45, 49–55, 70, 71, 73, 74, 105, 111, 113, 115, 117, 134–38, 147, 148, 181, 223: birth of, at time of Destruction of Temple, 110, 179–81, 188, 190, 199; calculation of coming of, 126, 176; centrality of, in Barcelona agenda, 60, 103; in Eden, 116, 129; in Judaism, 92, 113, 119, 127, 132, 134, 173, 183, 211, 214; longevity of, 70–71, 114, 182; mortality of, 130–31, 218; pre-existence of, 48, 140; as saviour, in Christianity, 116, 193, 218; suffering, 112, 123; unfulfilled claims of all aspirants to status of, 120–21, 211
Messianic feast, 46, 161, 162
Metaphor, 184
Metatron, 114
Methuselah, 45, 114; in Eden, 129
Michael, 122
Midrash, 42, 43, 48; authority of, 115; style of, 141
Ministering angels, 122
Milḥemet Ḥovah, 76
Minorites. *See* Franciscans
Miriam the Hairdresser, 30, 157. *See also* Mary
Moabites, 154, 218
Mishnah, 104, 205, 221
Mohammed, 121, 132
Moloch, 155–56
Moon: talking, 160
Moors, 40
Moses, 21, 104, 111, 117, 122, 139, 166; as Suffering Servant, 112
Moses ha Darshan, 13, 185–86
Moses Gerondi, 79. *See also* Naḥmanides
Moses of Coucy, 21
Moses ibn Musa, 169
Moslems, 132–133

Naḥmani. *See* Naḥmanides
Naḥmanides, Moses, 11, 12, 13, 14, 21, 22, 28, 39–78, 83, 84, 88, 92, 94, 102–49, 179, 182, 204, 217, 222; life of, 79–80; rationalism of, 62–63, 217; *Sefer ha-Gemul*, 116; *Sefer ha-Ge'ulah*, 54, 119, 126, 127; *Sefer Ha-Zekhut*, 107; *Torat Adonai Temimah*, 142, 144
Nasi: right of, to license judges, 107
Nathan (rabbi), 35, 104, 167
Nazis, 31
Nebuchadnezzar, 166
Neo-Platonism, 43
Neubauer, A., 112, 113
Nimrod, 122
Noah, 36
Noahide laws, 159, 218–19
nolad, 181, 200

Odo of Châteauroux, 22
Og, King of Bashan, 36, 161, 162
Old Testament, 23
Onqelos ben Qaloniqos, 27
Ordination, 106, 107
Original Sin, 51, 52, 74; denial of, by Naḥmanides, 118

Pablo Alvarez, 123

Pablo Christiani, 22, 39, 41, 42, 45, 47, 48, 51, 52, 61, 65, 66, 67, 68, 69, 70, 73, 74, 76, 80, 82, 97, 101, 102–50, 179, 182, 217
Pacios Lopez, A., 82, 187, 222, 223
Palestine, 80
Papal notary, 187
Pappa (Rav), 157
Pappos ben Judah, 26
Paracelsus, 221
Patripassian heresy, 34
Paul, 139
Pedro de Luna. *See* Benedict XIII (pope)
Pedro III (king of Aragon), 144, 179, 222
Peire of Berga, 133
Peire de Genova, 108, 109
Peniscola, 94
Persia: rule of, over the Jews, 106
peshat, 46, 112, 184
Peter of Castellnou (bishop of Gerona), 59, 77, 98, 117
Pfeffercorn, Johann, 216
Pharaoh, 51, 117, 118, 122
Pharisees, 24, 205
Philo, 46
Phinehas, 209
Pico della Mirandola, 43, 88
Pines, S., 145
Plato, 46
Pope, 53, 153, 154, 160
Prophecy, 179
Protestantism, 19, 20
Preaching Friars. *See* Dominicans
Provence, 103
Pugio Fidei (book), 41, 43, 58, 90, 222
Purgatory, 160, 219
Purim, 210

qal va-ḥomer, 223

Rabba bar bar Ḥana, 158
Rabbi, 104. *See also* Judah the Prince (rabbi)
Rabbi (title), 106, 107
Rabinowitz, A. H., 115
Rabbinowitz, R. N., 216
Ralbag. *See* Levi ben Gershom
Ramban. *See* Naḥmanides, Moses
Rankin, O. S., 13, 102–46; on time-span of 400 years, 131
Rashbam, 46
Rashi, 13, 28, 46, 97, 175, 185, 209, 219; on Birkat ha-Minim, 161; on Jesus, 166; on study of the Bible, 167
Rationalism, 62–63, 72, 87, 220–21; of Naḥmanides, 217
Rav (title), 106, 107
Rava, 222
Raymund de Peñaforte, 39, 41, 58, 64, 65, 80–81; part of, in investigation of Talmud, 98, 101, 102; on Trinity, 143, 144
'rebellious elder', 223
Reconquest, 40
Regné, Jean, 146, 217
Renaissance, 43
Resurrection of the dead, 46, 123
Reuchlin, Johann, 216
Ritschl, A., 216
Roman Empire, 53
Rome, 113, 141; confused with Tortosa, 180, 222; power of, not due to Jesus, 121
Rosenne, Shabtai, 219
Rosenthal, Judah, 23, 37, 163, 216, 219
Roth, Cecil, 13, 57, 66–68, 103, 106, 114, 121, 133, 141, 144, 217
Ruth, 154

Sa'adiah Gaon, 62, 112, 126, 128, 130
Sacrifices: abolition of, 194, 212
Sages: authority of, 154, 167
Salomon Ysach, 222. *See also* Solomon Maimon
Salomon Trecensis, 166, 219. *See also* Rashi
Salvation, 53
Samuel, 111, 136
Samuel (Mar), 131
Samuel ha-Levi, 169
Samuel bar Naḥmani (rabbi), 183
Samuel ben Solomon of Château Thierry
Sanhedrin, 107, 185
San Mateo, 91, 198
Sarachek, J., 116
Saraval MS (of Naḥmanides' *Vikuaḥ*), 76, 131
Saul (king), 133
Schwarzschild, Steven S., 219
Second Coming of Christ, 53
Seder 'Olam Rabba, 126, 128
Sefer Madd'a, 222
Sefer Mitzvot Gadol, 21
Selden, John, 218
semikhah. *See* Ordination

Seraḥ (daughter of Asher), 129, 130
Serpent, 51
Sheba ben Bichri, 130
shemittah, 223
Shiloh, 41, 56, 105, 134
Shofetim, 131–32
Shochat, A., 220, 222, 228
Simeon ben Yoḥai, 31
Simon, M., 218
Simlai (rabbi), 115
Sinai (Mount), 161, 165
Sir Leon, *See* Judah ben Isaac
Soferim (Talmudic tractate), 222
Solomon (king), 84, 109, 129
Solomon ben Abraham Adret (Rashb'a), 79
Solomon Maimon, 90, 198, 200, 222. *See also* Salomon Ysach
Solomon Yitzḥaki. *See* Rashi
Steinschneider, Moses, 76, 77, 78; and date of source MS of *Vikuaḥ*, 131
Strack, H. L., 112
Suffering Servant, 41, 42, 43, 57, 73, 112
Swift, F. Darwin, 111
Syllogisms, 87, 88, 171

Talmage, Frank, 46, 217
Talmud, 24, 91, 104, 168, 189; accusations against, 25, 91, 153–67, 189, 197; authority of, 47, 115; censorship of, 25, 132, 216; Geronimo's theory of, 89, 187, 189, 205; in Paris Disputation, 19–30
Tanḥuma (rabbi), 140
'Tanna of the House of Elijah', 172, 221
Targum, 112, 183
Tela Ignea Satanae (book), 76
Temple: destruction of, 104, 105, 106, 110, 111, 114; Second, 105, 106
Ten Commandments, 159
Theology, 48
Thibaut de Sezanne, 163
Tithes, 223
Titus (emperor), 27, 167
Todros ibn Jehia, 169
Todros Al-Constantin, 169
Toledo, 114
Toledot Yeshu, 28, 113
Toleration, 85–86
Torah, 153, 154, 175, 189, 193, 218
Tosafot, 21, 28, 33, 219
Trinity, 14, 56, 58, 63, 64, 65, 68, 143–46

Uranos, 36
Urim and Thummim, 179

varatio, 85
vav-consecutive, 105
Vidal ben Benvenista, 93, 169, 170, 172, 174, 177, 180, 184, 185, 222
Vivo Meldensis, 164, 219. *See also* Yeḥiel of Paris
Vows, 158, 166

Wagenseil, J. C., 76
Walter (archbishop of Sens), 22
Weisse, C. H., 216
'wilderness of the peoples', 127
William of Auvergne (bishop of Paris), 22, 23
Wiliam of Conches, 144
William of Saint Thiery, 144
Wolfson, H. A., 144
World: destruction of, 174

Ya'avetz, 129
Yeḥiel ben Joseph, of Paris, 11, 20, 21, 23 38, 44, 61, 76, 80, 111, 153–67, 218
Yelammedenu, 140
Yolande (queen), 81
yom, 126, 128
Yom Tov Karkosa, 169
Yose (rabbi), 106
Zedekiah (king), 166
Zeira (rabbi), 217
Zeraḥiah ha-Levi, 79, 169, 172, 222; sermon of, 171, 220–21. *See also* Ferrer (rabbi)
Zerubbabel, 105, 124, 125
zohama, 51
Zohar, 43, 44

Index of Quotations

Old Testament

Genesis
1:2 140
2:17 116
2:20 162, 176
3 118
3:8 46
3:22 116, 140
3:23 116
4:23 137
5:24 114
6:2 162
18:25 36
24:55 126
28:10 141
28:15 185
37:2 46
42:16 118
46:17 130
49:8 109
49:10 40, 56, 105, 106, 134, 149, 184, 190, 192

Exodus
3:6 139
8:1 111
8:16 123
13:6 217
13:10 126
15:6 136
19:20 154
20:7 154
20:22 154
23:2 154
31:3 141
32:14 158
33:11 139

Leviticus
8:35 155
18:6 121
20:2 155
25:29 126
26:12 138

Numbers
3:13 128
12:6 139
14:18 154
15:31 223

Deuteronomy
1:28 162
9:10 208
11:9 154
17:8 154
17:10 223
20:10 159
23:4 154
23:14 154
24:16 154
28:32 123
30 212
30:1–7 133
30:5 213
34:9 141

Joshua
7:25 156
9 158

Judges
5:11 168

I Samuel
9:18 177
12:11 136
20:25 133
28:3 136

II Samuel
20:16–22 130
23:8 136
23:18 136

I Kings
12:20 109

I Chronicles
4:18 130
5:2 109
11:11 136
16:7 135
16:22 125

II Chronicles
13:9 123
17:6 123

Ezra
2:2 124
3:2–13 124
5:1–2 124

Nehemiah
7:73 214

Esther
4:11 179
5:13 122
6:14 141

Psalms
7:9 175
18:36 136
21:4 149
21:5 116
35:10 169
47:10 125
49:2 126
51:17 171
72:8 121
76:2 214
85:7 171
90:2 181
95:7 148
105:15 125
110:1 135
118:15 136
122:5 168

Proverbs
12:3 84
15:35 181
27:1 181

Ecclesiastes
1:10 208
7:13 181
12:12 222

Isaiah
1:18 170
1:20 170
2:4 52, 121
5:27 168
8:20 168
9:6 192
10:34 179
11 212, 213
11:1 134, 179
11:2 140
11:4 121
11:9 121
11:12 132
27:10 117
41:6 175
41:8 112
42:4 131
44:1 112
45:1 125
45:23 171
49 212
52 212
52:13 ff. 112
52:13 122
53 149
54:9 158
56:5 168
63:12 136
66:1 130

66:7 183–84, 190
66:8 184
66:10 184
66:13 184

Jeremiah
3:22 171, 192
4:23 141
16 212
25:30 162
29 212
31:34 121
38:7 129
42 213

Ezekiel
20:35 126
28 212
28:18 117
37 212
39 212

Daniel
7:9 136
8:15 125
9:2 125
9:24 126, 181
9:24–27 124
9:26 124
10:20–21 122
12:4 128
12:11 125
12:11–12 126

Hosea
2:14 126
3:5 127

Micah
1:2 115
5:1 110
7 212

Zephaniah
2:3 198

Haggai
1:1 to 2:9 124

Zechariah
4:9 124
12:8 140

Malachi
3:19 160

New Testament

Mark
15:27 113

Luke
20:42 135

I Corinthians
11:12 139

Colossians
4:11 26

Targums

Onqelos

On Genesis
49:10 184

Jonathan

On Genesis
46:17 130

On Isaiah
66:7 183

Mishnah

Sukkah
3:13–14 219

Avodah Zarah
2:1 30

Avot
1:1 218
3:17 51
4:17 119
5:21 219

Tosefta

Sanhedrin
13 219

Ḥullin
2:22 26
2:24 26

Mekhilta

Baḥodesh
9 218

Sifre

Nitzavim
305 122

Babylonian Talmud

Berakhot
4b 219, 223
7a 218, 219
17a 139
28b 219
54b 36

Shabbat
63a 46
114a 161
145b 124
146a 161
151b 131

Eruvin
21b 219, 222

Yoma
9b 222
54a 124

Sukkah
43b–44a 219
45b 139
52a 113

Rosh Hashanah
16b 160
29b 219

Megillah
16b 210

Ḥagigah
14a 136

Yevamot
76b 218
82b 213

Nedarim
32a 210
32b 136
65a 219

Gittin
56b 26, 156

Sotah
13a 130
14a 112
47a 111

Bava Qamma
38a 219
113a–b 219

Bava Metzi'a
33a 209
59a 49
59b 35
86a 104

Bava Batra
3b 106
15a 136
73b 158

Sanhedrin
5a 106, 107
13b 106, 107
14a 106
22a 209
38b 136
43a 26, 97, 156
56a 218
67a 30, 156
67b 44
93a 122

97a 172, 183, 222
97b 176
98a 113
99a 223
105a 219
107b 26, 157

Makkot
23b 115

Avodah Zarah
3b 219
22b 51

Ḥullin
91b 122

Niddah
46b 224

Minor Tractates of the Talmud

Soferim
15 31, 159

Derekh Eretz Zutta
1 116, 129

Sefer Torah
1a 141

Palestinian Talmud

Berakhot
2:4 (5a) 199

Peah
2:6 (17a) 217

Ma'aserot
3:9 (51a) 217

Shabbat
16:1 (15c) 217

Midrashic Literature

Genesis Rabbah
2:5 140
8:1 140
25:1 114
94:9 130

Lamentations Rabbah
1:51 45, 179, 199
2:57 110

Ecclesiastes Rabbah
1:10, para. 1 208

Tanḥuma, Toledot
14 112

Midrash Tehillim
2:3 121
76:2 214

Pesiqta Rabbati
36:1 115, 123

Leqaḥ Tov, Genesis
49:10 134

Yalqut Shimoni
Isaiah, 476 112, 122
Hosea, 518 127
Ezekiel, 367 129
Beḥuqotai, 672 138
Tehillim, 869 137

Bereshit Rabbati (Albeck)
p. 131 183

Seder 'Olam Rabbah
27–28 124
30 106, 213, 223

Pirqei Hekhalot
6:2 117

Geonim

Otzar ha-Geonim
I, 2, p. 39 (Berakhot, 28) 219
Ḥagigah, 59–60 217

Jewish Medieval Literature

Abraham Ibn Ezra
on Genesis, 49:10 134
on Psalms, 110:1 135

Moses Maimonides

Comm. on Mishnah,
Introd. to Ḥeleq 131

Guide for the Perplexed
I:50 145
I:58 144–45
I:70 217

Mishneh Torah
Madd'a 206
Shofetim 131, 202
Shofetim, Mamrim, 3 207, 223
Shofetim, Melakhim, 11 222
Shofetim, Melakhim, 11:4 132
Shofetim, Melakhim, 12:2 202, 224

David Kimḥi
on Genesis 49:10 134
on Psalms 110:1 135
on Isaiah 52 112

Moses Naḥmanides
on Genesis, 2:17 116, 118
on Genesis, 3:22 116
on Isaiah 53 112–13
Sefer ha-Geulah, pt. 3 124, 125
Sefer ha-Geulah, pt. 4 120
Sefer ha-Zekhut, Gittin 4 107

Joseph Karo, Shulḥan Arukh, Oraḥ Ḥayyim
658:2 219

Christian Literature

Origen
Contra Celsum, 1: 55 112

Jerome
Comm. on Daniel, 12:10–11 128
In Isaiam, 59:12 218

Thomas Aquinas
Summa contra Gentiles, ii:25 216